IMAGES OF KABĪR

SOUTH ASIA INSTITUTE, NEW DELHI BRANCH
HEIDELBERG UNIVERSITY
SOUTH ASIAN STUDIES NO. XL

Images of Kabīr

edited by

MONIKA HORSTMANN

MANOHAR
2002

First published 2002

ISBN 81-7304-463-5

Published by
Ajay Kumar Jain for
Manohar Publishers & Distributors
4753/23 Ansari Road, Daryaganj
New Delhi 110002

Printed at
Lordson Publishers Pvt. Ltd.
Delhi 110007

CONTENTS

Editor's Preface

An international symposium commemorating the six-hundredth anniversary of Kabīr was held in Heidelberg in 1999. This symposium was an opportunity to bring together recent research on one of north India's greatest devotional poets. There was no intention to re-open the debate on Kabīr's date. The idea of a symposium was first suggested by Kedarnath Singh. Almost all the papers presented on the occasion are included in this volume, with the exception of contributions read by Purushottam Agrawal (whose paper appeared in the meantime in *Hindī*, 1, 2000), Mridula Ghosh and Linda Hess. Namwar Singh's paper was previously published in *Indian Literature*. The Sahitya Akademi's kind permission to reprint it here is gratefully acknowledged.

Ulrike Stark cooperated both in the organisation of the symposium and in the preparation of this volume, with spirit and efficiency. Claudia Ramsbrock helped patiently with the typing of the manuscript. The symposium was generously funded by the Deutsche Forschungsgemeinschaft, the Stiftung der Universität Heidelberg, and the Deutsche Bank. The editor gratefully acknowledges their generous aid. The gathering was hosted by the Internationales Wissenschaftsforum of the University of Heidelberg. The hospitality of this institution as especially represented by its Executive Secretary, Theresa Reiter, is gratefully remembered.

The editor has refrained from trying to make the various modes of transcription used by the authors unassailably uniform. For pre-modern names, diacritic marks have been given; for modern names, this has been left to the discretion of the authors. Names and other words current in English generally appear in their English spelling. Urdu and Persian words have been transcribed according to the system used by John T. Platts (*A Dictionary of Urdū, Classical Hindī, and English,* 5th impression, repr., London 1974).

Introduction

Kabīr is a vital presence in India. A good part of scholarly writing within and without India has sought to explore who he was and how text-critical methods might be helpful in establishing a core of sayings that, with some degree of probability, could be attributed to him individually. This type of research came almost to a conclusion by the year 1974 when Charlotte Vaudeville wrote her seminal study on Kabīr.[1] In 1993, this was made definitively clear by her last book on Kabīr, in which she conclusively brought together the relevant evidence so far available.[2] This study identified the limits of the historical study of Kabīr as a person and establishing any one authentic text of Kabīr's sayings. Within those limits, however, it had been possible to put Kabīr studies on firmer ground and to produce texts as well as translations without which any progress in studying him would have been inconceivable. Meanwhile, an earlier streak of interest in Kabīr had somewhat receded into the background and now receives renewed interest. It addresses the question of the life of Kabīr in society at large and within its various cultural components. This is the kind of interest first represented in a major way by Kṣitimohan Sen, who since 1908 had collected songs of devotional singers as they were part of the living tradition of Bengal.[3] The questions underlying this and related interest are, with respect to Kabīr: How do people from one or another section of society express their own conditions and feelings through recourse to Kabīr? How do contemporary thinkers relate to him? How does he challenge contemporary writers? How do we react on someone who takes him at his word? Does Kabīr still scandalise us or have we developed a mechanism of tucking him safely away as an academic or purely aesthetic issue, or, do we misuse him as a handy political tool and thus dwarf his literary, aesthetic and religious stature?

---

[1] Charlotte Vaudeville, *Kabīr,* vol. 1, London 1974.

[2] Charlotte Vaudeville, *A Weaver Named Kabīr*, New Delhi 1993.

[3] For this, see Kshitimohan Sen, *Medieval Mysticism of India,* with a Foreword by Rabindranath Tagore. Trs. Manmohan Ghosh. 1st Indian ed. of the 2nd ed, 1935, Delhi 1974, p. X.

Renewed identification with this quest led to a notable blurring of professional boundaries. The distinction between the seemingly objective outside position of the scholar and the subjective position of creative writers and social activists can no longer taken for granted. This is especially the case with writers who have been actors in, and witnesses of, recent developments in India in which the communal debate or the unrelieved plight of the Dalits was felt to run against the spirit of Kabīr. This recent development, however, only highlighted that the alleged distinction between an outside and inside approach to this engaging author is hardly tenable. A good number of contributions to this volume, on personalities or groups who appropriated Kabīr in creating their own worldviews, or by scholars who engage in a social activism, stand testimony to this. Shukdeo Singh, renowned for his textual studies on Kabīr and Raidās, focuses on the struggle of the Sants for self-assertion in the face of brahmanical dominance.

How did the past and how does the present take the challenge of Kabīr's teachings and his poetical genius? This issue touches upon intercultural perception as much as on that prevalent within India. It seemed therefore appropriate to review, first of all, how Kabīr figured in earlier scholarship and how this informed our image of him. Pradeep Bandyopadhyay, in a topical paper from the perspective of the history of science and ideas, puts forth how westerners of the colonial period imposed their own concepts on Kabir. This resulted in an anachronistic image of him, or in one insulated from the social context in which he lived. This problem, unsurprisingly, looms large for a figure so potently urging one to review one's own quest. Bandyopadhyay points out what ideologies account for the image of Kabīr as an enlightened religious reformer. With missionary thinking and an evolutionist optimism that mankind would eventually embrace Christianity play a prominent role, Kabīr was considered a kindred spirit. A view of him as a social reformer of nationalistic preoccupation was only a step away.

The early tradition of Kabīr and the Kabīr-panth

The privilege of discovering Kabīr as an object of study was that of Angelo de Gubernatis in 1878. He presented to the public his findings about the Capuchian friar Marco Della Tomba, who had discovered Kabīr for Europe in the latter half of the eighteenth century. Charlotte Vaudeville reminded us of this again in her book of 1974, and it is partly in response to her that David N. Lorenzen unfolds his pioneer research on Marco Della Tomba's writings. Amongst these are not only translations of the Kabīr-panthī *Mūlpañjī* and *Jñānsāgar*, but also a description of the Kabīr-panthīs of his time and their religious system as contained in the *Jñānsāgar*. Against this, Lorenzen also refutes Vaudeville's contention that what he calls a Rāmāyaṇa version is a Kabīr-panthī text whereas it is, in fact, the earliest known western translation of Tulsīdās's *Rāmcaritmānas*.

As for attempts to constitute a Kabīr text that might claim auctorial authenticity, the past few decades have been dominated by two major research projects. One was Pārasnāth Tivārī's attempt (1961) to establish a representative text, under the title *Kabīr-graṃthāvalī*;[4] the other was Winand M. Callewaert's project of filming Sant manuscripts, which led to the discovery and recovery of some of the most ancient compilations containing Kabīr's works, and his longstanding endeavour to approach anything that may distantly, if at all resemble a critical edition.[5] Both projects have after perseverance and intense labour churned up the insight that despite the wealth in Kabīr texts there is no way of establishing an authentic auctorial Kabīr text. Kabīr's words have remained a living and productive tradition that split early in different recensions and, both alongside and intertwined with these, oral ramifications. A written text of Kabīr, based on the manuscript tradition, therefore represents a historical step in the midst of ever-fertile traditions. In this volume, Winand M.

---

[4] Published in Allahabad.

[5] This process has, as far as the songs attributed to Kabīr are concerned, come to a conclusion by the publication of his *The Millennium Kabīr* Vāṇī. *A Collection of* Pad-*s*. In collaboration with Swapna Sharma [and] Dieter Taillieu, Delhi 2000.

Callewaert thus confines himself to constitute a textual corpus of the written traditions as they existed around 1556, all the while being aware of the fact that that text status does not correspond to any one living regional tradition.

In an attempt to identify the linguistic status of the Kabīr text shared by the early tradition, Stuart McGregor seeks to isolate the various linguistic strata in the sixteen *sākhī*s that all of them have in common. In this ancient textual segment he finds a broad basis of Khaṛī bolī with a probably popularly-used mixture of Braj Bhāṣā and Avadhī, the last-mentioned language buttressed by a well-developed literary tradition in its own right in the area of Kabīr's origin.

Kabīr and the literati

Kabīr continues to fertilise creative writing and cultural vision. We offer four examples of these. One is a critical reflection by Namwar Singh, another a piece of creative writing by Kiran Nagarkar; the third, by Kedarnath Singh, is a review of poetry thematic of Kabīr; and the last one, by Monika Horstmann, is a study of a cultural vision in which Kabīr figures as an exemplar.

Namwar Singh raises the issue of how Kabīr's and other low-caste authors' precarious social circumstances related to what they experienced as transcending the world. Singh perceives in Kabīr a sorrow of inevitable loneliness, the loneliness of one who feels at once the reality of the Divine and the separation from the Divine. He relates Kabīr's painful day-to-day experiences to this fundamental sorrow, but he circumspectly does not allow the world and the beyond, after which Kabīr strived, to be added up against each other in that account of sorrow.

Kiran Nagarkar transports Kabīr in his radicalism into our own present. Has, to us, Kabīr become 'like Gandhi', he asks, 'dead and gone and forgotten except when you needed a handy cliché or platitude to talk about the oneness of all faith'? His provocative text compels his readers to question how they meet Kabīr's challenge.

Kedarnath Singh, in whose own oeuvre stands out a long poem addressing Kabīr's fate in modern India and what in the present time the quest for salvation may mean,[6] reviews the reception of Kabīr in contemporary Hindi literature as it started half a century after the rediscovery of Kabīr for modern readers by Kṣitimohan Sen and Rabindranath Tagore.

Horstmann reconsiders Hazārīprasād Dvivedī's portrait of Kabīr and argues that his image of him was determined by Dvivedī's own attempt to conceptualise the image of man that would be able to stand the test of contemporary challenges. It is in line with such humanist concerns that he constructed Kabīr's biography.

Kabīr in cultural context

The first to draw the attention of twentieth-century scholarship to the tradition of Kabīr in its living cultural context was Kṣitimohan Sen. Kabīr and, for that matter, the Sant tradition in general, need to be seen in the context of the Nāth and Muslim traditions. The first to clearly elucidate Kabīr's relationship with the Nāth tradition were Pītāmbardatt Baṛthvāl and Hazārīprasād Dvivedī. Mariola Offredi in her paper reviews the various scholarly positions concerning Kabīr's links with the Nāths and then probes the esoteric doctrines of certain Nāth texts, variously edited and studied earlier or, more recently, by herself. Although the manuscript tradition of Nāth texts postdates Kabīr, it must be ascribed to a period anterior to him and is therefore usable as a historical antecedent of the Kabīr tradition. Offredi's analysis brings home to her readers Kabīr's great indebtedness to the Nāth doctrine.

Daniel Gold, too, studies the Kabīr tradition in the Nāth milieu, which in his case is that of the householder Nāths of southeastern Rajasthan. The communal religious practice of these Nāths unfolds in their *bhajan* gatherings. Their Kabīr songs are, however, liable to a sexual interpretation which relates them to the tantrik tradition. The ascetic Nāths of the same milieu notably abstain from the *bhajan* gatherings of their householder brethren. The Kabīr tradition thus forms a trajectory to the wider tantrik tradition such as that of the Bīsnāmīs. Gold shows the ways

[6] For bibliographical details, see his article, p. 113.

in which texts are negotiated among various groups, negotiations that the text as written word would in no way disclose outside its specific living setting.

Kabīr's reception in the Muslim milieu has so far received fairly little attention, apart from the fact that his Muslim credentials were acknowledged. Peter Gaeffke sketches the image of him in Muslim writing from the *Ā'īn-i Akbarī* to Urdu writing in 1947. Sadiqur Rahman Kidwai shows how Kabīr inspired Urdu poets. Thomas Dahnhardt studies Kabīr again in a specific socio-religious setting. The legacy of him helped link Muslim and Hindu traditions. Dahnhardt focuses on an instant of this, namely, the recruitment of Hindus in the Sufi tradition of the Naqshbandiyya Mujaddidiyya since Shaikh Aḥmad Sirhindī (1564-1624), which culminated in the late nineteenth century in the initiation of the Kāyasth Rāmcandra Saksenā who became a Mujaddidiyya master. The unifying spirit behind this event was the Kabīr tradition in the hands of the Dharamdāsī branch of the Kabīr-panthīs.

Bahadur Singh's study of a local Kabīr tradition squares with the findings on the textual divergence within the written tradition on the one hand and their differing from the many internally varying living Kabīr traditions on the other. It is not the wording but rather the spirit that they share and that safeguards their existence. This can only happen because Kabīr fulfills a purpose for specific groups, as this is the case for the Dalits whose relationship with the Kabīr tradition is the topic of both Nancy M. Martin and Maren Bellwinkel-Schempp. Martin sees the Meghvāls of Rajasthan, who sing the songs of Kabīr, empowered by his message. Martin, whose approach is also informed by the Liberation Theology, finds that theirs is an empowerment to dignity, not to rebellion against their Dalit status. Bellwinkel-Schempp focuses on the Kabīr-panthīs of Kanpur and traces their contribution to the Dalit discourse since the early twentieth century. A well-defined Kabīr-panthī identity, dissociated from the Devī worship thus far common with the Kabīr-panthīs, was formulated in the begining of the century. Later it was overshadowed by other forms of Dalit self-assertion, as initiated by Ambedkar, the strong local movement of Svāmī Achūtānand and the foregrounding of Raidās.

The findings presented in this volume resist the construction of any one Kabīr. They present particular Kabīrs according to their cultural contexts. These Kabīrs are refractions of a persona both persistently and powerfully present and evasive.

The Uses of Kabīr: Missionary Writings and Civilisational Difference

Pradeep Bandyopadhyay

This paper reviews the different conceptual frameworks and contexts in which Kabīr has been assessed in recent scholarship. The focus is on attempts to characterise Kabīr as a religious figure and not on studies primarily concerned to assess the literary value of his work. It is concerned first with some of the writings of British scholars, primarily the missionaries and other Christians, and uses this as a base to briefly consider some problems in inter-civilisational studies. The main claim is that Kabīr has been harnessed to a variety of uses, both religious and political, and no doubt this will continue to be the case. In any case, given the almost insurmountable difficulties facing historians or text-critics seeking warranted knowledge of Kabīr's life or the 'stratification' of the writings attributed to him, we are unlikely to be able to sort out the real Kabīr from the many 'Kabīrs' available to us. In this situation, I suggest that there is a persistent tendency to 'anachronism' in the form of reading in Kabīr a prototype or early anticipation of some current ideological or philosophical position; or else as having approximated some Western or 'modern' religious and political judgements, so that Kabīr is assimilated to a civilisational-cultural context not his own. I include in the discussion of Kabīr also remarks on the Kabīr-panthīs, where relevant.

Kabīr in British Missionary Writings

Kabīr and the *panthī*s, and bhakti as an 'innovative' development in Hinduism, are treated as a distinct topic from the mid-nineteenth century in Christian writings in English on Indian religions and sects. H. H. Wilson, G. A. Grierson, and M. Monier-Williams may be cited. Wilson's *Sketch of the Religious Sects of the Hindus* was published in 1846 by the

Bishop's College Press in Calcutta. Grierson wrote on Kabīr and his followers in several contributions to the *Journal of the Royal Asiatic Society* (1907/8) and, at some length, in *The Modern Vernacular Literature of Hindustan* (1889), probably the first systematic study of the literature in vernacular languages by a British scholar. Monier-Williams refers to Kabīr in several well-known works including *Hinduism*, a manual in the series Non-Christian Religious Systems, first published by the Society for Promoting Christian Knowledge (SPCK) in 1877 and reprinted several times, and in *Brahmanism and Hinduism* (1891). In these writings, the focus is on the emergence of bhakti as a new development in the religious life of Hindus and most attention is given to the Vaiṣṇava groups, described as 'sects'; Kṛṣṇa-bhakti is singled out as indicative of both a personal and an incarnate theism. Kabīr, often in tandem with Nānak, is discussed in this general identification of a personalised, devotional monotheism. The contrast drawn is between the earlier philosophical monism or pantheism and the better appreciated Vaiṣṇava monotheism, albeit contaminated by idolatry, mythology (which is often found to be 'lascivious' and 'gross') and superstition. This amalgam of Kabīr and the Vaiṣṇavas is sustained by the occasional reference to Rāmānand and his order and the traditional association of the two, along with emphasis on the significance of the name Rām in Kabīr's songs and poetry. A typical example of this, dependent mainly on Wilson and Grierson, is the following in R. W. Frazer's *A Literary History of India* (1898): [1]

> In the 'Sabdabali' or 'One Thousand Sayings of Kabīr', the Vedantic doctrine of Maya, the Jain, the Buddhistic, and Brahmanic doctrines of compassion toward all life were brought side by side with the monotheistic conception of Vishnu.

---

[1] R. W. Frazer, A *Literary History of India*, reprint, New York 1970 [[1]1898], pp. 345-6.

The author then quotes a prose rendering by Wilson of Kabīr's dismissal of fasting, bathing and other religiously enjoined rituals and pilgrimages, that ends with the lines: 'Every man and woman that has ever been born is of the same nature with yourself.'

Monier-Williams mentions Kabīr in his manual for the SPCK in a chapter titled 'Medieval and Modern Sects'. This immediately follows a discussion of 'Doctrine of Devotion (*bhakti*) as Developed in the Puranas and Tantras'. In this discussion, referring to the tantras, he writes:[2]

> Most of them are mere handbooks for the use of practisers of a kind of witchcraft, which to Europeans appears so ineffably absurd that the possibility of any persons believing in it seems in itself almost incredible. Whole Tantras teach nothing but what may be called the science of employing unmeaning sounds for acquiring magical power over friends, and for destroying enemies and rivals.

But with insight he goes on to suggest that:

> When they are better known, their connection with a distorted view of the Sankhyan philosophy, and with some of the corrupt forms of Buddhism, will probably be made clear.'

Coming to the medieval sects, Monier-Williams indicates that we are moving toward light, after the 'darkest and worst phase, Saktism or Tantrism'.

> This general degradation of religion through what is called the left-hand form of worship—or devotion to the female counterpart of Siva—led to the springing up of various reforming sects.... It is a subject which opens out on an almost unbounded field on which to expatiate, and volumes might be written before exhausting it.

---

[2] M. Monier-Williams, *Hinduism*, London 1906 [[1]1877], pp. 141-2.

With this view of the origins of bhakti, he draws attention to 'the exaggeration of the principle of devotion and love (bhakti), so that even caste was subordinated to it'. There follows an enumeration and discussion of six Vaiṣṇava *sampradāyas*, of which the second is that of the Rāmānandīs, under which heading he writes:

> This Kabīr became the founder of a distinct sect. He assailed idolatry with great boldness, and ridiculed the religious practices of his fellow-countrymen, though he allowed adoration to be paid to Vishnu or Rama, as names for one god. He promulgated a high moral code, declaring that life was a sacred gift of God, and that the blood of men or animals ought never to be shed by his creatures. He laid great stress on truthfulness, and advocated retirement from the world for attainment of control over the passions.

Monier-Williams closes the brief section with a few lines on Nānak Śāh who is said to be indebted to Kabīr for his 'pantheistic' opinions. In a footnote we are informed that the *Ādi-Granth*, the 'first book' of the Sikhs, was 'promulgated about the time of our Reformation'. This sounds a keynote which resonates through subsequent Christian writings on Kabīr and Nānak.[3] Monier-Williams had completed this work before the rise of the Singh Sabha movement toward the close of the nineteenth century.

---

[3] An interesting observation on this theme is in R. C. Zaehner, *Hinduism*, London 1962: 'In some ways the *bhakti* movement is comparable to the Protestant Reformation in Europe; the centre of interest passes from the hierarchical act of sacrifice and the hierarchy which mediates it to the laity to a direct and personal relationship between the worshipper and his God. As a natural corollary to this the language of the liturgy which only the priests could understand was replaced by the vernacular, and the singing of vernacular hymns gradually supplemented and replaced the priestly liturgies. Here, however, the analogy ends, for though there was often hostility to the old order as represented by the Brahmans, no clear break was ever made with it... but what the *bhakti* sects conspicuously lacked was the deep moral earnestness and the grave preoccupation with sin that marked the main stream of the European

To this point the understanding of Kabīr is in the context of bhakti—especially in its Vaiṣṇava form—as part of a Hindu reformation leading to rejection of caste and idolatry, the discovery of a personal monotheism (or a pantheism), non-violence, and as overcoming philosophical Brahmanical monism on the one hand and the licentiousness of the Tāntrikas.

In the subsequent period, we see progressively a greater understanding of Kabīr's distinctive role and an increasing appreciation of his 'Reform' stature and independence from the 'lower' or 'darker' layers of Hinduism. The writings of Westcott and Farquhar in the first decades of the twentieth century, and those of Estlin Carpenter and Keay, take us to the peak of Christian appreciation—through the use of contrastive concepts drawn from European theology and philosophy of religion, viz., monism/pantheism/monotheism; impersonal Absolute/personal God, etc.

To understand better the relief felt by missionary scholars in the presence of the bhakti tradition in the vernacular languages with its emphasis on love, devotion and adoration, one may note the observations of another British missionary in lectures delivered before a lay audience around 1902 on the Vedanta:[4]

> Humility, a sense of dependence, reverence, prayer, obedience, repentance: these things are all impossible. Love either to God or to our neighbour is equally so. Love *from* God is the same; for the poor Soul is alone in a loveless universe. The conception is appalling. So much for the Vedanta.

Reformation.' On Kabīr, he has this equally pertinent comment: 'Kabir was a Muslim by birth, and though he early abandoned the Muslim faith, he retained the strict monotheism of Islam and a strong aversion to the caste system.... It seems to have been Kabir's intention to found a religion that was inhibited by neither dogma, nor scripture, nor social framework' (p. 183). Zaehner was a convert to Catholicism.

[4] J. Murray Mitchell, *The Great Religions of India*, reprint, New Delhi 1990 [Edinburgh 1905], pp. 76, 94, 91-2, 82-3.

A while later the distressed missionary bravely broaches the dreaded tantras:

> Mystery, magic, and sheer folly mark all the books; but there are two branches of the worshippers—those of the right and those of the left hand; and the books of the latter branch overflows with all that is base and disgusting. I simply cannot describe the mode of worship for the reason expressed by the Apostle Paul in Ephesians, v.12.

But he also has something to say about bhakti, repeating a theory propounded a few decades earlier by Indologists like Albrecht Weber but subsequently refuted by R. G. Bhandarkar:

> Again there is the doctrine of *bhakti* or *devotion*—affection fixed on God. This does not occur in early Hinduism. The Vedas speak often of *sraddha* or trust in the gods; but they hardly recognise the emotional part of religion. The doctrine of *bhakti* comes in abruptly. We think that, if not originally drawn from Christianity, it was developed by contact with it. The Hindus, ere long, carried the doctrine to very extravagant lengths.

Finally, at the conclusion of a few paragraphs on the 'sects', he comes to Kabīr:

> The doctrine of the Divine Unity had deeply impressed him, but he could never get rid of his early Hindu beliefs regarding transmigration, the avataras and several other points. One high characteristic of Kabīr's teaching is its moral purity. It denounces caste, ridicules the Shastras, and denounces Brahmanical arrogance. Idolatry, it says, is sinful.

Evidently, there was much misunderstanding. In the next period there is remarkable change. G. H. Westcott innovated by devoting an entire book to *Kabir and the Kabir Panth*, published in 1907 by the Christ Church Mission Press, Cawnpore. Significantly, he starts his account with a *Chronological Table* of parallel figures, Hindu and Christian. Rāmānand is placed in the same row as Wycliffe; Gorakhnāth beside Erasmus; Kabīr beside Luther, and Nānak beside Cranmer. The parallelism of Reformation and Reformers is neatly exhibited. The study was based on field investigations among Kabīr-panthīs and a fairly thorough study of the relevant texts including the 'traditions'. The opening sentence sets the assimilative analogy: 'Kabīr has been fittingly described by Sir W.W. Hunter as the Indian Luther of the 15th Century.'[5]

Westcott follows the suggestion of his predecessor Colonel Malcolm that there was an association with the Sufi order in Kabīr, whose intention was to break down the barriers separating Hindus from 'Muhammadans'. This interpretive axis was part of the Congress nationalist ideology of a Hindu-Muslim syncretic culture in post-medieval times. He finds evidence that Kabīr was a theist and not a pantheist. He advances two grounds that are still the subject of, perhaps unresolvable, debate and makes a startling claim. One, that the pantheism attributed to Kabīr results from teachings given by his Hindu followers at a later date, and two, he rejects the judgement that all that is contained in the *Bījak* represent Kabīr's personal views. He then makes a claim that is highly significant for the assimilationist move:[6]

---

[5] This Reformation analogy by Hunter may be compared to that drawn by Max Weber, who briefly mentions Kabīr in the context of an 'orthodox restoration' of Hinduism following a long period of expansion and consolidation of heterodoxy, i.e. Buddhism and Jainism. Weber places Kabīr among other bhakti sects and as a disciple of Rāmānand. But instead of Luther, Weber finds Kabīr-panthīs more akin to the Quakers. On account of their pacifism, it would appear that he noted the centrality of the interior word (*śabda*) in Kabīr. His references are primarily to Grierson's papers and it is evident that Weber did not have access to any writings attributed to Kabīr, but he was indeed a keen student of Reformation theology, in particular that of the Protestant sects, viz., Calvinists, Baptists and Quakers. Weber is categorical; no 'inner worldly asceticism' could arise. One may speculate on whether Kabīr would be an instance of a rarely instantiated position in Weber's conceptual typology: the inner-worldly mystic! Cf. Max Weber, *The Religion of India*, New York 1958, pp. 312-13.

[6] G. H. Westcott, *Kabir and the Kabir Panth*, reprint, New Delhi 1986

> There is a reason to believe that insufficient care has been taken in studying the context in which certain sayings occur; reason to fear that Kabīr has been credited with the argument of Maya whom he at all times ruthlessly condemns.

This judgement is evidently dependent on the strong claim that Kabīr was both a Muslim and a Sufi—although his followers relapsed into being Hindus. The good Reverend, for good measure, points to the 'picture of Kabīr which forms the frontispiece of this volume ... (which) represents him as having Muhammedan features, and his grave at Maghar has always been in the keeping of Muhammedans'. After quoting an account of Kabīr's teachings from Nābhājī's *Bhaktamāla*, he presents us with a summary of Kabīr's doctrine that is remarkably like that of a Reformation Protestant:

> This short account describes a man who has no great sympathy with Brahmanical teaching, who believed in a personal God and in salvation by faith rather than by good works, and who delivered a message regarded as God's message, to Hindus and Muhammedans alike (p. 25).

Here we have a Lutheran reading with the Reform theology of justification through faith neatly at the centre, with a Weberian notion of 'emissary prophecy' as the link between creator and creature. The teachings of Kabīr remind Westcott of Scripture, and he surmises that those with knowledge of the matter will probably find numerous references to Sufi teachings. Kabīr's teachings are summarised in a 'free' prose translation:

[Cawnpore 1907], p. 22.

> God is one: the Hindus are therefore at fault in their worship of many gods. These are in truth the creation of Maya; they have their origin in sin and are themselves the cause of sin in others.
>
> . . . . .
>
> The Hindus bathe in sacred streams, go on pilgrimage to sacred places, bow down to images of brass and stone, and think that in so doing they are honouring God. In this they are mistaken. What God desires is purity of heart; to rest in symbols that should lead men to God is to be guilty of idolatry.
>
> . . . . .
>
> Muhammedans repeat prayers and texts of scripture which they cannot understand; Hindus believe in gods who destroy men, sport with milkmaids and assume the form of animals. All such religion is vain. (pp. 31-2)

These remarks include several 'tropes' of Protestant theology and missionary debates with Hindus, e.g. 'resting in symbols' as 'idolatry', 'sport with milkmaids', a frequent motif in the many mission glances at Kṛṣṇa, and the upright Christ versus lascivious Kṛṣṇa. The scope of *māyā* as embracing 'sinful origin' and being a 'cause of sin' derives in part from a confusion between the claim that the web of *māyā* engenders illusion and error (*bhrama*) which is common enough in *advaitavāda*, and the quite distinct claim that belief in *māyā* is a false belief, which is evidently Westcott's own judgement. Westcott also sets the pattern for later commentators as regards the relation of Kabīr to his professed followers, the Kabīr-panthīs. The latter are judged to have altered his teachings, accommodating to the dominant Hindu culture. They have adopted several practices which Kabīr denounced.

At the turn of the century, Christian theological reflection was significantly influenced by two intellectual developments. The first was the growing influence of the theory of evolution, initially amongst natural scientists, but also as a paradigm for social evolution. The relatively novel intellectual disciplines of anthropology and comparative religion were consolidating their academic stature and also influencing the literati and 'educated public opinion'. The evolutionary paradigm was dominant in both disciplines.[7] The imperial mission was to aid 'backward peoples' to attain the civilisation of the Europeans. The missionary movement was at its peak and the study of non-Christian religions, rich in details, was often presented as a sequence of progressive development. Second, the rapid growth of Biblical studies and Near Eastern archeology had introduced the 'Higher Criticism'—the examination of Christian religious texts and history with the attitudes and methodologies of the historical and social sciences. The joint effect was a growing rift between 'liberals' and 'evangelicals' (some of whom, in the United States, later self-styled themselves 'fundamentalists') about both theology and the Christian appreciation of other religions. One effect of this can be observed in the writings of J. N. Farquhar, especially in the three works for which he is best known: *The Crown of Hinduism* (1913), *Modern Religious Movements in India* (1914), and *An Outline of the Religious Literature of the Hindus* (1920).

Farquhar developed an original approach to the religions of India in terms of the new liberal theology which addressed the moral qualities of a religious tradition as a criticism of comparative evaluation on the one hand, and in terms of religious evolution in that all religions were seen as more or less developed responses to common religious quests and

---

[7] The influence of the evolutionary perspective can be gauged by comparing Max Weber's last writing on the comparative sociology of religions with his earlier work. Weber was careful in his earlier writings on religion, especially the papers on the Protestant sects, to avoid an evolutionary framework, given his general methodological claims in favour of the construction of conceptual 'ideal types' and the emphasis on 'charisma' and 'prophecy' as sources of innovation and change. But the summary study he wrote as part of what became *Economy and Society* indicates the evolutionary impact of the comparative religion of the early twentieth century, especially in his discussion of 'early' or 'primitive' religions and the use of developmental contrastive 'types' such as spirits/gods, magic/religion, priests/prophets, ethical/exemplary etc. This final summary was later translated and published as *The Sociology of Religion*, Boston 1993.

concerns. One was enabled to identify the 'progressive' and the 'backward' *within* a given religious tradition. This was based on the emerging theological doctrine of partial revelation, of which Christianity was the fulfilment. Thus after a judicious and well-informed study of the main tenets and practices of Hinduism, clearly identifying what was morally progressive and what was outdated for modern conditions, in an evolutionary sense, he could propose Christianity as the 'crown' or fulfilment of Hinduism. Here is a typical paragraph:[8]

> Christ thus provides the necessary religious foundations for a society characterised by equality, freedom and strict justice. Social evolution all over the world is steadily tending in the direction of these Christian ideals, and the needs of modern men will inevitably increase the rate of the movement. Universal intercourse necessarily demands a universal society, complete social liberty, and a social morality of depth and strength sufficient to bear the unparalleled strain of the new state of affairs. Nothing but a conception of human brotherhood which contains within itself these liberties and obligations is equal to the creative task. Thus Christian society is the evolutionary goal of all living forms of society and of all social unrest and agitation of our day.

The attitudes expressed above are not as dated as may appear on account of its missionary origins. If we were to 'secularise' the references to Christianity and human brotherhood, in this passage, it would have a contemporary ring.

After noting the functional coherence of the 'Indo-Aryan' system, Farquhar indicates that it was strongly conservative over centuries. 'With the exception of the results produced by the doctrine of *ahimsa*, there is no

---

[8] J. N. Farquhar, *The Crown of Hinduism*, London 1913, p. 202 (reprint 1971, Oriental Books). This contains a long chapter 'The Divine Social Order' on the caste system and its various functions which includes evolutionary anthropological theories along with themes like the Aryan invasions, the organisation of conqueror-conquered relations, the ethnic basis of horizontal caste exclusiveness, etc.

thought of reform.' The significant reforms arise only later, in the context of 'certain rather important movements arising from criticisms of idolatry'. This leads him directly to a consideration of 'another atmosphere' in the north during 'Muhammedan supremacy'. Religious change is clearly associated with the conditions created by Muslim rule. Here Kabīr and Nānak make an appearance and are commended, but not their followers.

> Through the instrumentality of Kabīr, who seems to have been half a Muḥammadan, the stern monotheism of Islam and its hatred of idolatry passed into Hinduism and took organized form. The followers of Kabīr to this day are a separate Hindu sect who do not visit Hindu temples, but worship in their own buildings without images... It is a very remarkable fact that these sects have failed to influence Hinduism in general. Outside the small groups of their own members they have had very little influence indeed. Even in their own midst they have found it difficult to maintain the pristine ideal.[9]

Farquhar's hero appears later, in the person of Rammohan Roy, whose portrait appeared on the frontispiece of his next book on modern religious movements.

In this book Farquhar returns to Kabīr who 'was greatly influenced by Mohammadanism as well as by the Vaishnavism of his teacher Ramananda'. He notes two great departures from ordinary Hindu practice: Kabīr took very seriously the doctrine that knowledge of God is not dependent on caste, and refused to submit to the rule of the Brahmin priest; secondly, Kabīr 'also ridiculed Hindu mythology, denied the doctrine of incarnations, affirmed that all the Hindu gods were dead, and forbade the worship of idols'. It is his characterisation of Kabīr's role that distinguishes Farquhar, for his knowledge of Kabīr appears largely dependent on Westcott's work. He returns to brief considerations of Kabīr's religious influence when he surveys modern reform movements—

---

[9] Farquhar, *The Crown of Hinduism*, pp. 332-3.

as a cited source amongst the Radhasoamis and the Sikhs. As indicated earlier, in Farquhar's judgement the true reform amongst Hindus finds its expression in the Brahmo Samāj and the impact of Rammohan Roy, at least on the 'educated' Indians—in effect the new elite sponsored by British educational and administrative policies. Not surprisingly, therefore, he discusses the Radhasoami Satsang and the Sikhs in a chapter with the telling title, 'Reform Checked by Defence of Old Faiths'. The Radhasoamis use writings attributed to Kabīr, along with those of other 'Hindu saints'. In Farquhar's view the theology of this sect is mostly Hindu, and it stands near Vaiṣṇavism and is perhaps most clearly allied with the teachings of Kabīr.[10]

> This is reflected in the practice of the sect. While they profess to find all truth in the books of their own gurus, they do use the writings of certain Hindu and Muḥammadan saints, and amongst these they give Kabīr the highest place.

But in spite of some 'modern' elements ('Love is emphasized in the teaching of the sect in such a way as clearly to reveal its Christian origin; for it goes far beyond the old ideas connected with bhakti. Works of faith and charity, the spirit of service and prayer, are laid down as necessary duties.') he deplores the persistence of Hindu elements like the adoration of the guru because 'everything that has touched him is charged with his sanctity and influence.' This leads to certain 'disgusting practices' which are indicated indirectly with due circumspection. Turning to the Sikhs, Farquhar first notes that with the decline of spiritual religion among them, there is the overpowering process of 'drifting back to ordinary Hinduism'—a fate that has befallen every other reformed Hindu sect. But, writing as he was at the peak of the Sikh Sabhā movement, which he attributes to the 'new forces set in motion by the British Government, Christian missions and the Samajes', he views the future with

[10] J. N. Farquhar, *Modern Religious Movements in India,* New Delhi 1977 [1914], pp. 170-2.

considerable hope. He commends Macauliffe's translation of the *Ādi-Granth* and the reforming spirit.[11]

> By word and action they have shewn that they wish to revive the spirit of their military organizer, the tenth guru. They want to reincarnate the courage, the freedom and the independence of these days. They wish to be truly Sikhs. They realize that they must resist Hinduism as well as the Arya Samaj, if they are to escape from caste and the other social evils of the Hindu system.

The pessimistic sense that progressive reform movements in Hindu society are recidivist, and that the followers fail to maintain and individualise the original reform impulse and traditional Hindu practices and rituals, is a persistent motif in both Christian and ostensibly secular Western writings. It reappears as a major theme in the well-known work of F. E. Keay, *Kabir and His Followers*.

Keay's book is adapted from an academic dissertation and is free of overt missionary interest and quick analogies with Reformation figures or doctrines. He provides copious citations from poems by Kabīr (or attributed to him) in the *Ādi-Granth* and the *Bījak*, but no references are drawn from the Rajasthani sources.

The book is well known and is still read. After assessing the Kabīr legends, an attempt is made to discern the historical Kabīr, and ends with a sketch of Kabīr's religious beliefs. This sketch notes the uncertainties, the shifting moods and apparent inconsistencies in belief and ends with the line: 'He spoke out his mind fearlessly, and never made it his object

---

[11] Farquhar, *Modern Religious Movements*, pp. 340-2. Farquhar does make an observation on the Radhasoamis that is significant with hindsight: 'The practice of the sect is summed up in the phrase *Surat Sabd Yoga*, that is, union (*yoga*) of the human soul (*surat*) with the spirit-current or word (*sabda*). The methods employed are unknown: for they are imparted by the guru to the disciple under a vow of secrecy...' (p. 168). This draws our attention to the subsequent scholarship on the place of Kabīr's background in the doctrines and practices of the Nāth-Yoga and Buddhist tantrik traditions.

merely to please his hearers.'[13] Keay uses language drawn from Christian religious literature and discourse and briefly surveys the issues that arise given that frame of reference. Was Kabīr a monotheist or a monist? Did he have a doctrine of Creation? What was his judgement of idolatry, caste and asceticism? Keay is pleased with Kabīr's rejection of these traits, taken by most Western writers of that period as core elements of Hinduism. But he then, equally, emphasises Kabīr's continuing belief in *karma*, transmigration and *māyā*, and notes with approval that Macauliffe translated the word *māyā* as 'mammon', 'because it stands in Kabir-verse for what in Christian theology are called "the deceits of the world and the flesh"'. He also notes the female imagery used by Kabīr in speaking of *māyā*: 'an evil woman, a witch, who entangles men with her deceit.' But no mention is made of the specific *kanak-kāminī*, *mohinī* metaphors associating woman with the entrapments of lust and harlotry, drawn from a rich and extensive tradition of Hindu literature. Kabīr's moral righteousness, the centrality of death and the transitory nature of living-in-the-world, bhakti (understood as loving faith and devotion), the need of a guru, the spiritual value of the fellowship of the sants, and finally the doctrine of the power of *śabda* are all discussed with citations from the verses. This last is rendered as Divine Word, and Keay comments that it 'is not so much in evidence in the verses of Kabir himself as in the later writings of the *Kabir Panth*'.

But what makes Keay an indispensable source is his research on the followers, especially the then current doctrines of the organised Kabīr-panthīs. The doctrines of the Panth 'display a great "advance" on the teaching of Kabir':

> No doubt, modern leaders of this sect could prove by means of a 'doctrine of development' the agreement of their teaching with his system. There may be passages even in his genuine works here and there which might countenance some of the present teachings of the

[13] F. E. Keay, *Kabir and His Followers*, Calcutta and London 1931, p. 50.

> sect; but taken as a whole, it certainly differs greatly from what Kabir taught.[14]
>
> Not only has the sect now elaborate rites which are binding on its members, but the use of the rosary, and the practices which Kabir condemned, are now recognised as not only lawful but important. Moreover a sacramental system has been developed which is far removed from the ideas of Kabir.[15]

This last remark suggests an analogy in keeping with the assimilative understanding displayed in these writings, viz., that the 'sect' though born in high Reform zeal has now sunk into Counter-Reformation practices and casuistry! With deep regret Keay concedes that:

> Though Kabir did not directly preach the abolition of caste, he spoke against it, and the logical outcome of his teaching would be that it should cease. But in this direction, as in the case of other reformers in India, his efforts met with little success.[16]

Civilisational Difference and Assimilationist Interpretation

This overview indicates some persuasive themes. First, the judgement that the religious experience and literature of the Hindus is on the one hand diverse, but also, on the other hand, subject to distinct stages of a

---

[14] Keay, *Kabir and His Followers*, p. 143.

[15] Keay, *Kabir and His Followers*, p. 144.

[16] Keay, *Kabir and His Followers*, p. 109. Keay rounds out his study with a return look at Westcott's bold analogy, but with a different sense of its relevance: 'Kabir has sometimes been compared with Martin Luther; and though the comparison is not altogether a close one, it does help in some way to indicate the position Kabir holds.... He stands chiefly for the development of the non-idolatrous ideal of the bhakti movement, to which he certainly gave a great impetus. It is a tragedy that so few who have come under his influence have been able to live up to the ideals he set before them.' (p. 167-8)

progressive nature. The bhakti stage is indicative of a major developmental shift toward a religiosity recognising a personal commitment to a personal deity. Second, there is the theme of the emergence of an ethical or moral dimension to religiosity, relative to the traditional, more pervasively ritualistic/sacramental practices, involving the rejection of 'idolatry'. Third, appears a theme of universal access to salvific liberation independent of Brahmin mediation, and thus a rejection of *varṇa/jāti* rules and regulations, at least in religious matters. Fourth, these observers have emphasised the anticipation or expression of a 'theology of grace' and the corresponding centrality of faith in the bhakti movement, i.e the admission of distinction and separation of God and his creatures (humankind), with a consequent recognition of the insufficiency, for deliverance, of exclusively human methods. All these orientations, expressed in a mutually consistent manner, lead to a positive evaluation of bhakti as a stage or social movement, and of Kabīr as a major, relatively early figure, even whilst admitting his singularity, his harshness, and the apparently contradictory and shifting contours of his beliefs and doctrines. This was a period of reform and improvement, and these were figures who challenged the received tradition and were religious innovators. The analogy with the Reformation is pertinent in this regard.

The absence of organised religious wars, and uprisings against ruling authorities and orthodox Brahmanical religious and social institutions—all contrasting with the European experience—is not noted. Attention is not drawn toward the cultural milieu and the associated thought patterns and normative understandings regulating religious life. The social, political and cultural management of heterodoxy, dissent and 'alternative' religiosities over the preceding centuries is not investigated beyond noting narratives in which there is mention of sectional attempts by Hindu priests and Muslim mullas to denounce Kabīr and to get him condemned by the political authorities—apparently failed attempts.

This lacuna was partially redressed in the decades during and after the 1920s, in the context of an active nationalist political movement and related researches into the history and development of the vernacular languages and their literatures. Grierson and Keay had written on the historical development of Hindi language and literature, but the engagement of Indian scholars in this research programme brought about a sharp shift in our understanding of Kabīr in particular, and the set of bhakti figures in general. This entire process, continuing into the present, may be understood as a process of 'indigenisation': involving a 'decolonisation' of intellectual resources after a century of education regulated by the infamous Macaulay Minute. The source of the stimulus for this change lies, in part, in research into the antecedents of Bengali literature, vigorously explored since the closing years of the nineteenth century. These studies influenced Kshiti Mohan Sen, and through him Rabindranath Tagore, but the enquiry into Indian mysticism undertaken by this group was still governed by modes of thought shaped by the assimilationist ferment of the currents dubbed the 'Indian Renaissance' by British Orientalists[17] and their Indian epigones. However, in the hands of Hazariprasad Dvivedi it fertilised Hindi studies on Kabīr, reinforcing understandings already suggested by Pitambar Datt Barthwal. Subsequent developments re-orienting Kabīr studies are well known. For present purposes, we need only to focus on the deep dependence they demonstrated of Kabīr's formative experience, understanding and deployment of language on the doctrines and practices of the Nāth *sampradāya*, and in particular their specific yogic theories and corresponding practices for the realisation of self-transcendence and transubstantiation, and liberation from the web of *māyā* and corruption (material and moral) including the fear of mortality and its corporeal effect. It remained for Shasibhushan Dasgupta to demonstrate both the substantive presence of the Nāth yoga tradition in Bengal, and its ambivalent relation to the much older Bengali tradition of tantrik Buddhism around the spiritual leadership of the Siddhas, and the quest for the attainment of the *siddhi* state of being, a state realisable in corporeal form.[18] These currents of religiosity, though perhaps 'obscure' during the

---

[17] In recent years 'Orientalism' in Indian studies has been much criticised, but the focus has been on the 'construction of Hinduism' or on 'caste'; the notion of an Indian 'renaissance' around Rammohan Roy, however, is also an Orientalist construction which still awaits 'deconstruction'.

[18] S. B. Dasgupta, *Obscure Religious Cults*, reprint of 3rd ed., Calcutta 1976

nineteenth century, had a substantial influence during and after the eleventh century, and are related to the diffusion of tantrik Buddhism to Tibet by Bengali monks and considerable Tibeto-Bengali cultural interaction in those centuries. In a later study Dasgupta demonstrated the linkage between the Siddhas and the much earlier Mahāyāna traditions including works ascribed to Nāgārjuna.[19] This non-brahminical popular religious mode was *nirguṇa* in its understanding of the ultimate ground of Being and the condition of transcending *māyā*. It attached great significance to the repetition of *śabda*s or *mantra*s that were deliberately 'meaningless' (which may be understood as 'free' of the semantic connotations of the *saguṇa* phenomenal world, both social and natural) so as to aid in the concentration required to reverse the flow of certain 'powers' and corporeal 'fluids' (material and subtle) away from the downward channels to the upward channel, thus leading the *kuṇḍalinī* to release through the *brahmarandhra*. Such *śabda*s in their repetition also served to remind the practitioner of the 'void' nature of that which is beyond the phenomenal.

It is not necessary to elaborate these considerations for present purposes. Only three significant conclusions of Shashibhushan Dasgupta need to be reaffirmed. One is his insistence that there is a common matrix of shared understandings and conceptualisations underlying an entire spectrum of religious practices and communities embracing Buddhists, Śaktas, Śaivas and Vaiṣṇavas and including the Nāths, Bauls, and Dharma cult of rural Bengal. This common matrix was one of yogic and tantrik ideas about self-transformation, transubstantiation, transfiguration affecting the totality of corporeal, psychic and 'subtle' sheaths of human being. Second, the shared feature of also transforming the ordered semantic space of the language used. Hence the inversions of standard conventional images and icons, which relate to the inversion of reverse-flow of 'powers' and fluids sought through well-defined practices

---

[[1]1946], pp. 229-50 and Appendix A, pp. 345-66.

[19] S. B. Dasgupta, *Introduction to Tantrik Buddhism*, Berkeley 1974 [[1]1950].

including concentrated meditation. Third and most important, the dependence of the understanding of religiosity, conduct, and inner mental conditions in terms of a homology between the human body (in this larger and specific Hindu sense which includes all non-physical dimensions of individual human being) and the cosmos or manifest 'body' of the ultimate source of being. That this complex of thought-forms and practices is distinct from mainstream, orthodox 'brahmanical' social practices and institutions can be easily assumed, since these beliefs, categories, and practices are clearly *asocial* in both content and implication. They are matters of interior attitudes, mental orientations, and personal practices, performable individually, domestically or in small circles. One could withdraw from the 'normal' social order surrounding one as in a traditionally understood 'renunciation', or remain embedded in the social world—inner-worldly—but dispositionally distanced, in quest of an interiorised transcendence (metaphorically, one would be 'living-as-if-dead'). It would be more appropriate to view Kabīr as having attempted a singular version of the latter: a mode of being rendered possible in, and by, a civilisational matrix that has its own distinctive grammar of generative possibilities. But if this particular modal possibility is generalised through an invitation to universal participation, as the sole 'true' realisation, exclusive of other 'erroneous' modes trapped in *bhrama* and *māyā*, it would meet with both direct and indirect impersonal resistance. Eventually, it would be re-positioned as a distinctive *sampradāya* consonant with the cultural grammar that generated it. This appears to be what has happened to the followers of Kabīr.[20]

The suggestion I am making is that we recognise in the study of different human civilisations that they are distinct at several constitutive levels. An analogy with language may be used as a 'model': languages have lexical, semantic and syntactical features, and their structure

---

[20] The most telling observation in this regard, is the Kabīr-panthīs' participation in the well-ordered procession of bathing during the Kumbhamelā. Agehananda Bharati, *Hindu Views and Ways and the Hindu-Muslim Interface*, Santa Barbara 1982, p. 79.

therefore is complex, where first-order rules and constraints have to be distinguished from second-order and third-order rules and constraints. Lexical borrowing is relatively easy and 'enriches' a language; semantic shifts and transformations occur but less flexibly, and laden with chains of connotations that vary between languages; syntax is deeply resilient and syntactical changes are rare, and few, if any, examples of syntactical syncretism are available. Comparative linguistics seeks its results in the search for linguistic universals at various structural levels and domains of the complex phenomenon that is language. Without suggesting that 'civilisations' or 'cultures' are structured exactly as are languages, it is possible that they have features that are structured as 'codes' or modalities at distinguishable levels. These may be, for example, distinct 'modes' of philosophising, at the level of form, rather than the substantive semantic content of philosophical doctrines.[21] The accounts given of the coming-into-being of what there is, are variant across different civilisations, and the 'syntactical' difference this makes affects the 'semantics' of the religiosity and the 'lexicals' of terms, concepts, associated artifacts, social and personal practices, etc. This is why the assimilationist risk is real and not fanciful. As a human being and a scholar one can, of course, 'learn' the operative 'codes' and constitutive rules of different civilisations, just as we can learn the grammars and lexicons of different languages, but it requires an effort that goes beyond lexical translation skills, itself a difficult task.

How is this relevant to Kabīr? I think in at least two recognisable ways. First we have the problem of Kabīr as both poet and mystic. It is entirely appropriate that the 'text' of Kabīr be read in various translations

---

[21] One recent example of such a methodology applied to the study of Indian philosophy is David B. Zilberman, *The Birth of Meaning in Hindu Thought*, Dordrecht 1989. The issues I am pointing out are also at the centre of cross-cultural inquiries in many domains, from linguistics through philosophy to comparative jurisprudence. The research programme implicit in the suggestion is discussed, amongst others, by Fritz Staal in *Universals: Studies in Indian Logic and Linguistics*, Chicago 1988.

by people of different cultures and civilisations, and his singularity, originality and style will elicit positive reader-response. A powerful poet lives through translation, across cultural and civilisational divides. The appropriation of Kabīr through these means will be variant, depending on the culture, ideology, literary sophistication and personal situation of the reader. However, if one is to assess Kabīr's mysticism and the content of his religious message, further demands are placed on the reader, beyond the literary-aesthetic experience. The *ulaṭbāṃsī* verses will need to be read not merely as playfulness and startling imagery but also as *sāndhā-bhāṣā* or coded references to tantrik and yogic understandings of overcoming *māyā* and mortality. The summum of mystical experience as an experiential mode of egoless-ness may be a common experience of all mystics, but such claims, correct or not, do not erase the discursive and methodological contexts that are different. Second, there has been in the recent period much use of Kabīr in the furtherance of political and social reform agendas. These discussions have a strongly assimilative character. In their specific way they are not much different from the missionary and 'orientalist' uses. The quest for a social reformer Kabīr is much like Kabīr as a Reform theologian—the ideological cloth is different, but both are woven out of threads and use designs located in the historical experience of Western civilisation. The long shadow of apocalyptic and eschatological concerns in the Judeo-Christian traditions, and in Eastern Mediterranean monotheisms more generally, itself dependent on a particular account of Creation, Fall, and Redemption, have no parallels in Hindu-Buddhist civilisation. Their secularised ideological representations are also incommensurate with modes of envisioning 'welfare' and 'justice' in the human condition in the Hindu-Buddhist historical context. Of course Islam did make available some of the shared understandings, the distinctive religious grammar or code, of the Eastern Mediterranean monotheisms, and it is precisely this context that allows Kabīr to realise and present a path to mystical understanding and experience that interiorises to an even greater extent than in his Nāth and bhakti sources. But he remains a liberator in the larger sense of the mystic, rather than an activist of institutional social change. The 'diamond' he sought, and recommended to others, was the object of a quest made possible by the good fortune of a human birth. Single-minded pursuit and internal purity was required, if one were to avoid the fate of the fly in the molasses. Changing the quantity or distribution of the molasses would not get it flying. The criticism and rejection of *mūrti-pūjā*, canonical learning, pilgrimage, ritual purifications, Brahmin pride, all had to do with avoidance of *bhrama*, erroneous understanding of the way out of bondage to *māyā*, and consequent triumph over mortality and *saṃsāra*. Many of those subject to these 'false beliefs' would surely have been low-caste people seeking solace and *puṇya* with little grounds for the 'false pride' of the Brahman or *qāẕī*. But Kabīr taunts them all. He seems to have a strong conviction that in following such practices one is squandering a fortune. The low-caste and impoverished are not exempt. The universality Kabīr took as evident was that of human birth, the necessary condition for the supreme bliss and self-transcendence. Denial of this equality is combated with the force of his sarcasm, vivid analogies and irony. But proposals for self-assertive individuality and legalist claims to material opportunities and enjoyments would, I suspect, be viewed by Kabīr as tragic *ahaṃkāra*.

It is important that we take Kabīr at his word and in his context. He extends an invitation to an experience and a mode of being-in-the-world that both liberates us from *māyā* and *moha*, and is supremely blissful.

was required, if one were to avoid the fate of the fly in the molasses. Changing the quantity or distribution of the molasses would not get it flying. The criticism and rejection of *karm-kand*, canonical learning, pilgrimage, ritual purifications, Brahmin pride, all had to do with avoidance of *bhram*, erroneous understanding, of the way out of bondage to *maya* and consequent triumph over mortality and *samsara*. Many of those subject to these 'false' beliefs would surely have been low caste people seeking solace and *phal* with little gainsaying the 'false pride' of the Brahman or *qazi*. But Kabir faults them all. He seems to have a strong conviction that in following such practices one is squandering a fortune. The low-caste and impoverished are not exempt. The universality Kabir took as evident was that of human birth, the necessary condition for the supreme bliss and self-transcendence. Denial of this equality is combated with the force of his sarcasm, vivid analogies and irony. But propositions for self-assertive individuality and legalist claims to material opportunities and endowments would, I suspect, be viewed by Kabir as tragic *ahamkara*.

It is important that we take Kabir at his word and in his context. He extends an invitation to an experience and a mode of being-in-the-world that both liberates us from *maya* and *moha* and is supremely blissful.

Marco Della Tomba and the Kabīr-Panth

David N. Lorenzen

The Italian Capuchin friar Marco Della Tomba, born in 1726 as Pietro Girolamo Agresti, arrived in Pondicherry in 1757. From there he travelled to Chandernagore and in 1758 set out for Patna and the small state of Bettiah on the border of Nepal. Apart from two years spent in Chatrapur and several short stays in Patna, he was mostly in Bettiah until his return to Italy in 1773. He returned to north India in 1786, and died at Bhagalpur on 18 March 1803. He was one of many Capuchin friars who joined the Franciscan Mission to north India, Nepal and Tibet during the eighteenth century. Most of these friars, like Marco, came from the Marches region of eastern central Italy.

Marco's papers are now stored in the Vatican library. In 1878 Angelo de Gubernatis published some of them, with his own forty-two page introduction, as *Gli scritti del padre Marco della Tomba, missionario nelle Indie orientali*. In spite of this, however, Marco's writings have since been mostly ignored. My own curiosity was sparked by Charlotte Vaudeville's brief discussion of Marco's contacts with the Kabīr-panth in her 1974 book on Kabīr.[1] Otherwise, the only scholarly discussions of his work are two articles mostly concerned with the identification of two Aśokan pillars mentioned by Marco[2] and, more interesting, a 1989 article by Umberto Nardella about eighteenth- and nineteenth-century studies of the Hindi language by Italian friars and

[1] Charlotte Vaudeville, *Kabir*, Oxford 1974, pp. 5-6.

[2] Chiara Silvi Antonini, 'Della "Piccola descrizione dell'India Orientale o Induistan" di Marco Della Tomba', in: Ugo Marazzi (ed.), *La conoscenza dell'Asia e dell'Africa in Italia nei secoli XVIII e XIX*, vol. 1, tomo 1. Napoli: Istituto Universitario Orientale, 1984; H. Hosten, 'Padre Marco della Tomba and the Asoka pillars near Bettiah', *Journal of the Asiatic Society of Bengal*, 8.3, 1912, pp. 109-13.

scholars.[3] An important source on the eighteenth-century Franciscan Mission, but not Marco himself, is Luciano Petech's (1952-56) seven volume collection of selected writings by various Italian friars (including the well-known Jesuit, Ippolito Desideri) who stayed mostly in Nepal and Tibet, rather than in India.

Among the friars of this mission who worked mostly in India several others besides Marco deserve further study. One of the earliest was Francesco Maria da Tours, a Capuchin friar of French origin who left for India in 1680 and died in Patna in 1709. According to Nardella, he is the author of a Hindustani and Latin dictionary.[4] Another is Marco's Capuchin companion, Giuseppe Maria da Gargnano (born Bernadino Bernini). He arrived in north India in 1739, staying in Chandernagore, Patna and Bettiah before arriving in Lhasa in 1742. He eventually stayed in Bettiah from 1749 until his death in 1761. Marco was there in 1758-1759 and returned in 1761 when Giuseppe Maria was dying. Giuseppe Maria is the author of two imagined religious dialogues between a Christian and a Hindu. One of these was written in 1751 in both Hindi and Italian versions.[5] Another companion of Giuseppe Maria, the friar Cassiano Beligatti da Macerata, wrote a biography of Giuseppe Maria that was published in 1767.[6] Finally there is the Capuchin friar Costanzo da Borgo San Sepolcro, who joined the mission in 1775. In the year 1787, he recopied the Hindi version of Giuseppe Maria da Gargnano's Christian-

---

[3] Umberto Nardella, 'La conoscenza dell'Hindi e Urdu in Italia nei secoli XVIII e XIX', in: Aldo Gallotta and Ugo Marazzi (eds.), *La conoscenza dell'Asia e dell'Africa in Italia nei secoli XVIII e XIX,* vol. 3, tomo 1, Napoli: Istituto Universitario Orientale, 1989, pp. 5-72.

[4] Nardella, 'La conoscenza', p. 10.

[5] Nardella, 'La conoscenza', p. 54.

[6] Cassiano da Macerata, *Memorie Istoriche della virtù, viaggj, e fatiche del P. Giuseppe Maria de' Bernini da Gargnano...* Verona: Moroni Press, 1767. I have been able to locate a published copy of this rare book in St. Bonaventure University Library in New York. A typescript of the book together with an English translation is found among the papers of Henry Hosten in the Vidyajoti College Library in Delhi.

Hindu dialogue and added his own word-for-word and regular prose translations of the text into Italian.[7]

In terms of its proselytistic objectives, the eighteenth-century Franciscan Mission to Tibet, Nepal, and north India was largely a failure. Despite the fervid religious dedication of the friars, and the investment of many years of effort and much money, the number of Christian converts remained small. The missionaries' own accounts of their struggles against Hindu and Buddhist idolatry make it clear that even these few converts were in constant 'danger' of returning to their original Hindu beliefs and practices. After the mission stopped sending new friars to India in the early nineteenth century, most of the miniscule Christian communities it had created withered away, although the community established at Bettiah still survives.[8]

More significant than the successes and failures of these Franciscans to convert the Hindus, from our point of view at least, are the writings that the friars left about what they saw and what they thought about what they saw. These writings represent one of the first deep cultural encounters between India and the West. More interesting still, Marco and most of the other Franciscan friars operated in areas where British armies had not yet entered and at the time that the political influence of the British was still in its initial stages, even in Bengal. It is not unfair to see these friars both as independent agents, free from any

---

[7] Most of this information is based on Luciano Petech, *I Missionari Italiani nel Tibet e nel Nepal* (vol. 2 of Nuovo Ramusio), Roma: Libraria dello Stato, 1952-6, part 1. I have obtained a microfilm of Costanzo da Borgo San Sepolcro's manuscript and have prepared a draft translation of this text. A much revised edition of this Hindi dialogue was published at Bettiah in 1907, but this volume appears to no longer be available anywhere. See also FlugentiusVannini, *Hindustan-Tibet Mission*, New Delhi 1981.

[8] Father Jose Kalapura, S. J., has recently written a Ph. D. dissertation for the Sociology Department of Jawaharlal Nehru University about this community. The responsibility for the community was transferred to the Jesuits in 1922. The surviving documents of the community were then transferred to the archives of the Capuchin Ashram in Agra. The present-day members of the community regard Giuseppe Maria da Gargnano, under the name Joseph Mary Bernini, as their founder.

direct imperial entanglements, and, at the same time, advance scouts preparing the way for the coming penetration of Western culture into the region.

One of Marco Della Tomba's most remarkable feats was to translate several religious texts written in different Hindi dialects, and at least one written in Sanskrit, into Italian. Several of these translations are included in de Gubernatis's edited volume. While reading these translations, I discovered something quite unexpected. Among the compositions that Marco translated were two chapters of a work identified as the *Ramaen.* De Gubernatis included the chapter entitled 'Libro di Lanka' in his collection, but he omitted and does not name the other chapter. De Gubernatis claims that this *Rāmāyaṇa* is different from the famous *Rāmcaritmānas* composed by Tulsīdās. In his introduction, de Gubernatis discusses the importance of Tulsīdās's text and notes that Growse had published an English translation of this text the previous year (i.e. in about 1876 or 1877). Then de Gubernatis says (pp. xlvi-xlvii): 'But another *Rāmāyana* existed, associated with the Kabīr sect in the northeast provinces of India, at Bettiah. This Kabirian text was the one that our Marco had in his hands.' ('Ma un altro *Rāmāyana* esisteva presso la setta dei Kabiri nelle provincie nord-est dell'India, a Betia; questo testo kabirico ebbe nelle sue mani il nostro Marco....')

Taking her lead from de Gubernatis, Charlotte Vaudeville correctly recognized the importance of Marco to the study of the Kabīr-panth, but also accepted his mistaken identification of Marco's *Rāmāyana* as a Kabīr-panthi text. She says: 'Padre Marco did in fact translate into Italian a particular *Ramaen* (*Ramayana*) in eight (and not seven) books which appear to be a "Cabirist" (i.e. Kabīr-panthī) version of the Ramayana legend, in which Rama appears as a great penitent and ascetic resembling the Buddha.'[9] In his 1989 article on the early study of Hindi

[9] Charlotte Vaudeville, *Kabir,* Oxford 1974, pp. 5-6. It is not clear why Vaudeville made this comparison between Rām and the Buddha. She repeats the same statement almost verbatim in her later book, *A Weaver Named Kabir*, Delhi 1993, p. 15.

by Italian scholars, Umberto Nardella explicitly accepted Vaudeville's judgment about the text's Kabīr-panthī associations.[10]

On reading through Marco's translation, however, I was surprised to find almost nothing that could connect it with the Kabīr-panth apart from a couple of references to the god Kāl (pp. 129, 135 and 141). Becoming curious, I began a line by line comparison of Marco's 'Libro di Lanka' with the Lanka chapter of Tulsīdās's *Rāmcaritmānas.* It immediately became clear that Marco's translation was in fact based directly on Tulsīdās and not on any otherwise unknown Kabīr-panthī *Rāmāyana*. Even the references to Kal are present in that text. Most likely, Marco's unpublished translation of a second chapter of the *Ramaen* is also based on Tulsī's text, although I have not yet had the opportunity to confirm this in Marco's papers in the Vatican library.

What all this means, of course, is that Marco deserves the credit, by a wide margin, of being the earliest translator of major parts of Tulsī's *Rāmcaritmānas* into a European language. Marco's translation of the 'Laṅka-kāṇḍ' into Italian was done in 1764.[11] In the bibliography of Charlotte Vaudeville's book on the sources of the *Rāmcaritmānas*, the oldest listed European translation of a substantial section of this text is a French translation of the 'Sundar-kāṇḍ' by Garcin de Tassy, published in 1847, eighty-three years after Marco made his 'Laṅkā-kāṇḍ' translation. The first English translation of a substantial section of Tulsī's text is one of the 'Ayodhyā-kāṇḍ' by Adalut Khan, published in Calcutta in 1871. A few years later, in 1876, F. S. Growse published some excerpts of an English translation in the *Journal of the Asiatic Society of Bengal.* Growse's complete English translation was first published from Allahabad between the years 1877 and 1881.

In Nardella's 1989 article (p. 66), there is a facsimile reproduction of the first page of the original manuscript of Marco's translation of the 'Libro di Lanka'. From this, one can see that the manuscript contains not only the translation but also the original Hindi text in *kaithī* script. This was presumably copied for Marco's benefit from an older manuscript sometime not long before 1764. Although there exist many older

[10] Nardella, 'La conoscenza', pp. 24-6.

[11] Nardella, 'La conoscenza', p. 25.

manuscripts of Tulsīdās's *Rāmcaritmānas,* Marco's still belongs to an early stage of the manuscript tradition. According to Vaudeville, the earliest dated manuscript of Tulsī's text is one in the collection of the Maharaja of Banaras, dated 1704 VS.[12] Evident differences between Marco's text and the now standard Gita Press edition of the *Rāmcaritmānas*—for instance, the long interpolation in Marco's Lanka text between *dohā 16* and *sorṭhā* 16—suggest that a closer study not only of Marco's translation, but also of his original Hindi text, would be a worthwhile exercise. As is well known, a good critical edition of Tulsīdās's text is an important task that still has not been attempted.

At least two of the Hindi texts Marco translated from Hindi into Italian—the *Mūlpañjī* and the *Jñānsāgar* (or *Gyānsāgar*)—are associated directly with the Kabīr-panth. Both translations are included in de Gubernatis's collection. Marco had established close contacts with members of the Kabīr-panth in Bettiah, a region where the panth is still popular, and some of these Kabīr-panthīs evidently introduced him to their sectarian literature and encouraged him to read these texts. Nardella includes facsimile first pages of Marco's manuscripts of both these texts. As in the case of the 'Libro di Lanka', the manuscripts contain copies of the original Hindi texts in *kaithī* script together with the translations. The *kaithī* script of all three texts is quite similar, but it seems likely that they were copied by three different persons, all of whom were Indians. Perhaps these same persons helped Marco with the translations. In this work they may have used the local Bhojpuri of Bettiah as their common language, but the Hindu-Christian dialogue composed by Marco's colleague, Giuseppe Maria da Gargnano, in 1751 is written in a form of Hindustani quite close to modern standard Hindi.

Of these two Kabīr-panthī texts, the best known is the *Jñānsāgar.* It was first edited and published early in this century by Yugalānand Bihārī as the first in his eleven volume *Kabīr-sāgar*. It has been in print

[12] Manuscript 072 in the Kabīr Caurā library manuscript collection bears the date 1663 VS at the end, but this is probably a mistake for 1863 since the date 1862 VS appears elsewhere in the same manuscript. See David N. Lorenzen, *A Catalog of Manuscripts in the Kabir Chaura Monastery,* expanded edition, Mexico City: El Colegio de México, 1998, pp. 61-2.

almost continually ever since. The collection of about 250 manuscripts stored in the Kabīr Caurā library in Banaras contains two copies of this text (nos. 240 and 242): one dated sometime between 1870 and 1879 VS (i.e between 1813 and 1822 CE) and one dated 1794 VS (1737 CE). The fact that the *Jñānsāgar* is more clearly associated with the Dharmdāsī branch of the Kabīr-panth, rather than with the Kabīr Caurā branch, probably explains why more manuscript copies are not found in this library. A comparison of parts of these two manuscript texts with Yugalānand's published text, the Hindi text of the facsimile first page of Marco's manuscript, and Marco's published translation, shows that the textual variants among all of them are relatively insignificant. Furthermore, a close comparison of the translation with the Hindi text shows that, while Marco sometimes misinterprets the original text—mistakes that are not surprising given the difficulties and ambiguities of the language—on the whole his translation is accurate. It is also clear in many places that Marco gives a decidedly Christian twist to the translation of some Hindi terms such as his rendering of *mukti* as '*gloria permanente*'—but what else should one expect from a Christian friar in this period?

In addition to his translations Marco wrote several essays about the religion of the 'gentiles', i.e. the Hindus, and on his own adventures in India. Several of these are included in de Gubernatis's collection. One entitled 'Diversi sistemi della religione dell'Indostano e regni circonvicini' (pp. 69-98), written in 1766, sets out Marco's appreciation of the basic beliefs and practices of the Hindus and their various sects including the Kabīr-panth and the religious system of the Sikhs. About the followers of the Kabīr-panth, he says the following (pp. 94-7):

> There is a sect or type of religious persons called *Cabiristi*, who are followers of a certain Cabir, a man considered to be a great saint who performed many miracles. They say that he was the spiritual master of Alexander the Great. About this sect I could say a great deal, because they are in great esteem and number. Since, however, I have translated line by line their book called '*Sat naus Cabir*' [i.e. the *Jñānsāgar*], one can read about them there without my having to repeat the same things here. At the end of this book, is found another of their books, called the *Mulpancì* [*i.e.* the *Mūlpañjī*] (road of the root), in which their systems can also be examined.

> These fakirs are seculars [*i.e.* monks who follow a rule]. They wear a necklace of small beads of wood, this being their distinctive mark, and some other symbols on their foreheads. They eat neither meat nor fish, being rigorous followers of the opinion that all the animals belong to the same species. For this reason they do not even kill their lice and take care to not step on the ants on their path, etc. They have permission to eat greens and pulses, in spite of the fact that these plants bear fruits, because they say that need supercedes rules.
>
> They do no believe in any particular God, but argue that God is nothing other than the generative power [*virtù*] of all the things of this world. In order to prove this principle, they are obliged to say nefarious things. In making their profession of faith, they swear to retain their semen [*in materiam decidentem*] and keep it in hand, promising not to release it, and, if released, to eat it. They have, however, wives and children. This sort of fakirs are not very improper [*impertinenti*]. ... This sect of *Cabiristi* do not establish monasteries, but are otherwise like secular [monks].

There are one or two comments that need to be made about this passage. First is the identification of Kabīr as the spiritual master of Alexander the Great. During the eighteenth century, among the best known sources of knowledge about India were the classical accounts of Alexander's raid into northwestern India, what is now Pakistan. Marco and other early European visitors were always on the lookout for local evidence to corroborate and expand the story of Alexander's Indian adventures. Marco's own fascination with this topic is also evident in his mistaken association of the Aśokan pillars that he saw in Bettiah with Alexander. Marco had undoubtedly heard the well-known legend of Kabīr's encounter with the Afghan Sultan named Sikandar Lodi. The name Sikandar is, of course, a Persian form of Alexander. This, I would guess, is at least one of the sources of Marco's evident confusion about when and where Alexander was in India.

Another curious feature of this passage is Marco's description of the marital and sexual habits of the Kabīr-panthīs. Today Kabīr's followers are divided into two clearly separate groups: the lay *bhagat*s who marry and follow the lifestyles of their respective castes, and the celibate sadhus who both wander about and live for more or less long periods in the monasteries of the Panth. Only a few *mahant*s of the Dharmdāsī branch are allowed to be full-time religious professionals and also marry. Unfortunately, there is very little direct evidence of the existence of Kabīr-panthī monasteries and sadhus before the latter part of the eighteenth century. Kabīr-panthī tradition, on the other hand, claims that even Kabīr himself had become a sadhu. Marco's description seems to conflate the two categories of *bhagat*s and sadhus. According to him, the Kabīr-panthī men are nominally celibate but in fact marry and have children. Also, he claims, they do not live in monasteries. All this is difficult to square with the present-day customs of the Panth.

Another problem is Marco's curious description of the sexual practices of the Kabīr-panthī men. Although the Italian and Latin of the passage is ambiguous, my Italian friends insist that it must refer to some sort of control over seminal emissions. The traditional Indian practice that first comes to mind is, of course, the *vajrolī-mudrā* of Haṭha Yoga, but the descriptions of *vajrolī-mudrā* never suggest that one should eat one's own semen. One can only assume that here Marco misunderstood what his informants had told him.

The rest of Marco's account of the *Cabiristi* is devoted to their concept of God and the creation. It appears to be based mostly on his own translation of the *Jñānsāgar*:

> Their visible God is a certain *Naraen* [=Nārāyaṇa]; and in addition another who is called *Nirangen* [=Nirañjan], that is, the instrument by means of whom God wills the creation of the world. When [Nirañjan] found that he was not capable of this task, he asked for the help (as is described in their book the *Mulpancì)*, with the permission of Naraen, or God, of one of his [=God's?] sixteen sons. God granted permission to one of the sixteen sons, called *Curumb* [=Kurmā], and to him God gave the order to give Nirangen the eggs to create the world. This Curumb had four heads, and his body was nine strides in length. Before [Nirañjan and Kurmā] would accept each other, a great battle was held in which Nirangen cut off three of Curumb's heads. Afterwards, with these three heads he formed the five elements, that is, the four elements and the void. From these all the rest of the things of this world were created one by one. In the battle Nirangen sweated a great deal, and from his sweat he formed the sea and the fish, and from

> other drops of sweat he formed another ninety-four crores of earth. He made the sun and the moon and 900,000 stars, that are all of the essence of God himself, because they arose from the three heads of Curumb, son of God. [They also have] many other stories that one should know. Having done this, Nirangen remained there thinking, not knowing how to populate the three worlds, that is, heaven, earth and hell. Then he went to God and performed penance for 768 years. God told him to go to Nacarnour, where he would find a virgin with eight arms, whose name was the eternal *Bavani* [=Bhavānī]. This virgin contained in herself the root of 84 lakhs of souls (one lakh is equal to one hundred thousand), from which creatures of different sorts would be produced. For this reason Nirangen went there and saw the virgin. Fearing to lose her, he swallowed her alive. God became angry because of this and gave Nirangen a punishment, of having to eat 125,000 souls every day for as long as the world endures, and even so never getting satisfied. Then God, being inclined against Nirangen, agreed to a request by Curumb who demanded vengeance for the loss of his three heads. God then created a certain Giorjit [?=Jogajit] to go and kill Nirangen. They fought a great battle, but Curumb threw him down, and removed the swallowed virgin from his belly. Then Nirangen considered his deeds, and from this thought Cal [=Kāl] arose, the king of death.

This curious myth is an accurate enough reflection of what is written in the *Jñānsāgar*, but the text gives only one of several quite different Kabīr-panthī accounts of how the world was created. All the alternate accounts feature the God Nirañjan, also called Kāl, as the effective creator of the physical universe. Although Nirañjan is the name of the supreme God in much *nirguṇī* literature, and even in some early songs attributed to Kabīr, in Kabīr-panthī texts this god is a secondary, partly evil, figure who is subordinate to the supreme Satpuruṣ and to the Satguru and his various incarnations. But that is another story.

In Marco Della Tomba, then, we have one of the first Europeans to live for an extended period in north India, the first European translator of Tulsīdās's *Rāmcaritmānas*, the earliest European scholar of the Kabīr-panth and its literature, and one of the earliest Europeans to write about the people, places, monuments, and religious beliefs and practices of northern India. I am currently working on a more complete study of

Marco Della Tomba and some of the other Christian friars of the eighteenth-century Franciscan Mission to north India and hope to be able to say more about them in the not too distant future.

Kabīr's *pads* in 1556

Winand M. Callewaert

The Popularity of Kabīr in 1556

In 1556 Akbar ascended the Mughal throne in Agra, two generations after Kabīr may have died in Banaras. For the dates of Kabīr (traditionally he is said to have lived for 120 years, till 1519), I am rather inclined to accept the dates proposed by David Lorenzen: c. 1450-1518. Even 68 years may have been a relatively long life for a (poor) weaver in Banaras in those days. The first attested written documents with his sayings/songs are dated 1572, written no doubt within the ongoing oral tradition. I argue that

> (1) Kabīr very soon was 'appropriated' by interested parties (from the Gorakhnāthīs and the Rāmānandīs in the seventeenth century to Brahmins like Hazari Prasad Dvivedi in the twentieth century) for their own ideological purpose or benefit. The corpus of songs with Kabīr's name increased accordingly. This may be compared with the situation of Mīrābāī (c. 1503-46) who may have composed one hundred songs: at the end of the twentieth century there should be as many as 5,197 songs in her name.[1]

> (2) Among the *pads* in the *Vāṇī* of Kabīr we can earmark those that may have been popular in the repertoires around 1556, that is two generations after the death of Kabīr and one generation before the first manuscripts still preserved now were written. Norm is here defined as 'occurrence' of a *pad* in Punjab and/or Rajasthan.

---

[1] See W.M. Callewaert, 'The "Earliest" Song of Mira (1503-1546)', *Annali*, Istituto Universitario Orientale, Napoli, vol. 50. 4, 1990, pp. 363-78.

When all is said and done, the question remains, how could Kabīr become so charismatic that many devotees, possibly during his lifetime and definitely after his death, were happy to insert his name as *bhāṇitā* in their own compositions and let those songs circulate with his name, not their own? What was his genius that eventually was changed into a social consciousness strongly influencing later generations? If in the twentieth century many singers may perhaps not even know who Kabīr actually was, why are they so happy to include their own compositions in the repertoires that are performed in his name? What we have here is a social strategy by which certain ideas are promoted using the charismatic name of a person who died long ago, who may not even have supported the ideas that are now spread in his name. If the singers in Rajasthan recorded by Bahadur Singh[2] are sponsored by Brahmins, as they are, their songs will not be as outspoken in their criticism of Brahmins as Kabīr was. It is the search for that charisma that keeps haunting me and encourages me to look for a 'Kabīr' we may still be able to define, that is the person who was popular in 1556. The only way to do that is to look at the songs that were popular in 1556[3] and may have a chance of having been composed and sung by him.

---

[2] See pp. 191-8 in this volume.

[3] This exercise in no way shows disrespect for the translators of Kabīr who find inspiration and aesthetic joy in what 'he' wrote.

List of extant manuscripts and texts

These are available with me on film. I give also the date of the manuscripts and the number of *pads* of Kabīr found in them:[4]

MANUSCRIPTS (IN CHRONOLOGICAL ORDER)		NUMBER OF *PADS*
M	*Mohan Pothī* of 1570-72	50 (2 are not in the *Ādi-granth*)
F	Fatehpur manuscript of 1582	15
AG	*Ādi-granth* of 1604	220 (89 are 'unique')
S	*Pañca-vāṇī* manuscript of 1614 (S. Sharma)	370
	The *Pañca-vāṇī* manuscripts S, A, V have more or less the same *rāg*-order, and that corresponds more or less to the Nāgarī Pracāriṇī Sabhā (hereafter: Sa) edition of Śyām Sundar Dās	
A	*Pañca-vāṇī* manuscript of 1675	393
Gop	*Sarvāṅgī* by Gopāldās of 1627 (MS of 1724)	352 (10 are 'unique')
Raj	*Sarvāṅgī* by Rajab (ca. 1620?; MS of 1744[5])	151 (4 are 'unique' and 22 not found in Gop)
V	*Pañca-vāṇī* manuscript of 1658	348

[4] For a detailed description of these manuscripts and their characteristics, see Winand M. Callewaert and Mukund Lath (eds., trs.), *The Hindī Songs of Nāmdev* (Orientalia Lovanensia Analecta 29), Leuven 1989 (also Delhi 1989), pp. 82ff.

[5] See MS E in Winand M. Callewaert (ed., tr.), *The* Sarvāṅgī *of the Dādūpanthī Rajab* (Orientalia Lovanensia Analecta 4), Leuven 1978, p. 93; for the date of the Rajab *Sarvāṅgī*, pp. 73 ff.

J	manuscript of 1681[6]	222
C	manuscript of 1660/1669	185

	Editions	Number of *pads*
Sa	Sabhā edition of 1928 by Śyām Sundar Dās [Rajasthani manuscript of 1620?]	403 (7 are not found in my MSS)
Tiv	Parasnāth Tivārī, 1961 [earliest MS dated 1684]	200 (49 are not found in my MSS)
MP	Mātā Prasād Gupta, 1969	403 (-19 given in footnote = 388)
YU	Yugeśvar [3rd edition], 1996	403
[Bij	Shukdeo Singh, 1972 [earliest MS dated 1805]	115 (32 *pads* also in our edition)]
W	my total (some occurring only in 1 MS)	593

[6] For the unique position of manuscripts C and J, see Callewaert and Lath, *The Hindī Songs of Nāmdev*, pp. 102 ff.

'Stemma' of the manuscripts and repertoires

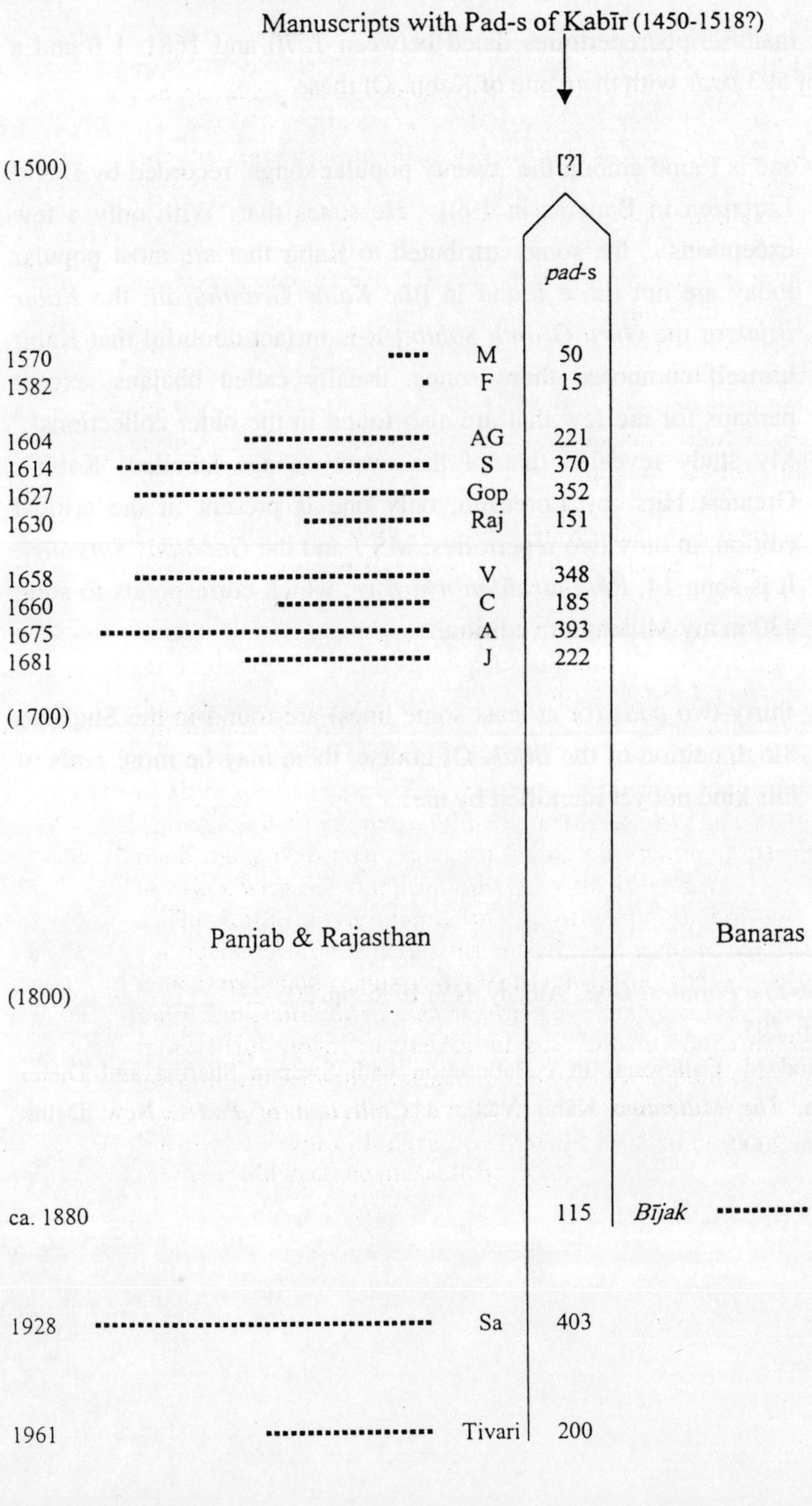

Available manuscripts and later editions

In the manuscripts/repertoires dated between 1570 and 1681, I found a total of 593 *pads* with the name of Kabīr. Of these

- only one is found among the 'twenty popular songs' recorded by David Lorenzen in Banaras in 1991.[7] He states that 'With only a few exceptions.... the songs attributed to Kabīr that are most popular today are not those found in [the *Kabīr Granthāvalī*, the *Kabīr Bījak* or the *Guru Granth Sāhib*.] It is in fact doubtful that Kabīr himself composed these songs, usually called bhajans, except perhaps for the few that are also found in the older collections'.[8] My study revealed that of the twenty songs labelled 'Kabīr's Greatest Hits' by Lorenzen, only one is present in the critical edition, in only two repertoires: MS J and the *Gopāldās Sarvāṅgī*. It is song 14, *Rām nirañjan nyārā re*, which corresponds to song 430 in my Millennium edition.[8]

- Only thirty-two *pads* (or at least some lines) are found in the Shukdeo Singh edition of the *Bījak*. Of course, there may be more *pads* of this kind not yet identified by me:

---

[7] *Praises to a Formless God*, Albany, NY, 1996, pp. 205-23.

[8] Ibid., p. 205.

[8] Winand M. Callewaert in collaboration with Swapna Sharma and Dieter Taillien, *The Millenium* Kabīr Vāṇī*: A Collection of Pad*-s, New Delhi: Manohar 2000.

W	*Bījak*
9	19
53	84
68	26
76	*Kaharā* 10
77	75
82	95
97	36
[102	99]
139	38
146	79
[148	39]
179	111
182	16
185	2
187	24
206	15
236	87
[253	35]
[256	35]
257	54
261	60
271	89
280	97
300	73
303	85
363	72
387	*Gyān cautisā*
416	106
429	108 [W512]
477	37
486	103
512	108 [W 429.1]

- Of the total of 403 *pad*s in the Sabhā edition (of 1928), as many as 396 are found in our manuscripts. The authenticity of the date ascribed by S. S. Das to his first manuscript (1504) is doubted by most scholars, but it is an important manuscript clearly belonging to the Rajasthani tradition (c. 1620?).
- Of the 200 *pad*s selected by Tivārī for his edition, only 151 are found in the manuscripts consulted by us. In his zeal to copy as many versions as possible, Tivārī collected also the verses of Kabīr found in printed (uncritical) editions. Of eleven kinds of sources, only four are manuscript 'recensions'.
- Initially, Vaudeville selected 165 from these 200 *pad*s of Tivārī for her translation project:[9] 'The remaining 35 *pads* had to be eliminated on grounds of doubtful authenticity, since none of them are found in any of the more ancient and reliable collections.' Eventually, she translated only 80 of them; of these only 72 are found in the manuscripts we consulted. I have high esteem for her judgment regarding Kabīr, but it should be pointed out that she also selected *pad*s which are found only in Tivārī (Tivārī, nos. 45, 46,151, 160, 163, 170, 179, 182, only in the *Bījak* or the *Ādi-granth*) and not at all in our edition.
- Of the 220 *pad*s found in the *Ādi-granth,* only 131—some are similar only for half lines—are found in the manuscripts we consulted. Of these 129, as many as 45 *pad*s are classified under a different *rāg* when compared with the (Rajasthani) manuscripts we consulted. Of these 45 *pad*s, 19 also have a different *rāg* in one or more Rajasthani manuscripts. Earlier, I was inclined to suggest that these 19 may be a little more suspect as they possibly travelled along more obscure lines of transmission. But now it appears from a detailed comparison that they all occur in several repertoires: 1 *pad* in 9 repertoires (the highest score!); 2 *pad*s in 8 repertoires; 4 *pad*s in 7 repertoires; 8 *pad*s in 6 repertoires and 4 *pad*s in 5 repertoires!

[9] See Charlotte Vaudeville, *Kabīr-vāṇī*, Pondicherry 1982, p. xxv, n. 29.

Selecting pads on the basis of occurrence

Below I give the complete list of *pads* and of the manuscripts in which they occur.

Depending on the occurrence in a number of repertoires, I have marked *pads* as more or less 'popular' around 1556, that is one generation after the death of Kabīr (see also below, *Alphabetical list of 'selected' pads).* Three asterisks (*) indicate a high probability of belonging to a very early core, because these songs are found in

- the *Ādi-granth* and/or *Mohan Pothī* [1]
- at least one *Pañca-vāṇī* manuscript [2]
- at least one *Sarvāṅgī* 3]
- at least C and/or J [4]

Two asterisks are given if a song is included in three of the above, including *Ādi-granth* and/or *Mohan Pothī,* while one asterisk is given if the song is found only in three of [1] [2] [3] [4], but not the *Ādi-granth* and/or *Mohan Pothī.* Thus looking at the occurrence of a *pad* in repertoires of both Rajasthan and Punjab, we have

- 48 *pads* with ***: found in Punjab and in most Rajasthani repertoires
- 97 *pads* with **: found in Punjab and in some Rajasthani repertoires
- 95 *pads* with *: found only in Rajasthan.

See also below, for the*** markings in the alphabetical list of *pads*.

Ten 'repertoires': no *pads*

	S	A	V	J	C	Gop	Raj	AG	M	F	

Nine 'repertoires': 2 *pads*

***	S	A	V	J	C	Gop	Raj	AG	M	—	78, 408

Eight 'repertoires': 12 *pads*

***	S	A	V	J	C	Gop	Raj	AG	—	—	30, 34, 41, 121, 127, 315
***	S	A	V	J	C	Gop	Raj	—	M	—	439
***	S	A	V	J	C	Gop	—	AG	M	—	410, 459, 486
***	S	A	V	J	—	Gop	Raj	AG	M	—	372
***	S	A	V	—	C	Gop	Raj	AG	M	—	402

Seven 'repertoires': 46 *pads*

**	S	A	V	J	C	Gop	Raj	—	—	—	2, 3, 31, 33, 50, 51, 52, 77, 115, 130, 211, 269, 270, 317, 405, 415, 436, 437, 461, 487
***	S	A	V	J	C	Gop	—	AG	—	—	27, 65, 92, [109], 114, 221, 253, 261, 268, 310, 406, 419, 440, 444
*	S	A	V	J	C	Gop	—	—		F	64
***	S	A	V	J	—	Gop	Raj	AG	—	—	95, 367
***	S	A	V	J	—	Gop	—	AG	M	—	363
***	S	A	V	—	C	Gop	Raj	AG	—	—	413
*	S	A	V	—	—	Gop	Raj	AG	M		46, 28ß
**	S	A	V	—	—	Gop	Raj	AG	—	F	126, 131
***	S	A	—	J	C	Gop	Raj	AG	—	—	338
***	S	—	V	J	C	Gop	—	AG	M		204
***	S	—	V	J	C	Gop	—	AG	—	F	473

Six 'repertoires': 90 *pads*

*	S	A	V	J	C	Gop	—	—	—	—	24, 48, 54, 105, 106, 107, 110, 151, 180, 208, 214, 215, 262, 273, 286, 321, 332, 339, 412, 414, 429, 442, 474, 475, 477, 481, 482, 484, 485
	S	A	V	J	C	—	Raj	—	—	—	93, 455
**	S	A	V	J	C	—	—	AG	—	—	1, 5, 8, 129
	S	A	V	J	C	—	—	—	—	F	443

*	S	A	V	J	—	Gop	Raj	—	—	—	81, 87, 88, 91, 140, 231, 326, 327, 355, 359, 366, 370, 379, 394, 399
***	S	A	V	J	—	Gop	—	AG	—	—	97, 381, 398
*	S	A	V	—	C	Gop	Raj	—	—	—	36, 38, 67
***	S	A	V	—	C	Gop	—	AG	—	—	29
***	S	A	V	—	C	—	Raj	AG	—	—	12, 15
**	S	A	V	—	—	Gop	Raj	AG	—	—	23, 84, 138, 149, 178, 212, 251, 271, 275, 281, 420
	S	A	V	—	—	Gop	Raj	—	—	F	59
**	S	A	V	—	—	Gop	—	AG	M	—	20, 47, 145, 285, 388, 390
**	S	A	—	—	—	Gop	Raj	AG	M	—	334
	S	—	V	J	C	Gop	Raj	—	—	—	222, 340
***	S	—	V	J	C	Gop	—	AG	—	—	200, 325, 448
***	S	—	—	J	C	Gop	Raj	AG	—	—	224
*	—	A	V	J	C	Gop	Raj	—	—	—	68, 162
*	—	A	V	J	C	Gop	—	—	—	F	329
***	—	A	V	—	C	Gop	Raj	AG	—	—	53
***	—	A	—	J	C	Gop	—	AG	M	—	416

Five 'repertoires': 95 *pads*

	S	A	V	J	C	—	—		—	—	89, 333, 467
*	S	A	V	J	—	Gop	—	—	—	—	90, 100, 104, 311, 354, 356, 357, 358, 361, 362, 368, 382, 383, 386, 389, 393
*	S	A	V	J	—	—	Raj	—	—	—	4
**	S	A	V	J	—	—	—	AG	—	—	60, [102]
	S	A	V	J	—	—	—	—	—	F	85
*	S	A	V	—	C	Gop	—	—	—	—	37, 71
*	S	A	V	—	C	—	Raj	—	—	—	7

**	S	A	V	—	—	Gop	Raj	—	—	—	18, 22, 28, 42, 73, 76, 82, 83, 137, 141, 142, 148, 150, 182, 186, 191, 192, 209, 220, 236, 237, 245, 246, 276, 298, 377
**	S	A	V	—	—	Gop	—	AG	—	—	19, 96, 113, 123, 139, 147, 249, 297, 395, 397
**	S	A	V	—	—	Gop	—	—	M	—	135
	S	A	V	—	—	Gop	—	—	—	F	62, 133
**	S	A	V	—	—	—	Raj	AG	—	—	177, 188
	S	A	V	—	—	—	—	AG	—	F	258
*	S	A	—	J	C	Gop	—	—	—	—	345, 348, 470, 490
*	S	A	—	J	C	—	Raj	—	—	—	472
*	S	A	—	J	—	Gop	Raj	—	—	—	58
*	S	—	V	J	C	Gop	—	—	—	—	320, 323, 343, 441, 476
***	S	—	V	J	—	Gop	—	AG	—	—	312
**	S	—	V	—	—	Gop	—	AG	M	—	288
***	S	—	—	J	—	Gop	Raj	AG	—	—	172
*	—	A	V	J	C	Gop	—	—	—	—	9, 167, 168, 407, 469
***	—	A	V	J	—	Gop	—	AG	—	—	360
*	—	A	V	—	C	Gop	Raj	—	—	—	13, 49
*	—	A	V	—	—	Gop	Raj	AG	—	—	346
**	—	A	V	—	—	Gop	—	AG	M	—	55, 464
**	—	—	V	—	—	Gop	Raj	AG	M	—	74
	—	—	—	J	C	Gop	—	AG	M	—	152

Four 'repertoires': 93 *pads*

	S	A	V	J	—	—	—	—	—	—	319, 422
	S	A	V	—	C	—	—	—	—	—	10

	S	A	V	—	—	Gop	—	—	—	—	16, 44, 63, 103, 108, 112, 117, 119, 120, 124, 125, 128, 143, 144, 153, 181, 190, 201, 233, 238, 241, 242, 243, 244, 252, 256, 259, 267, 274, 278, 313, 328, 335, 337, 371
	S	A	V	—	—	—	Raj	—	—	—	26, 43, 185, 187, 193, 197, 198, 199, 257, 387, 454
	S	A	V	—	—	—	—	AG	—	—	94, 146, 176, 316
	S	A	—	J	C	—	—	—	—	—	428, 491
*	S	A	—	J	—	Gop	—	—	—	—	101
**	S	A	—	J	—	—	—	AG	—	—	384
	S	A	—	—	—	Gop	Raj	—	—	—	189, 247, 263, 266
	S	—	V	J	C	—	—	—	—	—	322, 331, 445
*	S	—	V	J	—	Gop	—	—	—	—	365, 396
	S	—	V	—	—	Gop	Raj	—	—	—	173, 223, 336
	S	—	V	—	—	—	Raj	AG	—	—	206
	S	—	—	J	C	Gop	—	—	—	—	228, 353, 478, 480
	—	A	V	J	C	—	—	—	—	—	449, 452, 468
	—	A	V	—	—	Gop	Raj	—	—	—	164, 165, 450, 451, 466
**	—	A	V	—	—	Gop	—	AG	—	—	456
**	—	A	V	—	—	—	Raj	AG	—	—	203
	—	A	V	—	—	—	—	AG	M	—	462
*	—	A	—	J	C	Gop	—	—	—	—	303, 304, 380
**	—	A	—	J	C	—	—	AG	—	—	300
**	—	A	—	—	—	Gop	—	AG	M	—	307
**	—	—	V	J	C	Gop	—	—	—	—	457
	—	—	—	J	C	Gop	—	AG	—	—	111
**	—	—	—	J	—	Gop	—	AG	M	—	56

Three 'repertoires': 67 *pads*

	S	A	V	—	—	—	—	—	—	—	14, 25, 57, 116, 184, 202, 232, 234, 277, 294, 314, 318, 330, 435
	S	A	—	J	—	—	—	—	—	—	425
	S	A	—	—	—	Gop	—	—	—	—	40, 118, 132, 154, 194, 255, 264, 290, 296, 351, 453, 471, 488, 489
	S	A	—	—	—	—	Raj	—	—	—	260
	S	—	V	—	—	Gop	—	—	—	—	205, 207, 218, 219, 324, 424, 427, 432
	S	—	V	—	—	—	Raj	—	—	—	196
	S	—	—	J	C	—	—	—	—	—	175, 352, 434
	S	—	—	J	—	Gop	—	—	—	—	342, 378
	S	—	—	—	—	Gop	Raj	—	—	—	225, 226
**	S	—	—	—	—	Gop	—	AG	—	—	421
	—	A	V	J	—	—	—	—	—	—	292, 293
	—	A	V	—	—	Gop	—	—	—	—	32, 61, 136, 254, 272, 279, 423, 463
	—	A	—	J	C	—	—	—	—	—	158, 302
**	—	A	—	—	—	Gop	—	AG	—	—	159
	—	A	—	—	—	Gop	—	—	—	F	350
	—	—	—	J	C	Gop	—	—	—	—	122
	—	—	—	J	C	—	—	AG	—	—	35, 66
	—	—	—	J	C	—	—	—	M	—	401
**	—	—	—	J	—	Gop	—	AG	—	—	99
	—	—	—	—	—	Gop	—	AG	M	—	411

Two 'repertoires': 58 *pad*s

S	A	—	—	—	—	—	—	—	—	17, 45, 155, 235, 239, 248, 282, 299
S	—	V	—	—	—	—	—	—	—	341, 483
S	—	—	—	C	—	—	—	—	—	230
S	—	—	—	—	Gop	—	—	—	—	171, 210, 227, 229, 295, 431
—	A	V	—	—	—	—	—	—	—	156, 163

—	A	—	—	—	Gop	—	—	—	—	160, 213, 216, 284, 301, 306, 309, 349
—	—	—	J	C	—	—	—	—	—	6, 169, 170, 344, 369, 385, 418, 426, 438, 446
—	—	—	J	—	Gop	—	—	—	—	98, 430
—	—	—	—	—	Gop	Raj	—	—	—	495
—	—	—	—	—	Gop	—	AG	—	—	500
—	—	—	—	—	—	—	AG	M	—	75, 79, 80, 289, 308, 364, 373, 374, 375, 376, 391, 392, 403, 404, 417, 460, 465

One 'repertoire': 127 *pads*

S	—	—	—	—	—	—	—	—	—	174, 195, 433
—	A	—	—	—	—	—	—	—	—	157, 161, 166, 179, 217, 240, 250, 265, 283, 291, 305, 347
—	—	V	—	—	—	—	—	—	—	183, 458
—	—	—	J	—	—	—	—	—	—	69, 70, 287, 400, 409, 447, 479
—	—	—	—	C	—	—	—	—	—	11, 39, 72
—	—	—	—	—	Gop	—	—	—	—	492, 493, 494, 496, 497, 498, 499
—	—	—	—	—	—	Raj	—	—	—	501, 502, 503, 504
—	—	—	—	—	—	—	AG	—	—	505-593 (=88 *pad*s, + 17 only in AG/M) 512, 559, 560
—	—	—	—	—	—	—	—	M	—	21, 134
—	—	—	—	—	—	—	—	—	F	86

An analysis of this list reveals that there is no consistent occurrence of the same songs in the different repertoires/manuscripts. In other words: in vain do we look for a consistent set of *pad*s that may be found in all the repertoires. At times there seems to be a relation between the *Pañca-vāṇī* manuscripts, but then again that is contradicted when we look at other combinations of manuscripts. Three examples may be given here:

Song 8

Looking at the inversion of stanzas 1 and 2, we see a relation between *Pañca-vāṇī* manuscripts S/A and *Ādi-granth* against manuscripts C/J and *Pañca-vāṇī* manuscript V.

This 'relation' is contradicted many times, as can be seen in songs 109 and 390 below.

॥ राग गौड़ी ॥ S7
मन रे मनहीं उलटि समांनां ।
गुर प्रसादि अकलि भई तोकूं । नहींतर था बेगांनां ॥ टेक ॥
1 उलटे पवन चक्र षट बेधे । सहजि सूंनि अनरागी ।
आवै न जाइ मरै नहीं जीवै । ताहि षोजि बैरागी ॥
2 नेड़ै तै दूरि दूरि तै नेड़ै । जिनि जैसा करि जांण्यां ।
औलौती का चढ्या बलींडै । जिनि पीया तिनि मांनां ॥
3 अनभै कथा कवन स्यूं कहिये । है को चतुर बमेकी ।
कहै कबीर गुरि दीया पलीता । सो झल बिरलै देषी ॥
॥ राग गौड़ी ॥ A7
मनरे मनहीं उलटि समांनां ।
गुर परसादि अकलि भई तोकूं । नांतर था वेगांनां ॥ टेक ॥
1 उलटे पवन चक्र षट वेधे । सहज सुंनि अनरागी ।
आवै न जाइ मरै नहि जीवै । ताहि षोजि वैरागी ॥
2 नड़ै थै दूरि दूरि थै नेड़ै । जिनि जैसा करि जांन्यां ।
औलाती का चढ्या वलीडै । जिनि पीया तिनि मांन्यां ॥
3 अनभै कथा कवन स्यौं कहिये । है कोई चतुर बबेकी ।
कहि कवीर गुरि दीया पलीता । सो झल विरलै देषी ॥
॥ राग गौड़ी ॥ V7
मंनरे मंनहीं उलटि संमानांरे ।
गुर प्रसादि अकलि भई तोकूं । नहींतर था बेगांनां ॥ टेक ॥
1 नेड़ा थै दूरि दूरि थै नेड़ा । जिनि जैसा करि जांनां ।
औलौती का चढ्या बलीडै । जिनि पीया तिनि मांन्यां ॥
2 उलटे पवन चक्र षट बेधा । सुनि सुरति लै लागी ।
अंमर न मरै मरै नही जीवै । ताहि षोजि बैरागी ॥
3 अनभै कथा कंवन सूं कहिऐ । है को चत्रु बमेकी ।
कहै कबीर गुर दीया पलीता । सौं झल बिरलै देषी ॥

॥ राग गौडी ॥ J92

मनही मनरे उलटि समांनां ।
गुर परसाद अकलि भइ तोंको । नाहि तो हा बेगानां ॥ टेक ॥
1 नीरा तें दुरि दुरी तें नीरा । जीन जेसा उनमांनां ।
ओलोभी का चढ्या बलिडें । जीन पीया तिनि जानां ॥
2 उलटे पवन चक्र षट बेध्या । सहज सूंनि ल्यो लागी ।
आवे नहि जाइ मरे नहि जामें । ताहि षोजी बेरागी ॥
3 अनभे कथा कोंन सुं कहिये । ऐसा कोइ चतुर बेषी ।
कहे कबीर गुर दीया पलीता । सो झल बिरले देषी ॥

॥ राग गोड़ी ॥ C10

मनरे मन ही ऊलटि समांना ।
गुर परसादि अकलि भई तौंकौ । नहीतर था बेग्यांनां ॥ टेक ॥
1 नीरा थै दूरि दूरि थै नीरा । जिनि जैसा उनमाना ।
ओलौंती का चढया बलींडै । जिनि पीया तिनि जांन्यां ॥
2 उलटे पवन चक्र षट बेधा । सुनि सुरति ल्यो लागी ।
आवै न जाय मरै नहीं जीवै । तोहि षोजि बैरागी ॥
3 अनभै कथा कौंन सौं कहिये । है कोइ चतर बिबेषी ।
कहत कबीर गुर दीया पलीता । सो झल बिरलै देषी ॥

॥ गउड़ी ॥

1 उलटत पवन चक्र खटु भेदे सुरति सुंनि अनरागी ।
आवै न जाइ मरै न जीवै तासु खोजु बैरागी ॥
मेरे मन मन ही उलटि समाना ।
गुर परसादि अकलि भई अवरै नातरु था बेगाना ॥ रहाउ ॥
2 निवरै दूरि दूरि फुनि निवरै जिनि जैसा करि मानिआ ।
अलउती का जैसे भइआ बरेडा जिनि पीआ तिनि जानिआ ॥
3 तेरी निरगुन कथा काइ सिउ कहीऐ ऐसा कोइ बिबेकी ।
कहु कबीर जिनि दीआ पलीता तिनि तैसी झल देखी ॥

Song 109

In the manuscripts of this song we see a different 'relation' because of the 'missing' stanza 1.

Pañca-vāṇī manuscripts S/A/V and Gopāldās *Sarvāṅgī* (and *Ādi-granth*) against manuscripts C/J and no other *Pañca-vāṇī* manuscript.

The version found in the *Ādi-granth* shows similarities only in a few (parts of) lines.

॥ राग गौड़ी ॥ S84

यामे क्या मेरा क्या तेरा । लाज न मरतहु कहत घर मेरा ॥ टेक ॥
1 चारि पहर निस भेरा । जैसैं तरवरि पंषि बसेरा ॥
2 जैसैं बनियैं हाट पसारा । सब जग का सो सिरजनहारा ॥
3 ऐ ले जारे बै ले गाडे । इन दुषियन दोउं घर छाडे ॥
4 कहै कबीर सुनहु रे लोई । हंम तुम बिनसि रहैगा सोंई ॥

॥ राग गौड़ी ॥ A92

यामैं क्या मेरा क्या तेरा । लाज न मरहु कहत घर मेरा ॥ टेक ॥
1 चारि पहर निसा भेरा । जैसैं तरवरि पंषि वसेरा ॥
2 जैसैं वनियें हाट पसारा । सव जग का सो सिरजनहारा ॥
3 ये ले जारे वै ले गाडे । इंन दुषियंन दोऊ घर छाडे ॥
4 कहै कवीर सुनहु रे लोई । हंम तुंम विनसि रहैगा सोई ॥

॥ राग जंगली गोड़ी ॥ V83

इनमैं क्या मेरा क्या तेरा । लाज न मरत कहत घर मेरा ॥ टेक ॥
1 चारि पहर निस भेरा । जैसैं तरवरि पंषि बसेरा ॥
2 जैसैं बनियां हाट पसारा । सब जग का सोई सिरजंनहांरा ॥
3 ऐ ले जारे वै ले गाडे । इिन दुषिइिन दोऊ घर छाडे ॥
4 कहै कबीर सुंनहं रे लोई । हंम तुम बिनसि रहैगा सोई ॥

॥ राग गौडी ॥ J140

यामें क्या मेरा क्या तेरा । लाज न मरों कहत घर मेरा ॥ टेक ॥
1 बनिये हठ पसारा । सब जुग का सेइ सीरजाइ ॥
2 ये ले जारे व ले गाडे । इन दोषे दोउ घर छाडै ॥
3 कहत कबीर सुनहु रे लोइ । घर घर करि बुडो जिनि कोइ ॥

॥ राग गौड़ी ॥ C69

यामैं क्या मेरा क्या तेरा । लाज न मरो कहत घर मेरा ॥ टेक ॥
1 बनिंये हाट पसारा । सब जुग का सोई सिरजनहारा ॥
2 ये ले जारे वै ले गाडे । ईन धोषै दोउ घर छाडे ॥
3 कहत कबीर सुनांहु रे लोई । घर घर करि बूडै जिनि कोई ॥

॥ राग गौडी ॥ Gop89;7

रे यामैं क्या मेरा क्या तेरा । लाज न मरहि कहत घर मेरा ॥ टेक ॥
1 चारि पह निस भोरा । जैसैं तरवरि पंषि बसेरा ॥
2 जैसैं बनियैं हाट पसारा । सब जग का सो सिरजनहारा ॥
3 ए ले जारे वै ले गाडे । इनि दुषिइनि दोऊ घर छाडे ॥
4 कहत कबीर सुनहुं रे लोई । हम तुम बिनसि रहैगा सोई ॥

॥ रागु गउड़ी ॥ [AG325;11]

1 उपजै निपजै निपजि समाई । नैनह देखत इहु जगु जाई ॥
लाज न मरहु कहहु घरु मेरा । अंत की बार नही कछु तेरा ॥ रहाउ ॥
2 अनिक जतन करि काइआ पाली । मरती बार अगनि संगि जाली ॥
3 चोआ चंदनु मरदन अंगा । सो तनु जलै काठ कै संगा ॥
4 कहु कबीर सुनहु रे गुनीआ । बिनसैगो रूपु देखै सभ दुनीआ ॥

Song 390

In this song we see again another 'association':

> *Pañca-vāṇī* AV/*Ādi-granth* and M/ Gopāldās *Sarvāṅgī*
> against *Pañca-vāṇī*

M/AG invert the order of the refrain (*ṭek, rahāu*) and the first stanza, but that is no problem as this is common practice in the *Ādi-granth*. What is more interesting is the fact that here all available repertoires agree except for S. Both the order of the stanzas and the readings are variant in S.

॥ राग भैरु ॥
है हजूरि क्या दूरि बतावै । दूंदर बांधौ तो सूंदर पावै ॥
1 सो सुलतांन जु दोइ सुरतांनै । बाहरि जीता भीतरि आंणै ।
गंगन मंडल मैं लसकर करै । सो सुलितांन छत्र सिरि रै ॥
2 सुपिनै बिंद न देई चरणां । ता काजी कूं जुरा न मरंण ।
सो मुलनां जो मन स्यूं लरै । अह निसि काल चक्र स्यूं भिरै ॥
3 काल पुरिस का मरदैं मांन । तां मुलना कूं सदालंमां ।
जोगी गोरष गोरष करै । हीदू राम नाम उचरै ॥
4 मुसलमान कहै मेरे एक षुदाई । कबीरै कौ स्वांमी सब घटि रह्यौ समाई ॥

॥ राग भैरु ॥ A319
है हजूरि कत दूरि वतावै । दूंदर वांधें सूंदर पावै ॥ टेक ॥
1 सो मुलां जो मन स्यौं लरै । अहि निस काल चक्र स्यौं भिरै ।
काल पुरिस का मरदै मांन । ता मुलां कूं सदा सलांम ॥
2 काजी सो जो काया विचारै । अहि निसि व्रंह्म अगनि परजारै ।
सुपिनैं व्यंद न देई करनां । ता काजी कूं जुरा न मरनां ॥
3 सो सुलितांन दोइ सुरतानैं । वाहरि जाता भींतरि आंनैं ।
गगन मंडल मैं लसकर करै । सो सुलितांन छत्र सिरि धरै ॥
4 जोगी गोरष गोरष करैं । हींदू रांम नांम ऊचरै ।
मुसलमांन कै एक षुदाइ । कवीरा कौ स्वांमीं घटि घटि रह्यौ समाइ ॥

॥ राग भैरु ॥ V268
है हजूरि का दूरि बतावै । दूंदर बांध्यां सुंदर पावै ॥ टेक ॥
1 सो मुलनां जो मंन सूं लरै । अह निसि काल चक्र सौं भिरैं ।
काल चक्र का मरदै मांन । ता मुलनां कूं सदा सलांम ॥
2 सो काजी जो काया बिचारै । अह निसि ब्रह्म अगनि परजारै ।
सुपिनै ब्यंद न देई झरनां । ता काजी कूं जुरा न मरंनां ॥

3 सो सुलितांन जु दोइ सुरतांनै । बाहरि जांता भीतरि आंनै ।
गगंन मंडल मंहि लसकर करै । सो सुलितांन छत्र सिरि धरै ॥
4 जोगी गोरष गोरष करै । हींदू रांम रांम उचरै ।
मुसलमांन कै एक षुदाइ । कबीर का स्वांमी घटि घटि रह्या संमाइ ॥

॥ राग भैरू ॥ Gop55;8

है हजूरि क्या दूरि बतावै । दूंदर बांधैं सुंदर पावै ॥ टेक ॥
1 सो मुसलमांन जु मन सूं लरै । अह निसि काल चक्र सूं भिडै ।
काल पुरिस का मरदै मांन । ता मुसलमांन कूं सदा सलांम ॥
2 सो काजी जो काया बिचारै । अह निसि ब्रह्म अगनि परजारै ।
सुपिनैं ब्यंद न देई झरनां । ता काजी कूं जुर्हा न मरनां ॥
3 सो सुलितांन जु द्वै सुरतांनैं । बाहरि जाता भीतरि आंनैं ।
गगन मंडल मैं लसकर करै । सो सुलितांन छत्र सिरि धरै ॥
4 जोगी गोरष गोरष करै । हिंदू रांम नांम उचरै ।
मुसलमांन कहै एक षुदाइ । कबीरा कौ स्वांमीं घटि घटि रह्यौ समाइ ॥

॥ भैरउ ॥ AG1159-1160;11

1 सो मुलां जो मन सिउ लरै गुर उपदेसि काल सिउ जुरै ।
काल पुरख का मरदै मानु । तिसु मुला कउ सदा सलामु ॥
है हजूरि कत दूरि बतावहु । दुंदर बाधहु सुंदर पावहु ॥ रहाउ ॥
2 काजी सो जु काइआ बीचारै । काइआ की अगनि ब्रहमु परजारै ।
सुपनै बिंदु न देई झरना । तिसु काजी कउ जरा न मरना ॥
3 सो सुरतानु जु दुइ सरतानै । बाहरि जाता भीतरि आनै ।
गगन मंडल महि लसकरु करै । सो सुरतानु छत्रु सिरि धरै ॥
4 जोगी गोरखु गोरखु करै । हिंदू राम नामु उचरै ।
मुसलमान का एकु खुदाइ । कबीर का सुआमी रहिआ समाइ ॥

॥ भैरो कमीर नामा ॥ M24

1 सो मुला जु मन सऊ लरै । गुर उपदेसि काल सिउ जुरै ।
काल पुरखु का मरदे मानु । उसु मुला कऊ सदा सलामु ॥
हइि हदूरि कत दूरि बतावहु । दुदुरु बाधहु सुदरु पावहु ॥ रहऊ ॥
2 कादी सो जि काइिआ वीचारै । काइिआ की अगनि ब्रहम परजारे ।
सुपनै बिंदु न देइी झरना । तिसु कादी कऊ जरा न मरना ॥
3 सो सुलितानु जि दुइी सरतानै । बाहरि जाता भीतरि आनै ।
गगन मंडल महि असकर करै । सो सुलतानु छतु सिर धरै ॥
4 जोगी गोरखु गोरखु करै । हिदू रामु नामु उचरै ।
मुसलमान का ऐकु खुदाए । कमीरै का स्वामी रहिआ समाए ॥

There are very many more examples one could give to confirm the following: the repertoires reflected in the manuscripts we studied do not go back to one archetype of one generation before. These repertoires underwent changes several generations earlier and a comparison of these repertoires takes us to at least the year 1556. And, if a song is found in more repertoires, it has a better chance of belonging to a basic core of songs popular around 1556. It is hard to explain that a song popular around 1556 would become uncommon and would eventually continue to exist only in one repertoire.

Kabīr's songs have had a long life of nearly five centuries. The first major event in that life was not that they were written down, but that they travelled. They travelled in different directions and they travelled in different companies, in different memories. Of one thing we are certain: the songs of Kabīr very soon travelled west and became popular in Rajasthan and in Punjab. They were not popular in Vrindaban where a revival of devotion for Kṛṣna started after Caitanya came there around 1500.

Alphabetical list of 'selected' pads

For the *** markings, see above p. 53. Out of a total of 593 *pads* in my Millennium edition,[9] 240 *pads* have been marked:

48 ***: found in Punjab and in most Rajasthani repertoires
97 **: found in Punjab and in some Rajasthani repertoires
95 *: found only in Rajasthan.

अंजन अलप निरंजनं सार 394*
अंतरगति अनियन बांनी 191**
अंधे हरि बिन को तेरा रे 311*
अकथ कहांणी प्रेम की 180*
अच्यंत च्यंतये माधौ 71*
अजहूं बीच कैसैं दरसंन तोरा 429*
अपणै बिचारि असवारी कीजै 29***
अपणै मैं रंगि अपणपौ जांणौं 28**
अब क्या सोचैं आइ़ बणी 105*

[9] See above, fn. 8.

अब घटि प्रगट भये रांमराई	24*
अब मै जांणिबौ रे	188**
अब मोहि रांम भरोसो तेरो	111**
अब हंम सकल कुसल करि मांनां	23**
अलह रांम जीउं तेरे नांई	280*
अला अलष निरंजन देवा	396*
अवधू मेरा मन मतिवाला	19**
अहो मेरे गोबिंद तुम्हारा जोर	440***
आसन पवन कीये दिढ रहु रे	420**
इंहि तति रांम जपहु रे प्रांणीं	9*
इब तोहि जांन न देहूं रांम प्यारे	3*
इब मोहि नाचिबौ न आवै	315***
इहि बिधि रांम स्यूं ल्यौ लाइ	317**
उतिम कोई न मधिम कोई	470*
ऐक अंचभा ऐसा भया	389*
ऐक अंचभा देष्या रे भाई	15***
ऐक सुहागनि जगत पियारी	444***
ऐ जीव आइ र कहा गयौ	325***
ऐसा ग्यांन बिचारि रे मना	410***
ऐसा ग्यांन बिचारि लै	177**
ऐसा ध्यांन धरूं नरहरी	386*
ऐसा भेद बिगूचनि भारी	77**
ऐसी आरती त्रिभवन तारै	487**
ऐसी रे अवधू की बांणीं	231*
ऐसे लोगनि स्यूं का कहिये	149**
ऐसै मन लाइ लै राम रसनां	475*
कवीरौ संत नदी गयौ वहि रे	167*
कहा करूं कैसैं तिरौं	473***
कहा भयौ तिलक गलै जपमाला	142**
कहु पांडे सुचि कौन ठांऊं	307**
कहूं रे जे कहिबे की होइ	368*
काजी कौण कतेव वषांणै रे	53***
का नागौं का बांधै चांम	138**
काया मंजिसि कौन गुंनां	338***

का सिधि साधि करौ कछु नांही	137**
काहे कूं माया दुष करि जोरी	107*
काहे री नलनी तूं कुमिलांणी	58*
काहे रे मन दह दिसि ध्यावै	91*
किते ऐक सिव संकर गये उठि	36*
कुसल षेम अरु सही सलांमति	439***
कैसैं नगरि करौं कुटवारी	82**
कैसैं होइगा मिलावा हरि संनां	130**
कोई पीवै रे रस रांम नांम का	18**
कौण मरैं कौण जनमैं जाई	42**
कौण कौण गया रांम कौण कौण जासी	276**
क्यूं लीजै गढ बंका रे भाई	421**
गोकल नाइक बीठला	5**
गोबिंद तुम्हारे बन कंदलि	236**
गोबिंदा गुंन गाइये रे	129**
गोबिंदे तूं निरंजन तूं निरंजन	246**
ग्रह जिनि जांनौ रूरौ रे	88*
चतुराइ न चतुरभुज पइये	159**
चरषा जिनि जरै	13*
चलत कत टेढौ टेढौ रे	363***
चलन चलन सब लोग कहत हैं	114***
चल मेरी सषीरी वोलगन रांम राया	383*
चलहुं बिचारी रहौ संभारी	140*
चलि चलि रे भंवरा कंवल पास	469*
चलौ सषी जाइयै जहां	354*
चेति न देषौ रे जगु धंधा	262*
चौषौ बणिज ब्यौपार करीजै	273*
छाकि पर्‍यौ आतम मतिवाला	22**
जतन बिन मृगन षेत बिगारे	474*
जपि जपि रे जीयरा गोब्यंदौ हित चित	490*
जब थै आतम तत बिचारा	209**
जस तूं तस तोहि कोइ न जांनं	73**
जाइ परौ हमारा का करिहै	150**
जाइ पूछौ गोबिंद पढिया पंडित	182**

न कछू रे न कछू रांम बिना	485*
नकटी कौ ठंण गंणबा डांडूं	297**
नर जांणै अमर मेरी काया	110*
नर पछिताहुगे अंधा	484*
नरहरि सहजै जिनि जांनां	7*
नहीं छाडौ बाबा रांम नाम	459***
नैक निहारि हो माया बीनती करै	326*
न्रिंमल न्रिमलं रांम गुंन गावै	65***
न्रिगुंणं रांम न्रिगुंणां	74**
पढि ले काजी वंग निवाजा	55**
पवन पति उंनमनि रहैन षारा	203**
पांडे कौंन कुमति तोहि लागी	145**
पांडे वाद वदत है झूठा	162*
प्रांणी काहे कै लोभि लागि	271**
प्रांणी लाल औसर चले रे बजाइ	367***
प्यारे रांम मनहीं मना	48*
फिरत कत फूल्यौ फूल्यौ	300**
बलिया ल्यूं कब देषूंगी तोहि	356*
बहुत दिनन तैं मैं प्रीतम पाऐ	2**
बाबा करहु कृपा जन मारगि लोवो	200***
बाबा पेड छोडि सब डाली लागे	211**
बिनसि जाइ कागद की सी गुडिया	100*
बिरहंणी फिरै हो नाथ अधीरा	332*
बोलणां का कहिये रे भाई	95***
बोलौ भाई राम की दुहाई	20**
भगति बिन भौ जलि बूडत है	362*
भजि गोब्यंद भूलि जिनि जाइह	408***
भयौ रे मन पाहुंनरौ दिन चारि	366*
भाई रे चूंन विलौटां षाई	83**
भाई रे विरले दोस्त कवीर के	68*
भाई रे सकहु त तणि बुणि लेहु रें	321**
भोली मालनी हे गोंबिंदौ जागतौ जग देव	212**
मन के मोहन बीछुला	4*
मन न डिगै तातै तन न डराइ	398***

रांम चरंण जाकै ह्रिदै बस्त है	448***
रांम न जपहु कवन भ्रंमिं लागे	135**
रांम नांम ह्दै धरि त्रिमोलिक हीरा	382*
रांम नाम मनि भाईये रे	60**
रांम बांण अंणियाले तीर	126**
रांम भजै सो जांनियें	436**
रांम भणि रांम भणि रांम चिंतामणि	64*
रांम मोहि तारि कहां लै जैहौ	47**
रांम रस पाईया रे	92***
रांम रांम रांम रांम राम रमि रहियै	251**
रांम राइ तेरी गति लषी न जाई	215*
रांम विन संसार धंध कुहेरा	360***
राम अैसौ हीं जांनि जपौ नरहरी	481*
राम थोरे दिनन कूं का धन करंणा	106*
राम बिन तन की ताप न जाई	123**
राम रमत सब जरि क्यूं न जाइ	99**
राम राइ भई बिगूचनि भारी	339*
रे दिल षोजि दिल हर षोजि	285**
रे भाई दोइ कहां सो मोहि बतावो	51**
रे मंन राम नांमहि जांनि	379*
रे मन बैसि किते जिनि जासी	192**
रैनि गई जैसैं दिन भी जाइ	416***
लावौ बाबा आगि जरावौ घरा रे	298**
लोका जांणि न भूलौ भाई	46*
लोका तुम ज कहत हौ नंदन कौ नंदन	172***
लोका रे मति भोरा रे	486***
लोग कहै गोवरधन धारी	393*
वहुरि हंम काहे कूं आंवैंगे	168*
वाल्हा आव हमारै ग्रेह रे	357*
विषिया अजहू सुरति सुष आसा	84**
वै दिन कब आवैंगे माइ	358*
षालिक हरि कहीं दरहाल	286*
संतनि ऐक अहेरा लाधा	415**
संतौ आई ग्यांन की आंधी	224***

Kabīr's Language: Notes on Data from Selected Text

Stuart McGregor

Introduction

In the *Ādi-granth* text of verses ascribed to several northern Sant poets, including Kabīr, we see linguistic forms whose regional character lends some support to traditions of the poets' regional origins, or residence. Some verses assigned to Nāmdev, Trilocan and Pīpā illustrate fleetingly this kind of congruence between language evidence and historical or sectarian tradition. In the case of Kabīr, the significance of eastern language forms occurring in Kabīr texts as received is hard to assess, because of the notorious complexities of the MS tradition of his oral poetry. The materials in which the Kabīr tradition now exists are, first, those of the *Bījak* and the linguistically very different *Ādi-granth*, which had become available for study early in this century. In 1928 Śyāmsundardās produced his text of Kabīr *sākhī*s and *pada*s, which differed from the *Bījak* and *Ādi-granth* in its Rajasthani language coloration; then in 1961 Pārasnāth Tivārī's indispensable critical text, based on all these materials and others, appeared. Charlotte Vaudeville in her 1974 study of Kabīr (with translation of Tivārī's text of the *sākhī*s) suggested that further textual work should include studies of the language of each of the recensions or major groupings of the materials.[1] A step in this direction was taken in the same year by Georgii Zograf of St Petersburg in his article on verb structure in the *Gurū granth saloku*s (*sākhī*s).[2] Vaudeville also noted the fact that the number of Kabīr verses, whether *sākhī*s or *pada*s, found in all three recensions of the text is very small, and that these verses share common themes and similarities of literary character. They should thus stand near the core of the Kabīr

[1] Charlotte Vaudeville, *Kabir*, Oxford 1974, p. 68.

[2] Georgii Zograf, 'Glagol'naia sistema v shlokach Kabira', in: G. Zograf (ed.), *Problemy istorii iazykov i kul'tury narodov Indii*, Moscow 1974, pp. 192-210.

textual tradition. Accordingly, I have taken the *sākhī*s common to all recensions, which number only sixteen, as material for this paper on Kabīr's language. I could expect to have reliable material here, which should yield some evidence as to which types of language were originally represented in Kabīr's *sākhī*s, in what proportions, and used in what ways.

Local speech and literary language. Rāmcandra Śukla's concept of *sadhukkaṛī bhāṣā* as a mixed jargon in use among Sant poets may have owed much to the appearance of the Rajasthani-coloured Kabīr text in his time. However, other language styles were mixed too, so what reason was there to posit a distinct *sadhukkaṛī*? At a later period, language mixing was normal. We may think of the rhetorician Bhikhārīdās's references to local variations in Brajbhāṣā as used at assemblies of poets around 1750. Much earlier, around 1600, a similar if apparently smaller impact of local language appears in the Brajbhāṣā prose written at Orcha in Bundelkhand by Raja Indrajit. Conversely, Indrajit's prose reflects intrusions from Khaṛībolī also, as well as being receptive to local usage. Khaṛībolī had by then been established for centuries (under such names as 'Hindi') as the speech of Indo-Muslim communities in northern urban areas. A few references by Śamsu'l 'Uśśāq of Bijapur, perhaps a late contemporary of Kabīr, show its status in southern communities also: *'Ham hindī boleṁ sab ... je koi ache k͟hāṣe is bayān kere piāse, ve 'arbī bol na jāne na fārsī pahcāne.'*[3] Śamsu'l 'Uśśāq's usage with its postposition *kere* is that of an eastern area, where the Khaṛībolī of his community had been exposed to Avadhi influence. As for Kabīr, he had broken with Islam, but he, too, would hardly have broken with his local speech. It is certain, moreover, that given Kabīr's Sant identity he would have experienced the drawing together of Sufi and Nāth communities that had taken place by his time. If so, it was improbable that he was unfamiliar with the language and style of the Sufi poet Dāūd's *Candāyan* (1379), which became, as Badā'ūnī attests, widely popular in the fifteenth century. Thus the essential ingredients of Kabīr's language and style, as we identify them and see their participation in the expression of his meaning, were all to hand in his

[3] Cited by 'Abdu'l Ḥaqq, in 'Qadīm urdū', *Urdū*, vol. 26, April 1927, p. 185.

day. There is every likelihood that Kabīr's mixed language could have been built on a local base, a natural product of language conditions of his time and place.

Procedure

I have compared three published versions of Kabīr *sākhī*s: those of S.S. Dās and Tivārī in their editions of 1928 and 1961, both called *Kabīr-granthāvalī* [KG1 and KG2], and that of the *Gurū Granth* [Gu]. To study the divergences between these versions I have used Tivārī's extensive list of variants from the composite Rajasthan recension or tradition and from the *Bījak* recension. The relationships between the materials are complicated and often ambiguous, and suggest new aspects of the text or its transmission at almost every point of comparison. The best illustration of this in my material is found in Tivārī's v. 8 of section (*aṅg*) 15, with its variants. I therefore start by analysing in some detail the questions that arise from this verse, then summarise the evidence collected from the others. I then move to a discussion of the regional and supra-regional forms of language found in the sources.

Evidence from KG2, verse 15.8[4]. Four versions of verse 15.8, or of its separate lines, are found. The best version seems to be that of KG2. The versions of KG2, KG1 and one given in Gu 153 start with the same line, while another Gu verse, 144, uses line 2 of almost the same text as the KG versions as its own first line, and completes the couplet differently.

1. KG2 **jaisī upajai peṛa taiṁ <jau> taisī nibahai ori**
kauṛī kauṛī joṛatāṁ jorai lakha karori

'As the fruit is born on the tree,
so it remains to the end;

[4] References to Kabīr text are to Pārasnāth Tivārī's edition, *Kabīr-granthāvalī*, Prayāg 1961 (KG2).

Saving cowrie after cowrie,
man gathers millions!' (Vaudeville 1974: 229)

KG1 **jaisī upajai peṛa sūṁ taisī nibahai ori**
paikā paikā joṛatāṁ juṛasī lākha karoṛi

Gu 144 **kaüḍī kaüḍī jori kai jore lākha karori**
[calatī bāra na kachu milio laī laṅgoṭī tori]

Gu 153 **jaisī upajī peḍa te <jaü> taisī nibahaï oṛi**
hīrā kisa kā bāpurā pujahi na ratana karoṛi

It is clear that the verse has been corrupted within the Gu transmission and that KG1 and KG2 provide its original form. In KG1, however, the reading *paikā paikā* loses an assonance with the word *karoṛi* at the end of the line, and it also loses a word-play that is present in KG2 between *kauṛī* and *karori*. To that extent it is a suspect reading. We may next note that it is in the very line containing this suspect reading that the Rajasthani future form, *juṛasī* (corresponding to Hindi *juṛegā*), occurs.[5] We may therefore suspect that the form *juṛasī*, too, was not integral to some earlier or an original wording of the verse.

Looking next at line 2 in KG2 and the matching line 1 in Gu 144, we find that assonance on the retroflex consonant *ṛ* is consistent through the first half of the line in KG2, but in the second half of the line there, and in Gu 144, it gives way to an assonance on continuant *r* starting with the word *jori* (*jorai*) and running through to the last word, *karori*. Tivārī's variants imply consistent support for these *r* forms, agreeing with Gu 144, in his MSS of Rajasthan provenance. *r* forms, which are phonologically of Brajbhāṣā-Avadhī and not of Khaṛībolī-Rajasthani type, are thus well established in the Rajasthan tradition of Kabīr. Once this is demonstrated, we find confirmation of the status of the *r* forms in the KG2 rhyme of *karori* with the word *ori*, which in the collocation *nivahai ori* must represent H. *or*, f. The KG1 reading *karoṛi*, and the Gu153 form of this

[5] *Gurū Granth* contains one case of a future in *-sī*, Georgii Zograf, 'Glagol'naia sistema v shlokach Kabira', p. 198.

rhyme, emerge as inauthentic. Finally in this verse, if we consider the verb form *joṛatāṁ* which is well represented in the KG2 sources, and compare its flapped *ṛ* with that of the authentic *r* forms in the same line, *joṛatāṁ* may seem itself to be an alteration of a *r* form: perhaps brought into the text in a Rajasthani language environment to heighten the assonance of retroflex *ṛ* in the opening words of the line.

Looking at this single verse in this way suggests three aspects of the history of the Kabīr text: 1. the importance of the Rajasthan materials in its preservation, and especially of Tivārī's leading MSS; 2. the significance that the Gu readings can have, even in cases where the Gu transmission of a verse has gone wrong; and 3. the possible existence of a Rajasthanising tendency liable to affect transmission.

Evidence from other verses. I considered the other verses of the selected material in a similar way to verse 15.8. Out of fifteen verses, six seemed to show evidence bearing on the status of the Rajasthan materials and the Gu recension, or on the nature of interactions between them. Three tendencies could again be seen. (1) In five cases, a Rajasthan source or sources seemed to contain best readings, that is, readings having the strongest claim to authenticity at a particular point in the text.[6] (2) In four cases, Gu contained best readings or the best line order.[7] (3) In three cases, both the Rajasthan sources and Gu participate in what seems the best version of a sākhī, in respect of either line order or readings.[8] Thus the first two of these tendencies agree with the deductions demonstrated from verse 3, while the third is a separate, new consideration.

A great number of factors would of course have contributed over time to the discrepancies of our received texts: what successions of people may have recited or sung the verses? Who chanced to do so most memorably, and was heard for posterity? In what locations? To what audiences, assuming what freedoms of interpretation, making what

[6] 1.5, 15.8, 16.1, 16.3, 20.5.

[7] 1.5, 2.1, 15.8, 16.1.

[8] 1.5, 15.8, 16.1.

concessions in style or language? What range of attitudes informed the recording of oral verses? And among other imponderables, what external factors led to the loss of material already recorded?

Sikh and Panjabi language influence. Before leaving the question of relationships between sources, we should notice that the wording of the Gu recension seems occasionally to reflect Sikh presentational concerns. In verse 21.1 where the Rajasthan and *Bījak* materials speak respectively of 'encouraging' or 'instructing' others (*aurāṁ kauṁ paramodhatāṁ/ sikhalāvate*), the corresponding Gu phrase contains a noun, *upadesa*. This is not a word foreign to Kabīr by any means, but is revealed here by a dislocation of its grammar (*avaraha* <u>*kau*</u> *upadesa te*) as probably a divergence from a received source. It is is hard to explain this lapse in so simple a context, but perhaps a Sikh community interest has motivated such a change in Gu. In verse 2.1 on *viyoga*, the Gu reading *nām biogī* seems, as Tivārī judged, inferior to KG2 *rāṁm biyogī*. The symbolism of *viyoga* seems to have a fuller meaning in direct reference to Rām than in reference to the Name, an entity which removes the Satguru so specifically from the realm of the personal.

In at least one other case, the text of the selected verses shows a random Panjabi language influence. This is a use of the noun *tār* as feminine (*ṭūṭi gaīṁ tār*) 4.1. This reading is shared by Gu and a single Rajasthan MS, guṇ. A reading in Rajasthan MS ni may show either Panjabi or Rajasthani language. This is a direct object usage with postposition *naiṁ* corresponding to Hindi *ko*, 11.1.

Preservation of older language forms in Gu. Gu shows two types of older language usage that may prove on examination of a wider range of material to be significant. One is the construction of a noun in oblique case without postposition, illustrated in *andhai na lāgaï* 1.5 (corresponding to H. *andhe ko na lage or nahīṁ lagtā*). This type of usage is an inheritance from early NIA, and is already relatively rare in sixteenth-century Brajbhāṣā. It may be significant for our understanding of the Kabīr text that we find it more commonly in the Avadhi of

Tulsīdās's *Rāmcaritmānas*.[9] Second, there are two examples of colloquialised semitatsama loanwords, the nouns *mantu* and *jantu*. These forms seem more likely to represent fifteenth-century usage than do the tatsama form *mantra* and the Sanskritic *jantra* admitted by Tivārī to his text (2.1 and 16.1). It is worth noting that Tivārī gives no semitatsama variants of these forms from his Rajasthan materials (or from *Bījak*).[10]

Avadhi, Brajbhāṣā and Khaṛībolī forms

The last part of this paper deals with textual evidence for Avadhi, Brajbhāṣā and Khaṛībolī forms in Kabīr's usage. It must be said at first of both Brajbhāṣā and Avadhi forms that their identification is often difficult. Some Avadhi forms such as the perfective ending in *-eu*, or the possessive postposition *ker* (H. *kā*), can be referred easily to the eastern Hindi region, but others are ambiguous. This applies particularly to many cases of words where medial or final *r* corresponds to Hindi flapped *ṛ* (e.g. the verb roots *jor-* or *par-*, cf. H. *joṛnā*, *paṛnā*). These, and similar cases involving alternation of *l* and *r*, are often indistinguishable from Brajbhāṣā forms. The *l-r* alternation can also be found in early Hinduī (Khaṛībolī). We must endeavour while investigating regional aspects of Kabīr's language not to misinterpret manuscript forms which are in fact ambiguous, but are likely because of the supra-regional status that was achieved by Brajbhāṣā, to be taken as Brajbhāṣā items.

Indications of Avadhi usage in the text. Tivārī's verse 24.7 describes the world as a soot-filled dungeon whose residents are contaminated by karma, *kājal kerī obarī aisā yahu saṃsāra*. The postposition *kera* is

[9] E.g. in *abhimata birava pareu janu pānī*, II. 5.

[10] The forms *jantu, janta* are much more frequent in *Gurū granth* than *jantra*. Conversely *mantu, manta* are less common than *mantra*, but preference for the tatsama here can be assumed to be due to the religious and cultural associations of these words. Citations in Winand M. Callewaert, *Srī Gurū Granth Sāhib*, Delhi 1996.

specifically an eastern form, and the word *obrī*, which means 'small room', is still current today in the Avadh region. Gu, however, has a different reading, which employs the common modern Hindi expression *kājal kī koṭhrī* of the same sense. The full line in Gu reads *jagu kājala kī koṭhrī aṁdha pare tisa māhi*. The opening of this line has, today, a perhaps anachronistic clarity and a certain flatness, although the second half-line (with its Khaṛībolī pronoun, *tis*) does fill out the implication of the first quite pointedly. Moreover the reading *jagu*, with its final *-u*, does look like an older form. Yet the KG2 reading with its declamatory beginning seems a more effective and original utterance than the Gu reading, despite the conventionality of its own second half-line. We infer that Tivārī's preference for it is correct and that his reading of the verse is the one likely to go back to, or farthest towards, Kabīr.

Among other possible Avadhi items in the text is a variant in Gu on the noun *prema* 'love'. This word appears in the Rajasthan sources of verse 24.9 as *pirema* or *prema*:

KG2 24.9 **jau tohiṁ sādha pirema kī, tau pākā setī kheli**
kāṁcī sarasauṁ peli kai nāṁ khali bhaī na tela

'If you seek [the oil of] Love,
then use only ripened [seeds];
Crushing unripe mustard seeds
gives neither oil-cake nor oil!'
(Vaudeville 1974: 278)

Raj. variants in this verse	*pirema*, *prema*
Gu	*piramma*

The Gu reading is *piramma*, and elsewhere in Gu the form *pirama* occurs. Such semitatsama forms as these must of course have been liable to occur in any region. But it may be relevant in considering this Kabīr verse that use of the form *pirama* is attested in the early Avadhi *Candāyan*, of 1379. Dāūd describes Candā's asking her servant to recite an old tale of love, in the words: *cānda biraspati pāsa bulāī, pirama kahānī kahu mohi āī.*[11] We must admit that the Gu Kabīrian reading *piramma* represents the kind of vernacularised pronunciation that might be expected either in a Sufi context of popular speech in Bihar, or equally, in the speech of a Banaras Muslim of approximately the same time. Could *piramma* or *pirama* be the authentic reading of the Kabīr verse?

Let us consider this possibility in the light of the whole first line of KG2. Two items here, making up almost the whole of the line, are ambiguous as to their language identity, but there is one region and only one to which both may be referred: that of Avadh. These items are the sg. pronoun *tohiṁ* 'you' (found in Brajbhāṣā and Avadhi, but not in Rajasthani or Panjabi); and the figurative expression *pākā setī kheli* 'deal in a right way (with people)' (Rajasthani or Avadhi, but not Brajbhāṣā or Panjabi).[12] There is thus combined evidence in this verse suggesting rather strongly that Avadhi speech is at the base of its textual tradition. The only contra-indication I can see is in the fem. adjective form *kāṁcī* in line 2, where the long final vowel is hardly a metrical lengthening of short Avadhi *i*, and in that case *kāṁcī* probably represents a Brajbhāṣā usage.

Indications of Brajbhāṣā usage in the text. A clear impact of Brajbhāṣā usage is seen in the form of the oblique case marker *kauṁ* with its diphthong and nasality. The form *kāṁcī* appears as Brajbhāṣā rather than Avadhi in respect of its inflexional ending. The pronominal base *tā* found in verse 24.7 is characteristic of Brajbhāṣā. Dialectally ambiguous forms are found to penetrate the text in grammatical, phonological and lexical functions.[13] If only statistically, it is likely that some of these forms reflect a Brajbhāṣā influence. It is relevant to note that these forms are present in

---

[11] *Candāyan*, ed. by M.P. Gupta, Agra 1967, v. 172.

[12] The postposition *setī* is common in older Rajasthani (Sītārām Lāḷas, *Rājasthānī sabad kos*, Jodhpur, 1962-78, *s.v.*) but comparatively rare in older Avadhi. However Saksena (*The Evolution of Avadhi*, 2nd ed., Delhi 1971, p. 223) illustrates its use in a similar Avadhi expression of instrumental case type (*dayā setī*) to the *pākā setī* of our text.

[13] E.g. *tohiṁ* 24.9, *bhaī* 24.9; *r* forms; the noun *obrī*, and the verb *pais-* 'enter'.

two instances within a single verse, in Gu and KG1, where the text seems to have been simplified.[14] Insofar as simplifications in the received text may have been made after Kabīr's own time, and so increasingly within the period when Brajbhāṣā was becoming dominant, it would seem better to interpret ambiguous forms of this kind as Brajbhāṣā.

A variant in Gu calls for similar interpretation. In the expression *na kachu milio* Gu 144b the perfective *milio* could be taken as either Brajbhāṣā or Rajasthani, but occurring in *Gurū Granth* as it does, is more probably Brajbhāṣā.[15]

Khaṛībolī usage in the text. There is a pervasive Khaṛībolī quality to the text. It is shared by all versions and is visible in both phonology and grammar. It must be noted, though, that some forms showing a phonology that is properly Brajbhāṣā, such as the verb *lāgaï* (H. *lage*), can be seen to be repeatedly used even in the present very small selection of *sākhī*s. Such mixing of language is present in the Delhi poem *Kutub-śatak* (c. early sixteenth century) and perhaps became a feature of informal literary style.[16] Khaṛībolī forms are seen to dominate substantial portions of such verses as 17. 1 and 21.1. Occasionally, as I have mentioned also for Brajbhāṣā, Khaṛībolī forms appear in simplifications of a verse that have been made in the course of transmission, e.g. in 18.1 where the form *milaigā* replaces the older reading *pāiahi* of Gu, with change of construction (and a deterioration in metre). Finally, it is clear that despite the standing of Khaṛībolī in Kabīr's mixed language, there was a sense in which Khaṛībolī did not always hold pride of place, for there is one verse in the material which has no specific Khaṛībolī identity at all. Is it accidental, we may ask, that this is 24.9, showing the coincidence of Avadhi features which we have just been considering?

---

[14] 20.4

[15] Perfectives in *-yo* outnumber those in Khaṛībolī or Panjabi *-yā* in *Gurū granth*. Zograf, 'Glagol'naia sistema v shlokach Kabira', p. 203.

[16] There are many more cases of *lāg-* than of *lagg-* in the edited text. M. P. Gupta, Kutub śatak *aur uskī hinduī,* Calcutta 1967.

Conclusion

A provisional interpretation of the matters put forward in this paper is as follows. A Khaṛībolī style of language had pervasive currency in the place, and at the time of composition of the Kabīr *sākhī*s, and must have been strongly represented in them from the outset. A Brajbhāṣā usage, and a usage of Avadhi language, sharing various phonological and also grammatical features, were also current, and both must have been represented in the *sākhī*s at an early stage. We might venture to think of elements common to Brajbhāṣā and Avadhi as constituting a variable mixed style at a level of popular use. The position of Brajbhāṣā in the Kabīr transmission is clear in the extent to which Brajbhāṣā elements are present in both the Rajasthan materials and the *Gurū Granth*. A specific participation of Avadhi language in the composition of Kabīr's *sākhī*s is very probable. In further assessment of this question we should bear in mind the likelihood that Avadhi as a local speech was supported by a literary tradition of its own (as indicated in *Candāyan*).

The Sorrows of Kabīr[1]

Namwar Singh

I was introduced to the sorrows of Kabīr through 'Kafan' (The Shroud), perhaps the most famous short-story by Premchand. The initiation was done by Ghīsū and Mādhav, the father-and-son protagonists who, suffice it to say, belong to the leather-working caste, now one of the so-called Dalits—the oppressed. The duo has no more than four or five earthen pots by way of belongings. They have lived their lives hiding their shame behind tattered rags. Mādhav's young wife lies dead in the hovel but the father and the son, both widowers now, are now washing down their sorrow in the village liquor-shop with the money meant for the lifeless woman's shroud. But the memory of the dead body interferes with the pleasures of drinking. The bereaved son starts wailing and the father consoles: 'Why cry, son? Be glad that she is free from the mesh of Māyā. So fortunate was she that she could break free from the bonds of *māyāmoha*—worldly illusions and infatuations.' And they stagger to their feet and begin to dance and sing: 'Why do you flash your eyes so, o temptress!'

That is the moment of my introduction to Kabīr and Kabīr's sorrows. Death, salvation, illusion and above them all the dance of the two creatures from the lowest class of the society! Death dances, salvation dances and with them dances Māyā—illusion. It is again Kabīr who says elsewhere: 'This Māyā is like a liquor-seller—she keeps you crazed by making you drink.'

The dance is thrilling and the festivities of salvation wondrous! Ghīsū and Mādhav are singing their Kabīr, dancing their Kabīr and it appears that Kabīr himself is dancing with them and singing:

---

[1] This paper was previously published in *Indian Literature*, vol. 43.4, 1999. The Sahitya Akademi's kind permission to reprint it here is gratefully acknowledged. Some minor editorial changes have been inserted in the present version of the text.

Dance my soul intoxicated.
Mountains seas earth dance, the people dance laughing and crying.

It is a strange dance where laughter and tears co-exist. Did Shiva dance in such frenzied inebriation as he carried the corpse of his spouse Satī?

Ghīsū and Mādhav could hardly have known that Shiva. But it is strange that in their moment of sorrow they did not recall the Rām of Kabīr. They could only remember Māyā the temptress. There is a Māyā that belongs to Śaṅkarācārya but it is largely the property of pandits and philosophers. The common world only knows the illusory temptress and Kabīr too was confronted by her. For Kabīr, Māyā is not an abstract concept from philosophy but she is a concrete reality, a bitter truth. His Rām might be *nirguṇa*, without attributes, but Māyā to him is absolutely *saguṇa*, with attributes, present everywhere, all the time, corporeally. Let us recall this verse by him:

Maya is the greatest temptress we know.
She has ensnared purity, passion and ignorance in her hands
And struts about mouthing sweet words.
To Vishnu she is the consort Lakshmi, to Shiva she is Paravati.
To the priest she sits as the idol, at the place of pilgrimage
She is holy water.
She squats as Yogini with the Yogi, as queen with the king.
To some she belongs as a diamond, to some as a cracked cowrie.
She is a devout female to the devotee, a Muslim woman to a Turk.
The menial Kabīr is the Master's slave and she sold herself to him.

In short, Māyā is as universal and all-pervasive as Rām, if not more. She can reach where Rām has no place and she transforms herself to suit the venue— she is not called Māyā for nothing. But she sells herself to Kabīr whom she failed to enchant and got subjugated instead. At least that is what Kabīr likes to think. But one comes across a verse from him in which he confesses helplessly that he is trying to jettison Māyā but she won't let him go—the familiar case of the ascetic trying to rid himself of his blanket but the blanket clinging to him. This is how the verse begins:

> I am abandoning Maya but she doesn't get abandoned.
> Maya embraces me again and again.

What follows is a detailed delineation of Māyā. She is respect, honour, the sap and the taste. Incantation, penance, yoga are Māyā as well. Mother, father, wife, son, daughter etc. are Māyā and so are, of course, wealth and possessions, popularly called Māyā. When she is so rampant, who can escape her bondage? This helplessness is possibly the reason behind one of Kabīr's sorrows.

He has said a lot more about Māyā. The name of Rām recurs a number of times in *Kabīr bāni*—Māyā almost equally so. Kabīr has many relations with her. At times she is a whore, sometimes his sister in whom he confides his sorrows. First he says affectionately:

> Return to your house, Sister, your eyes are poison to me.

He goes on to point out the reason:

> Go where there is throne and silk, where there is incense and sandal.
> What use is living with me, I belong to a base caste.

And finally his sorrow:

> A weaver by caste, by name Kabīr, I wander in the forests forlorn.

If truth be told, the Kabīr who wanders dejectedly, uninvolvedly in the woods of the realm of Māyā is the real, genuine Kabīr. He confesses in one of his *sākhī*s:

> Ever since Māi, the Mother, gave me birth, I never found happiness.
> I searched branch to branch for joy, sorrow followed me from leaf to leaf.

'Māi' could also mean Māyā here.

Kabīr sedulously eschewed happiness and knowingly cultivated sorrow. This was his choice. He has hinted as much in another of his *sākhī*s:

Kabīr was headed towards happiness but ran straight into sorrow.
Go home, happiness, it is now me and the sorrow.

But this should not lead to suggest that Kabīr is permanently unhappy in his own sorrow. When he laments that Māyā is not leaving him, the hint is obvious that the world created by Māyā does not free him. In a way, Kabīr is seen to weep for the entire world. He says as much in a *sākhī*:

I cry for sansara, the world, but no one weeps for me.
The one who cries for me will be a discerner of the Word.

This is a kind of challenge to all those who are 'discerners of the Word' or lay a claim to discerning of the Word. It need not be said that it is only through the discernment of words that the real meaning of Kabīr's crying for the world can be caught—the world around him. Often such verses are wrapped in metaphysical metaphor; therefore they are interpreted on the regular metaphysical lines, for this is the easy way and does not require much mental rigour for the discernment of words. Take, for example, the following verse:

I shall no more reside in this village, O Master
Thy tithe-collectors are very cunning, O Rām
Here there is a living headman and there are five farmers
Eyes Nose Ears Tongue and Organ defy rules, O Rām
The Kshatriya landlord measures the fields badly, the Kayastha record-keeper demands bribes
He tampers with the maps and they all unite to trash me, O Rām
The headman is a liar, the policeman is terrifying, how dare a man rebel?
The minister is bad, unwilling to listen, one ties up and the other beats, O Rām
When the judge demanded to see the accounts, I was the heavy defaulter
The five farmers have absconded, so the living headman is in custody, O Rām
Says Kabīr, listen O Ascetics, praise God and prepare the boat
Pardon your slave this time, Lord, I shall discharge all my debts.

This verse is subject to textual variations and the fifteenth-century revenue jargon presents further difficulties. Chiefly it is a familiar bhakti verse of devotion which laments the wantonness of the sense with almost nothing uncommon about it. But it is made extraordinary by the metaphors drawn from atrocities perpetrated on the farmers of the day. Allegories from real life galore, but it is difficult to relate them to the actions and functions of the various human limbs they seek to allegorise. Who or what could be called the tithe-collector in the human body? And what could be taken as the landlord, the record-keeper, the minister and the police official? It is clear that social reality weighs heavy on the intended spiritual purport. The metaphysical meaning recedes and social reality rears its ugly head. The entire village administration is cruel and rapacious and combines to torture the hapless farmer who is left with no other option but to flee from his village.

This social sorrow is so excruciating that it disturbs an ascetic like Kabīr even in his spiritual moments. In a way, social reality infiltrates into spiritual territory. Thus it would appear that the sorrows of Kabīr have a concrete social base. That is why the pain behind 'I shall no more reside in this village, Master' is so acute.

The examples of the pressures of social reality on Kabīr are many. Though he totally rejects caste-discriminations, he can never forget that he is a weaver, not even in the sublime moment of spiritual experience. He weaves the name of Rām as a weaver and to weave a great name like that one ought to have a big enough loom. So he combines the three realms of heaven, earth and netherworld to fashion a loom, turns the entire world into a warp and thus completes the complex technicalities of his trade. This grand vision provides the verse 'O Weaver, weave the name of Hari' with its imagery. In the process, sometimes, he makes his Rām sit at a great loom. 'Who would weave now, O Mother, I am in love' is an extraordinary verse of a similar moment of spiritual experience. Singing it, Kabīr goes into an ecstasy and begins to dance; and then

> The warp dances, the woof dances, dances the old weaver's brush,
> Who would weave, O Friend?
> Kabīr sits on the loom and dances, the rat bit off the warp,
> Who would weave, O Friend?

The most interesting is 'the rat bit off the warp' part of the last line. This is an example of the irony in Kabīr's oeuvre. As the warp reaches ecstasy in dance, a nibbling rat brings it back to senses. What is this rodent? Is it the gnawing of a sorrow? How did the bandicoot creep into the loom? Whatever it might be, it is a curb, a check on both—the spiritual flight and the ecstasy.

There are so many verses of spiritual ecstasy in *Kabīr granthāvalī* and *Bījak* that reading them all sorrow is forgotten and the conviction gets strengthened that Kabīr ultimately found his Rām. One of such *sākhī*s claims: 'I got to know the perfect and threw off all my sorrow.' But concurrent are verses of separation, and they are more in number. When the supreme lover is not far off but within oneself, 'in all souls', then why this acute pang of separation?

The core of 'knowing' or 'acquaintance' can be comprehended once we resort to 'the discernment of the word'. This is an acquaintance which Kabīr calls *anubhav*, 'experience', a special experience, something like an interface. The revelation of mystics. The purport is that only one fleeting glimpse of the Supreme Being could be had. Like a flash or lightning and, like it, accompanied by an exploding sound. Therefore Kabīr calls it *sabda* or *śabda*, 'the word'. *Nāda*, sound, is the property of *ākāśa*, the firmament, space or cosmos. Thus one comes across in Kabīr such phrases as '*anahada garaje*', 'the unstruck sound thunders', and '*gagana damāmā bājīyā*', 'the kettledrum resounds in the sky'. The supreme element expresses itself only in the space, but it is both expressed and unexpressed as the space itself. As it is formless, it is only a name. It is called Rām for convenience's sake—but with the harsh precondition that it is without attributes. Now, how can one meet with his *nirguṇa*, the attributeless? Acquaintance is fine but a meeting—now that is a different thing altogether! Therefore Kabīr says: 'The meeting of words was consummated, not the meeting of bodies.' A long-distance conversation but no physical confrontation.

Sometimes Kabīr calls this acquaintance *jñāna*, or 'knowledge'. Not the 'simple', 'common' knowledge but special knowledge. It may be called 'inner knowledge', 'self-knowledge' or 'spiritual knowledge'. This knowledge has its joy and its sorrow. A kind of sorrowful joy. The Sanskrit term '*vedanā*' denotes both knowledge and sorrow—'*yā vedanā tad akhilaṃ khalu vedanaiva*'—'whatever is knowledge is actually all sorrow'. The roots of Kabīr's sorrow are to be found in that special, unprecedented knowledge. The sorrow which was not felt while abandoning Māyā was experienced when Rām was gained. If the Supreme Element is the firmament, then reaching and embracing is no playful task. It is not without reason that Kabīr says: 'No one ever found the lover laughing, it was only through crying that one found him'. That is why Kabīr repeats such a phrase as 'the devotion of Rām is painful'. And it is all the more painful if one tries to achieve the unachievable—a Rām without attributes!

But this does not mean that the attributeless Rām is an abstract philosophical concept. Like Māyā, the attributeless Rām is also quite 'material'—material and real. No less concrete than anything with attributes! The attributeless which shook the foundations of the temple and the mosque, which upset the Brahmin and the Shaikh and which brought the credibility of the Veda and the Koran into question could not be an airy nothing. The attributeless is a kind of 'knowledge' that Kabīr calls variously an arrow and a sword. This knowledge had pierced his own heart as an arrow, but to his detractors it was a flashing sword-blade. The knowledge that is 'neither Hindu nor Musalman', that repudiates the difference between the Brahmin and the Shudra could be nothing else but without attributes.

The negation of all established beliefs is attributeless and sorrow is only natural in such mighty negation. But this is not the sorrow of the faithless nor is it the terror of doubt. By accepting the attributeless, Kabīr attained the courage to deny everything else. Surely there is a deep acceptance in Kabīr who sings 'fearlessly of the attributeless'. This attributeless is no mystery but the sublime imagination of a visionary poet. It is the possible blueprint of all desirable values and dreams—Gajanan Madhav Muktibodh calls it a 'map'. The map is in the mind, but there are no tools to build a new world based on it—this is the sorrow. The helplessness is sorrow. This is also a 'sad dream' but not exactly the 'tragic vision' of Pascal. Like Kabīr, this sorrow is also unique—ironical, replete with paradoxes. The moments of heightened experience thus often find expression in his *ulaṭbāṃsīs*—verses of suggestive contradictions and paradox.

There is no doubt in Kabīr's mind regarding Rām and his Māyā. He never lost faith in his Rām and never compromised with the world of Māyā. He denied the world absolutely but decided to remain in it and continued to have debate and discourse with his detractors. Basing their argument on a *sākhī* which says: 'The firebird has burnt its nest and now dwells between the heavens and the earth—abandoning their duality for it has faith in neither.' Some scholars try to prove that Kabīr was like the legendary bird of fire who had built his nest in the middle of nowhere and his faith hung in mid-air, supportless. To me this interpretation seems absurd. Kabīr's head may have touched the sky, but his feet were firmly on the earth. His faith was never baseless. The Ghīsūs and Mādhavs of the bygone and the present era are the solid pillars of the attributeless of Kabīr and it is this attributeless which gives them the basis of their confidence.

Despite this definite social base Kabīr does not seem satisfied with it. He seems anxious to broaden his base. If he calls out 'listen, brother sādhus' to the kindred spirits, he beseeches the Mullas and the Priests as well. He does not appear amenable to taking a lonely road. It is another thing that he might sometimes find himself alone in the bustle.

Yet, it has to be acknowleged that Kabīr often appears dejected. Perhaps because he is not only a saint but a poet as well. There are a lot many saints who wander about with their tambourines. But the sorrow of Kabīr, who roams dejected, is explosive and destructive. It is the raging fire in the soul that has immense power to reduce this corrupt world to ashes. Kabīr's 'word' is fire, his sorrow revolt.

(Translated from the original Hindi by Vishnu Khare)

The Arsonist: The Last Days of Kabir[*]

Kiran Nagarkar

The Khans are a cultured and liberal Muslim family from Bombay, India. Zia, the younger son and protagonist has, however, grown up to be a fanatic Muslim under the influence of his Aunt Zubeida. His relationship with his older brother Amanat has always been ambivalent. Zia is currently studying economics at Cambridge, and has just received a book from Amanat as a birthday gift.

* * *

It was a week or ten days later while he was clearing his table that Zia came upon his brother Amanat's birthday gift. He had no intention of reading whatever it was, at least not till the summer vacation, but as a courtesy to his absent brother he was willing to open the package to find out the title of the book and its author. It was a novel called *The Arsonist* and it was written by Amanat Khan. The flavour of Zia's reaction was something like Oh God. He was amazed that his brother, his very own Amanat, was a published author (when the hell did he get the time, he was supposed to be sick, he was helping his father in the makeshift office at home, soliciting work for himself, designing flying saucers for Aerospatiale and for aliens) but he also felt uneasy. It was a complicated response. There was a touch of envy and jealousy, more than a few grains of trepidation and a desire to protect his brother from those predators called critics.

There was a picture of Amanat (he looked shy and charming) and a blurb about the book on the back-cover:

---

[*] This excerpt on the life of Kabir is a fabrication. It is almost untainted by historical fact. It is, instead, an attempt at imagining Kabir, and a fabulist's impressionistic account of what Kabir's life, which is mostly a mystery, may have been like.

> This is the unlikely story of a weaver. It should be an ordinary story, dull, prosaic and journeyman-like. What, after all, can happen in a weaver's life? So one would think.
>
> But this is no ordinary weaver. It is a man who weaves God. It is a spiritual and spirited adventure. It is a story of great ribaldry, exuberance and joy. It is also a metaphysical journey: man's eternal search for meaning and his attempt to make sense of his life and of the world around him. It has the mordant wit of a Guenter Grass, the compassion of a Camus and the wisdom of a Zen master.
>
> Khan is a novelist of rare audacity and daring. He would make the Buddha and Christ, not to mention all of us readers, sit up and rethink their beliefs and sacred dogmas. *The Arsonist* will shock and alarm the West as it will the East. It is the story of the camaraderie, love, bickering and friendship between a man and his God. The arsonist, as you must have guessed, is the story of the great mediaeval Bhakti mystic, Kabir.

It was the usual orotund and inflated hype that blurb-writers across the world employ. Oh God, he thought, how am I going to read this? What if it's really boring and dull? What would he tell Amanat? That I thought your book phony and pretentious? That's the trouble when someone from your family thinks he belongs to the tribe of artists. They fancy themselves as slightly superior beings, they put on airs, their hair grows long and curly, they become bohemians. They turn ethereal or they become Rodin-like salt-of-the-earth figures; they wear stone-washed or primary colours, everything about them is a statement and a scream, look at me, look at me, I'm an artist, I'm different and, mostly, aren't I wonderful. Oh God, why did Amanat have to write, and why did he have to send his book to Zia? At some point or the other, Zia might even have to read it, damn, damn, damn.

It was not curiosity that led Zia to the book that night, he just wanted to get over the queasiness, the uncertainty, the bad taste in his mouth, the apprehension. Nobody knew whether Kabir was a Hindu or a Muslim. Little or nothing was known about his antecedents, his parents or his birth. What was worse, Kabir's verse proclaimed from the rooftops that it didn't make a difference whether you were Muslim or Hindu. Call Him Ram, Rahim or by any other name, God couldn't care less. (This was, of course, blasphemy. Hadn't God told Mohammed that there is no God but Allah and all the others are false gods? But for the sake of art and that highly suspect thing called artistic licence, Zia was willing to overlook that for a second.) But who would want to read about Kabir? He was like Gandhi, dead and gone and forgotten except when you needed a handy cliché or platitude to talk about the oneness of all faiths.

It was a short book, just a hundred and seventy pages, and Zia read it in one sitting. It was worse, much worse than he had imagined, but in an altogether different sense. It woke him up at night. He was angry. He felt defiled. It was about a saint and yet it was degenerate and debased. He read it again. Now he knew it was an evil book, a travesty of all that he held sacred and sacrosanct. It transgressed almost every boundary of decency, civilized behaviour, humanity, ethics and morality. It seemed to hold up the worst in man and glorified it. It was brutish and brutalized the reader. It desecrated not just the Islamic notion of God but scoffed at the very concept of good and evil, at godliness, at the aspiration to raise oneself above one's animal instincts. It was full of dark and ambiguous things. It was ambivalent and you did not know what to make of it. It left you unsure and uncertain of everything you held dear in your life.

It was, there was no question about it, the work of Satan. You were drawn to it. It was as if you had lost all volition. You knew that you must stop, fling the book out, out, far, far away, and yet you kept burrowing further and further into it. The blurb was right. It was ribald, exuberant and joyous. It was lively, intriguing and utterly bewildering. It made God accessible and it devalued him. Yes, Amanat had had the gall to laugh at God.

What was Amanat trying to say, for God's sake? How could he write about life and death matters so urgently and grippingly and yet trivialize them? Zia began to have the awful suspicion that he had got it all wrong. Was Amanat trying to provoke the reader, throw him off balance, make him reassess all that he had taken on faith or for granted? Zia kept going back to the book.

If you had to choose between a woman you had met the day before and God, who would you choose? And the weaver said, the woman, is there any doubt about that?

And the *mullah* asked him, if you had to choose between a song and God, which would you pick? And the weaver said, the song, of course.

And the priest from the temple asked him, weaver, if you had to perforce choose one or the other, a beautiful sunset and God, what would your choice be? And he said, isn't it obvious, the sunset.

And they asked him how could he blaspheme so. And the weaver said, why sirs, God has eternity on his side, he can always wait. Will the woman, the song and the sunset wait for me?

And they asked in desperation, if you had to choose between sin and God, weaver, what would you choose? And he laughed and he said, sin, always sin. Sin is fun, sin is forbidden; sin is, what shall I say, so sinful. They should forbid God as they forbid sin, maybe he would become far more attractive then and we would all be drawn to him. What a bunch of cretins you have for your devotees, oh Lord, he laughed out loud: the fools would sever you from your creation.

* * *

What incensed Zia particularly were the conversations between the weaver and his disciples that occurred again and again throughout the book.

The weaver had announced some weeks ago that he was going to send his old mother on a pilgrimage to Gangotri in the Himalayas when she could barely walk. His pupils asked him how he could be so cruel. And he said why not? Did you expect me to look after her in her old age while she blabbers and drools and dirties herself instead of going into the fields?

Then the other day the weaver let on that he had sold his wife to the wine merchant. And his assistants and trainees asked him, how could you do this to the woman who cared for you and cooked your meals and bore your children? And he said, what use is she to me now? She's past childbearing, her breasts have begun to sag, her teeth are shaky and she's become a shrew.

What an ungrateful and selfish man this weaver is, they said. Surely he'll burn in hell forever and after. Does he have no conscience?

Speak not to me of conscience. Does God have a conscience? Does he not get rid of us when he's done with us, and isn't that the reason we find ourselves dead when we would rather live as long as he?

God is always asking us sods to give up something we like or someone we love. Why doesn't he stop making so many demands on us and give up something himself for a change? Ask him to give up his

Godhood. What would he do without it? Who would ever look at him then?

* * *

The apprentices took up a subscription and told the weaver's wife that they had decided to buy a small cottage for her and her mother-in-law. She was moved by their kindness but also a little surprised.

You think it's time I left the old man? she asked. He's certainly getting more and more irascible by the day.

It was Gunidas who broke the news gently to her. Ma, the Master's sold you to the wine merchant and is getting himself a new woman.

Did he now? the weaver's wife stamped her foot in mock anger. Has the scoundrel forgotten that the house is mine and he's a mere house-guest, albeit a rather long-standing one? Gunidas, my child, haven't you learnt after all these years that my husband is perverse? He has a topsy-turvy tongue and a bizarre imagination in which mirages and reality, nightmares and magic mingle and clash and twist the listener's mind out of shape. He will say anything to jolt and shock the gullible and the know-alls, who are not so different really, just to provoke them to think.

* * *

One afternoon when the weaver was taking his siesta, two of his pupils, Ismael and Ananda, rushed into the house and woke him up.

I hope you've found God or something as important, Ananda. For if you haven't, I'm going to beat the living daylights out of you.

Is it true, Ananda was still out of breath, that you were an ascetic and lived alone in the mountains?

Is that why you woke me up, you fool?

Answer the question, Master, Ismael said tersely. The other apprentices left their looms and gathered around the weaver.

I don't remember. It was a long time ago. What's it to you, anyway?

No ascetic with any self-respect would ever return to a normal life or go back to his wife and children, Ismael sneered.

I suppose I have no self-respect. Now may I go back to my nap?

Why, why would you come back when you were supposed to be the greatest Maharishi in the country?

Can't we talk about that some other time?

Now, the pupils said impatiently.

When I was your age, I set out in search of God. Not small gods and medium-sized gods but the big one, the Almighty himself. I was a pretty persistent sort and over the years I got a reputation as a holy man. They called me a sage and a seer. Some said I was a siddha and I had miraculous powers. I used to stay in the Himalaya in those days, some fourteen thousand feet above sea-level. It was my seventh year of standing on one leg. My eyes were closed and my mind was focused on *Brahman*. People from far and near, from neighbouring principalities and distant kingdoms, trekked into the mountains to fall at my feet and receive my blessings. Sometimes they would wait for days, even weeks, to see me, for there was no telling how long my devotions and meditations would last.

Why do people go to see holy men? Because they believe the enlightened one can make God bend down his ear all the way from heaven. For them a sage is a go-between and a middle-man and who knows, God may be on the take. But I promised nothing. If I had, as was rumoured, magical powers, I was keeping them to myself. And yet they kept coming, the great mass of pilgrims, the rich and the poor, men, women and children, the lame and the halt and the handicapped; those who needed their lives fixed and those who needed nothing. They came to sit in the shadow of saintliness and be touched by someone who, for all they knew, was privy to God's thoughts.

One day the blacksmith's wife came to see me with her son. He was of an indeterminate age, he could have been twenty-five or maybe he was close to forty. His mouth was open and there was a vacuous smile on his face.

Don't just stand there, you fool. Touch the Master's feet, the mother snapped at him.

He bent down and lay prostrate in front of me, his hands joined prayerfully for a full five minutes.

Bless him, Master, the mother told the weaver. I've seven daughters and one son. His name is Suraj. He's a good boy and his heart is in the right place but he's a little simple. He's slow to learn and gets a beating from his father almost every week.

Tell the blacksmith to beat iron and not the boy, I told her. The simple of heart, I suspect, are closer to God than all the subtle scholars of the world. Rise, my son. I put my hand on his head. May God be with you.

Likewise, he said and laughed as if he had said something vastly funny.

He would come by from time to time and watch me from a distance. I would forget him and then hours later realize that he was still staring at me.

It was the beginning of February and a cold nasty wind was blowing, the one they call the Intruder. It groped under your clothes and whistled inside your bones. The blacksmith's son came up to me and wrapped a shawl around my shoulders.

I thank you for your kindness, I told him, but I must return your gift, for I have vowed that whatever the season, however inclement the weather, I will endure it.

The blacksmith's son looked puzzled. Why would you do this, Master?

A small token, I smiled self-deprecatingly, of my devotion to God.

I have brought you some bread that my mother made, and raw chillies. They'll bring warmth to your shivering body.

That is kind of you, Suraj. I'm touched by your concern, but I'll not touch food for the next three weeks.

And why would you do this, Master? Are you unwell?

Nothing of the sort, I said. Just another small token of my affection for the Almighty.

Does it give God pleasure, then, when people starve or freeze to death? he asked innocently. Is that why people scourge themselves?

Oh no, no. The good Lord doesn't ask anything of us. It's just a way of showing my love for Him.

Is that why you stand on one leg?

Yes, that is the very reason.

You have a rather funny way of showing your love, Master. For if God wanted us to be one-legged, he wouldn't have given us two.

I smiled at his naiveté but decided to humour him. Maybe you've got a point there.

What else have you given up, Master?

Not much, really. I shaved my head, left my young wife and my child of two months. And my elderly parents. They didn't want me to go, since I was their only child and the support of their old age. Who will run the workshop and who'll look after us, they asked. God will, I told them. He takes care of his own.

What workshop? Are you too an iron-master?

No. I was chief weaver by appointment to the king. All the princesses and queens wore fabrics woven on my looms.

All this you gave up? No wonder they call you Maharishi.

Not much really. Just a trifle. I bade farewell to my job as the village *mukhiya*. The villagers said, who will save us when the floods come and who will listen to our troubles? And I told them power is an unquenchable thirst, and high office, a pair of shackles. I will have nothing to do with them. Everything I had desired, I parted with.

Surely then you must part with the Almighty too.

I laughed and asked him. Pray, why should I part with the Almighty?

Because you desire God more than anything else in the world.

I was nonplussed. Was this man just stupid or was he the devil incarnate?

You suggest that I would forsake the most precious thing in my life? I spoke with suppressed rage.

The blacksmith's son fell at my feet and clung to my ankles.

Mercy, Master, have mercy on me. I will not get up till you've forgiven an ignorant man with a loose tongue.

Rise blacksmith, I said, I bear you no ill-will.

Your love of God is indeed great, Master. Greater than any other man's, the blacksmith's son said and bowed. I'll take your leave now.

May God go with you.

He never showed up again. The weaver paused. It was I who visited him a week later. He was in the smithy and cleared some cast iron scrap off a bench to make room for me to sit and asked his mother to get me a glass of buttermilk.

What can I do for you, Master? he asked me.

Will you be my teacher, my guru?

Me? He seemed astounded by the suggestion.

Yes. You have more wisdom than all my years of searching for the Almighty have given me. You taught me that one can get a little too attached to selflessness. You taught me that at the end of the day a man must renounce renunciation itself.

The blacksmith smiled. I taught you, Master? You are pulling my leg.

I'm not, I told him emphatically. I've never been more serious. Be my guru.

He laughed then, a loud guffaw that shook the smithy. You've got to be joking, he said. Do you think I've nothing better to do?

* * *

People were always asking the weaver, even after he came down from the mountains, to guide them, hold their hand and light their path, to accept their children as disciples.

Everybody wants a guru to show them the way, the weaver said. It's not such a bad idea, I suppose. You cannot see without a guru. But then, more often than not, you cannot see beyond the guru, either. The guru is vision and the guru is blinkers. It is easy to forget that one is not searching for the guru but for God. Once you've found a guru, it's time to think of leaving him and make your own way.

If I could teach you anything, he told his pupils and apprentices, I would teach you irreverence. Irreverence towards your guru; irreverence towards all and sundry, but most of all, irreverence towards yourself and your solemnities. The day you take yourself seriously, you'll become a prophet or a saviour, but in reality you'll be nothing but a pretender or the false messiah.

I may have found the true path, if such a thing exists, but the truth like all of us has a short life span. Somebody must then find another path, and another truth. And the one will not cancel the other.

* * *

No. No more. If I read any more, Zia said, I'll cast myself into hell. And he read on.

But why is there so much suffering? One of the weaver's disciples, the one they called Gunidas, asked. He was so earnest and solemn in his quest for God, the weaver wanted to kick him down the stairs to get a laugh out of him.

Why does a child of two die of diphtheria, why do the poor starve while the rich only get richer, why is there is no justice, there was no stopping Gunidas, why is there no equality, no fairplay, why are there untouchables, why is there pain, Master?

What a silly question, the weaver said. Because God is evil.

Gunidas and his fellow-pupils were aghast. The Master was always being heretical, partly to shock them, partly because he liked to speak in puzzles and enigmas, but today he had gone too far, he had crossed all bounds even of irreverence. He had to be taught a lesson. They would all leave him.

Good riddance, the weaver said, I'll have some peace now.

But blasphemy is always tempting. It is, after all, the first expression of freedom. One by one, they came back.

We are here on one condition only. You'll stop being childish and not say something terrible to merely provoke and torment us. Is that a promise?

The weaver gave his word that he would never say anything shocking. He looked contrite. I swear by Satan I will not be heretical again.

It was pointless talking to him, they said, and walked out. You could never trust him.

Is Satan not the creation of God? he shouted after them. Are there departments up there, one for evil and one for good? You, Michael, you are in charge of all plant life. Gabriel, I'm shifting you to the department of plagues and the research institute for new and more horrific diseases. We haven't had anything grand, scary and deadly since smallpox. And you, Lucifer, the portfolio for evil, I'm entrusting it to you. I don't want any dirt to stick to me. You are the bad guy and I'm the good one. It's very primitive and simplistic but take my word for it, good against evil is the best theatre in the world. People will flock to see us. The bishops, qazis and rabbis will philosophize interminably about the tree of knowledge and the doctrine of free will. And how God in his wisdom created polarities and each human being must choose between him and evil. They'll love it, Lucifer.

Why does God get all the credit for good, the weaver asked, and why is all evil attributed to Satan? If God is the Creator he can handle both. You must decide who's in charge here, my friends. Only then can you understand that all polarities and divisions are sacrilege. God, if I may use one of these new-fangled academic terms, is the unified theory of the universe. Good and evil, Hindu, Muslim, Jew, Christian, Buddhist are all encompassed in Him. He's large enough and wise enough to accommodate all contradictions.

* * *

A pox on Amanat. Was he cocking a snook at God? Or was he suggesting something profound? But Zia couldn't even be sure what Amanat was up to. There was a passage almost towards the end of the book that Zia found outrageous and the most puzzling of all.

The weaver was an old man now. He had always said, we weave the fabric of life, the warp of space and the woof of time, and no design is like any other. That's the guarantee we give in our workshop, that every design is unique because it comes from straight above.

He had announced many a time that he had no intention, none whatsoever, of dying. I plan to carry on, he would say, get as old and bald and toothless as the Almighty himself. And yet, in his work nowadays, you could see the threads and colours of old age. He would occasionally miss a stitch or repeat one. Or worse, he forgot the pattern.

His students and disciples looked at each other meaningfully at such times. They smirked, they made faces about the half-deaf, half-blind and half-mad weaver who was their Master. He was only half the man he was, they said. The trouble was there was no telling which half you would meet. Sometimes if he happened to hear you, he raged and ranted. I am still more of a man, he would say, than all of you young bucks put together. My dong is longer than yours, my hard-ons are harder and they can outlast anybody else's.

They wouldn't have dared to in the past but now they laughed openly in his face.

Hey, cock-of-the-walk, the troublemaker Inayat picked up the old man's *kurta* so that you could see the bulge of his trailing genitals, let's go to the brothel and test the matter.

You think I'm going to pay for your pleasure? the weaver asked, perhaps to put Inayat off.

No, no. We'll all come along and pay for your pleasure.

Well, I'm busy, he said, I get more orders than I can handle. There are so many other weavers but the nawabs and rajahs insist that I design and weave all their fabrics. Just the other day, the Sultan of Persia sent a messenger saying that I must weave the world's most exquisite and expensive cloth for his son's wedding robe next year. I had to refuse. What could I do? I have only two hands and you people are a dead loss. Can't ever rely on you.

Don't give us that cock-and-bull story, old man, Charatram, usually the quietest of the weaver's apprentices, spoke. Why can't you admit that you can no longer get it up?

That evening, all seventeen apprentices and the weaver went to the whores' alley. They took a woman each for themselves and the prettiest, the one they called Sherani because she was a tigress in bed, they kept for the old man. The deal was that at the end of the session, Sherani would give a report to them about the weaver's sexual prowess.

When they were done, the pupils gathered in the courtyard but there was no sign of the weaver. Fifteen minutes, half an hour, two hours. They went and listened at the door. The weaver was still at it. Then there was absolute silence. It sounded ominous after all that panting and heaving. He's obviously overdone it and got a heart-attack. Must have burst a blood vessel. We went too far this time, they said when the door was flung open and Sherani came out swearing at the weaver in the most foul language imaginable. They had to admit that her vocabulary in such matters was infinitely more colourful than their own limited and repetitive oaths.

This is not a man, Sherani screamed, he's a tomcat, a billy goat, a sex-maniac. He's done it seventeen times and he wants to do it again. The bloody lech says you guys are paying for it, so why shouldn't he get his money's worth? And what about me? I'm as good as dead. He's done it so often, a bullock cart, even the Maharaja's chariot can pass through. Come on, cough up, each one of you. This is no laughing matter. I'm ruined for life.

That night they had dinner at an open-air roadside café: biryani and tangdi kebab. The weaver was feeling generous and they ate heartily. He was narrating in great detail his exploits with Sherani when he became short of breath. They made him lie down on a bench. He was pale and a grey-blue tinge was creeping into his face. They wondered if this was the end.

Charatram, the shy one, said, Master, you should have some sense at your age. Couldn't you have controlled yourself? Even we can't do it more than twice or thrice.

The Master could hardly speak but that didn't prevent him from laughing and spluttering. I held Sherani's breasts in my hands. They were full and heavy as papayas and I thought God was finally in my palms. I told her if I sleep with you—and I'm not sure I'm up to it today—you'll earn some money but not much. But if, on the other hand, we lie blissfully in each other's arms for a couple of hours and then you scream and shout that I'm a monster and forced sex upon you seventeen times, all my apprentices will pay you seventeen times as much. Sherani is a businesswoman. How could she not go along with my scheme?

They could have strangled the Master. Instead they laughed, called him a cheat and a liar. Why else would they love him so and follow him everywhere? He was really a child and he never tired of practical jokes. By now, the weaver's pulse was unsteady and his breathing was short and staccato. He looked at them, he smiled weakly and he fell silent. A few more breaths and the soul had flown out of him. They touched his feet and asked his blessings one last time. They sent Charatram to get the wood for his funeral pyre and told him they would meet him at the burning *ghats*.

But even as Charatram left, Inayat said, the Master is a Muslim and he should be buried. Adil, Rehmat and Suleiman agreed with him. A vehement argument broke out amongst the disciples, but the Muslim pupils were outnumbered by the Hindus and walked away in anger.

Charatram came back with a bullock cart loaded with firewood. The Hindu disciples arranged the pyre and laid the Master gently on it. They performed the last rites, and each one of them lit a torch. They poured the *ghee* and were about to light the pyre when Inayat, Rehmat and the others returned with a group of Muslim friends. They had knives in their hands. The Hindus and the Muslims were now evenly matched.

If you know what's good for you, Inayat said, give the weaver back to us.

Just you try and take him, Gunidas retorted.

There was only one way to decide the matter. They fell on each other. Scalps broken open, blood and guts, both the parties were doing pretty well when the weaver sat up.

Can't a man even die in peace? he asked.

The Hindus and the Muslims froze as in a tableau. What was this apparition? They fled in panic.

Come back, you fools, come back, the wispy figure called after them.

One by one they returned. Some of them stood at a distance just in case the succubus sprang at them.

You won't ever change, will you? For the first time in his life there was defeat and failure in the weaver's voice. Light me a torch, he told them.

They had to help him down the pyre. He stood unsteadily and took the torch from Charatram.

Come, he said, follow me.

His legs seemed to buckle and he walked drunkenly. He had, after all, just come back from the dead. It was three in the morning when they reached the marketplace. The weaver stood almost at the centre. He was silent for a minute or longer than that. He was not going to make it, they thought, but his voice rang out.

I stand in the market place,
A torch in my hand.
Whosoever will set fire to his house,
Come, join me.

Now, he's really gone off his rocker, his apprentices and disciples said to each other.

Bring me the town crier's drum, the weaver said.

Why not, Inayat thought, this might be fun. He went to the peepul tree where the drum rested when it was not in use.

Beat it, the Master said, wake up the whole world and the heavens too.

The townspeople came out of their houses, husbands, wives and children, patriarchs and mothers-in-law, dogs and cats and soon the whole town was gathered around the weaver. They looked a little eerie and unreal in the light of the torches.

I stand in the market place, the Master spoke again. His voice was steady and it seemed to echo off the walls of the houses.

I stand in the market place,
A torch in my hand.
Whosoever will set fire to his house,
Come, join me.

What the hell is the old man up to? Ismael asked. What's he trying to say?

Something symbolic and profound, Charatram said sardonically. Something totally beyond you and me.

It slowly began to dawn on the townspeople that the weaver was serious about his invitation. He was always a bit mad but this time he had definitely gone over the edge. They began to close in on him almost imperceptibly, the men followed by the women. There was something sinister about the way they moved as if the weaver's madness had touched them too. The pupils and disciples, all but Inayat, slowly shrank away. The villagers bent down and picked up stones, bricks and whatever they could lay their hands on. Some went back to their homes to get knives, axes, hammers and bamboo poles.

Inayat, they said, move away, lest you get hurt.

He shook his head but was sensible enough to distance himself from the Master. The weaver began to run, his right hand up in the air. The flame of the torch sputtered and zigzagged. The villagers were not about to let the mad old man burn their homes. They began to pelt him. The Master torched his own house. A stone opened his forehead, a bamboo cracked the bone of his left arm. The weaver did not stop. A boy with a catapult got his left eye. Some of the disciples shouted to the villagers not to hurt the Master but no one paid them any heed. Gunidas and Rehmat flung their torches up in the air, caught them and set their own houses on fire. The haystacks next to their homes crackled and sputtered and turned into fireworks. Sparks rose in the air like fireflies. Two of the houses were burning steadily, the conflagration making a crackling racket and rising high into the skies.

There was a battle raging between the Master's pupils and the villagers. The disciples were in a minority and even those who had merely stood aside and watched were attacked; some were grievously injured. The villagers had long realised that their houses were safe but that did not assuage their fury. They continued their rampage.

* * *

Are you happy now? Inayat asked the Master. Why burn our own houses? Makes no sense.

The wounded weaver said, fire purifies, my friend. It is our chance to start afresh, to alter the course of our lives. The trouble with men is that the past is always and ever with them, as it was with you, Inayat and Charatram and all your friends at the burning *ghats*.

Is arson, then, the end of all your weaving and questioning, whoring and poetry? Inayat sneered. Or perhaps that was his way of concealing his utter despair.

It needn't have been if even a few of my pupils had changed just a little. We are never fully God's because we are always bound to the world and its ways; to our children, wives, work, pleasures, old habits that don't die, to our pride and sacrifices, to our homes. Once we are homeless, once we have no past, once there's an end to me, me, me, and there's nothing to hold us back, once we are true orphans, then our only home is God.

And is your work done now, old man?

The weaver laughed, more like a cackle.

Hardly, he said, now we'll burn heaven and hell and smoke and flush out God.

Kabīr and Contemporary Hindi Poetry

Kedarnath Singh

The impact of Kabīr on contemporary Hindi poetry of the past thirty years or so) can be tracted in various ways. The fact is, this impact has never been explicit that or immediately perceptible. Further, I have no facts and figures to state how much of Kabīr is actually read by new poets: to the best of my knowledge, not even one article has been written on Kabīr by any significant poet of the new generation. Despite this, Kabīr has been a strong presence behind the entire range of contemporary poetry.

It is not possible to determine the exact date of the beginning of this dialogic relationship of contemporary Hindi poetry with Kabīr's poetry as such. I would guess that its roots can be traced to the 1950s. Phanishwarnath Renu's famous novel, *Mailā āṁcal* (1954), bears the obvious impact of Kabīr's folk tradition in many ways. Many songs of Kabīr echo through the whole texture of the novel. In Renu, this impact had seeped in through folk roots, so it has a freshness and vitality unknown to the bookish interpretations. Actually, as we know, folk tradition has played a great role in keeping Kabīr alive down the ages and not much has been written to highlight, analyze or define this development.

The major part of medieval Hindi poetry has no bearing on contemporary poetic idioms, and Kabīr is the only potent exception whose down-to-earth language, and the message it conveys, is relevant to our own time. Not only his poetry, but also his person stand tall as a major influence. Poetry, as suggested by a great Romantic poet, should resist 'having a palpable design on us'. Generally speaking, the essence of poetry lies beyond its immediate message. But Kabīr is one of those rare poets whose poetic essence lies woven into his poetic message. In some respects this situation is akin to the poetry of Bertolt Brecht. Needless to say, Kabīr and Brecht belong to different time and space frames. But what establishes an obvious link between them, is the fact that they both seem to be touching upon the danger zone of didacticism, which marks the end of poetic periphery, and it is important that this never happens at the cost of poetic merit. How actually this is possible can be examined separately.

In the last two or three decades, something like a movement has taken place in the field of music, which has popularised *'Kabīr sangīt'* or the singing of Kabīr poetry amongst the urban middle class. The singer Kumar Gandharva was the leading figure of this movement. His musical reception of Kabīr has something to do with contemporary Hindi poetry as well. But in the field of folk music, the emergence of some new groups of folk singers have almost revolutionalised the whole gamut of *'Kabīr sangīt'*. A singer like Prahlad Singh Tipanya, who tries to reach the original sources of singing of Kabīr's songs, has touched the imagination of some young poets. The most interesting thing is that these folk singers are, knowingly or unknowingly, combatting the rampant pop-culture. By fresh musical transcreation of Kabīr's poetry, they are trying to raise a counter pop-culture, the tunes of which correspond to the rhythm of our time.

In Hindi poetic tradition, Kabīr perhaps was the first of his kind to try to transform the human discourse of his time into poetry. What Buddha calls '*dukh*' or the misery of humankind, remains the main poetic concern of Kabīr as well. But his way of reaching the roots of this misery is different in nature from that of Buddha. He never hastens to put the answer before the reader. His poetry questions everything and argues with everybody. It is the kind of argumental poetry that makes you restless. This aspect of his poetic creation especially attracts the contemporary mind because one often finds the words of the great poet echoing one's own basic queries. His poetry plays the role of an objective critique of his time. This was a revolutionary departure in the Indian poetic tradition which took poetry beyond the dominant *ras-siddhānt* or pleasure principle.

There are many factors which bring Kabīr close to the contemporary poetic scene. The most important thing is his poetry itself. Kabīr's poetry at one point has been dubbed a 'by-product' of his spiritual pursuit. I do not know what is meant by 'by-product' or *'phokaṭ kā māl'*. But if it suggests that Kabīr wanted to attain something of a higher value and poetry flew unwittingly through it, it is not true. Kabīr was a rationalist in the true sense of the word. The rich intellectual content of his poetry is the greatest proof that he was a conscious poet, and we can say with certainty that its artistic quality negates the romantic theory of spontaneity.

In the field of epistemology, as also in the field of poetic creation Kabīr dismisses all indirect evidence in favour of direct perusal. In this process, he rules out the presence of Rām or even the supreme reality when he says,

How can I know Rām
I never saw him

This insistence on the importance of physical verification fascinates the modern mind and this is what accounts for the unique thrust of his poetry, which paves every gap between the signifier and the signified.

Not many attempts have been made to trace the linkage between Kabīr and contemporary poetry. It is an established fact that among the medieval poets, Kabīr is the closest to the modern temper, but this proximity was not sudden. Before Independence and even sometime after it, the poetic stature of Kabīr was questioned time and again, giving vent to many literary controversies. Many scholars, despite their open appraisal of Kabīr, still consider him alien to the Indian poetic tradition. Despite extensive social recognition, Kabīr is one of those poets, who is not provided with either the right kind of aesthetic structure or the appropriate critical milieu against which his poetry could be truly evaluated. A new kind of critical tool and a fresh value system are essential to place this unique poetry in perspective. This new critical approach has not yet shaped up, but a certain curiosity towards the creative output of Kabīr has certainly dawned during the last few years.

Some of the *chāyāvādī* poets did try to link their poetic movement with the mysticism of Kabīr, but their basic poetic temper has very little to do with Kabīr's blatant gusto. It is ironical indeed that Nirala, the most revolutionary of the *chāyāvādī*s, established a direct creative link with the Vaiṣṇava poet Tulsīdās, and not with Kabīr. The fact is that it is only in the poetry of those born around Independence that a dialogue with Kabīr takes place, merging with the contemporary temper. This culminates into something unique.

If I am not wrong, the progressive poet Trilochan was the first among the modern Hindi poets to establish a creative link with Kabīr. His famous poem, 'The Weaver of Kashi', exposes the orthodoxies of Hindus and Muslims and ridicules both.[1] This poem of fourteen lines hails Kabīr as a weaver, but the aspect especially highlighted is the rebel. The limitation of this poem is that here Kabīr does not actually outgrow the stereotype of a symbol. The poem is concerned with Kabīr's personality but not with his poetic vision. The poem was written sometime in the 1960s. After that, for a whole decade, Kabīr emerged neither at the centre nor at the margin of any poem. But at the end of the 1980s, contemporary poetry did seem to be establishing a new kind of relationship with Kabīr which deserves to be discussed at length.

One of the forerunners of contemporary Hindi poetry was Vijay Dev Narayan Sahi who, besides being a powerful poet, was an insightful critic. His anthology of poems, *Sākhī*, is in many ways a point of departure that establishes an intertextual dialogue with Kabīr.[2] Sahi was born in Benaras, precisely in the locality where the Kabīr Caurā stands. So there is substance in the hypothesis that as a child he registered the reverberations of Kabīr poems being sung and recited in those areas. Even the name *Sākhī*, which he gave to his anthology, has a Kabirian ring. Most of the poems of the anthology, too, have a direct or indirect reference to Kabīr. This is for the first time in modern days that the creative literature in Hindi seeks to establish a dialogue with Kabīr's psyche and draws parallels with his mental make-up and his poetic idiom to address a contemporary consciousness. Kabīr here is present like a racial legend, and the poet feels one with him somewhere deep down. Kabīr's pet address, '*sādho*' or '*sādho bhāī*', frequents Sahi's poetry and here it becomes quite difficult to decide who this '*sādho*' is. The fact is that in these poems the poet seems to be addressing Kabīr himself. In some poems, he talks to him as a man talks to his senior contemporary. Actually this is a poetic device that Sahi used for a close dialogic reception of Kabīr. The important aspect of the poem of this anthology is its skill of

---

[1] Trilocan, *Pratinidhi kavitāeṁ*, New Delhi 1985, pp. 106-7.

[2] Vijay Dev Narayan Sahi, *Sākhī: Machlīghar ke bād kī kavitāeṁ*, New Delhi 1983.

pouring in new echoes in a medieval form of address. This also bears evidence to the fact that the sensibility of a modern poet can be close to that of Kabīr.

An important poem of *Sākhī* is 'A Prayer: To Guru Kabīrdās'. The crux of this prayer is that the poet wants to revoke in himself the courage to speak the truth with the fearlessness of Kabīr, which is missing in the intellectual climate of today. To explain the inter-relationship of Kabīr and contemporary Hindi poetry, this anthology needs to be studied at length.

In many of the younger Hindi poets, too, some kind of intertextual dialogue with Kabīr can be easily traced. Some passing reference to him, some semiotic link, some suggestion, some idiom from Kabīr is creatively hooked up by these poets and placed in a new perspective. In recent times the use of Kabīr's name in anthologies like *Uttar Kabīr*[3] or 'Kabīr's Address' cannot be called incidental. (At this point, I may mention my own long poem, called 'Uttar Kabīr', which was written some six or seven years ago.) The establishment also is trying its level best to assimilate Kabīr. Many institutions have been named after Kabīr, but this displays not so much faith in Kabīr's poetry or philosophy as a tendency to cash in on his popularity. 'Uttar Kabīr' highlights the hollowness of the political reiteration of Kabīr. It also articulates Kabīr's agony over his transformation from a living man into monument or institution. Ironically, over the years Kabīr has become a dead stereotype. I feel that the growing attraction to Kabīr in contemporary Hindi literature in some ways represents a reaction to a growing tendency in Indian society to create stereotypes. One aspect of the inter-textual dialogue of contemporary Hindi poetry with Kabīr is this tendency of new poets to reflect Kabīr both in style and poetic idioms. They do so sometimes almost in the spirit of Lowells 'Initiations', and this is meaningful in many ways. Some recent poems of Uday Prakash are good examples of such creative imitation. No such fruitful imitations of other medieval poets have fallen in sight, perhaps because no other medieval poet actually comes so close to the contemporary poetic timbre. Kabīr is a rare poet in the sense that he

---

[3] Kedārnāth Siṃh, *Uttar Kabīr aur anya kavitāeṁ*, 2nd ed., Delhi 1999 (1st ed. 1995), pp. 132-41.

belongs as much to his own times as to ours. In times to come this bondage will intensify, as promised by some new poets and especially some poems by the young poet Gyanendrapati where he gives a new stylistic turn to the current poetic language by his playful variations on Kabīr's linguistic nuances. For most of the younger poets Kabīr is not just a major medieval poet but also a vibrant presence who is there with them in all their struggles against social discrimination, religious intolerance and human sufferings in general.

Hazārīprasād Dvivedī's Kabīr[1]

Monika Horstmann

Hazārīprasād Dvivedī (1907-79) is an outstanding figure in the field of Hindi literature and literary criticism, and an acclaimed authority on medieval religion and poetry.[2] His writings have been admired and widely used, but seldom have the basic assumptions on which his work rests been identified as crucial to his way of representing medieval personalities and their role in the religious and literary history of India. Dvivedī's basic assumptions seem to have unfolded without major breaks fairly continuously through his life.[3] Therefore, to single out his book on Kabīr, as I do here, may help highlight some of these assumptions rather than distort them in a myopic perspective. That book also commends itself for examination because it has recently attracted attention from the Dalit perspective and aroused severe criticism of the very assumptions on which Dvivedī's image of Kabīr is based.[4]

The straightforward utilitarian Indological, and especially the western Indological, understanding of Dvivedī's *Kabīr* is exemplified by a quotation from Charlotte Vaudeville's book of 1974:

> Barthwal had worthy successors in H. P. Dvivedi and Parashuram Chaturvedi, whose Hindī writings on the Nāth and Sant traditions constitute an important contribution to the religious and cultural history of medieval India.[5]

---

[1] A modified version of this paper was published in *Hindī* (2000).—References to H. P. Dvivedī's collected works (*Hajārīprasād Dvivedī granthāvalī*, ed. Mukund Dvivedī, 11 vols., 2nd ed. [[1]1981], New Delhi 1994) are by volume and page.

[2] Nirmalā Jain has recently underscored this in a statement which will probably meet with wide consent. See 'Racnā kā pūrv aur ālocnā kā paścim', *Haṃs*, August-September 1997, p. 140.

[3] There exists to date no critically documented study of Dvivedī's life and work.

[4] Dharmvīr, *Kabīr ke ālocak*, Delhi 1997, 2nd ed. Delhi 1998, pp. 73-96.

[5] Charlotte Vaudeville, *Kabīr, I*, London 1974, pp. 24-5.

In Chapter V of her book, Vaudeville relied heavily on those contributions. When she wrote, in a period that retrospectively can be identified as the heyday of research on bhakti, the focus of scholarly interest was to isolate the historical Kabīr from younger layers in the picture drawn of him mainly by hagiography. Vaudeville's assessment of Dvivedī's contribution is correct within that specific historical purport. It was, indeed, an express principle of Dvivedī that a writer should be familiar with the cultural milieu of the topic he wished to discuss. As one needs hardly mention, Dvivedī's oeuvre is rife with evidence of his profound interest in ancient and medieval cultural history and ethnohistory. That it was necessary to acquire familiarity with the cultural past, he emphasized in a letter to his mentor Banārsīdās Caturvedī, the editor of *Viśāl Bhārat*, in August 1940.[6]

This principle was not based on scholarly considerations alone, rather in that letter it already had a societal connotation. He thought that a writer in terms of true servant of literature would be driven by a deep urge to present his country and its inhabitants as 'beautiful and respectable', and in order to achieve this, he would also be driven to equip himself with the necessary historical knowledge. He thus established a link between the writer, his sincere analytical urge, and the vindication of his subject's dignity. Thus it was part of his project to seek an India 'beautiful and respectable', inhabited by human beings living a life of dignity.

Linda Hess has been the only one of the few scholars to address in detail the issue of the image that Dvivedī had presented of Kabīr. In a paper published in 1987, she noticed Dvivedī's biographical approach.[7] Although published five years after the publication of Nāmvar Siṃh's *Dūsrī paramparā kī khoj*,[8] she was hardly familiar with that impressive piece of literary criticism, for the volume of which her article forms part

---

[6] Dvivedī, letter of 26 August 1940, *Hajārīprasād Dvivedī ke patra*, pt. 1, ed. by Mukund Dvivedī, New Delhi 1994, pp. 72-3.

[7] Linda Hess, 'Three Kabir Collections: A Comparative Study', in: Karine Schomer and W. H. McLeod (eds.), *The Sants: Studies in a Devotional Tradition of India*, Berkeley and Delhi 1987, pp. 111-41, especially p. 134.

[8] 2nd ed. New Delhi 1989 [^{1}1982].

represents the proceedings of a conference which had taken place in 1978 but took nine years to come out.

Nāmvar Siṃh's book brings together personal and literary aspects of Dvivedī's work which must be considered in conspectus. Much indebted to his representation of Dvivedī, I will argue in what follows that *Kabīr* is a book on Dvivedī's dominant theme: the image of man in the twentieth century and its rootedness in the Indian national tradition. I will further argue that that image was shaped by autobiographical factors amongst which the most determining one appears to have been Dvivedī's encounter with Rabindranath Tagore. Last, I will emphasize the rather obvious, namely, that our understanding of Dvivedī the scholar, will gain if we also take account of Dvivedī the creative writer.

Kabīr was first published in 1942, twelve years after Dvivedī had joined Śāntiniketan. He had published three major books, *Sūr-sāhitya* (1936), *Hindī sāhitya kī bhūmikā* (1940) and *Prācīn bhārat meṁ kalātmak vinod* (1940), the second setting the key for a good part of subsequent scholarly writing on the history of Hindi literature. In May 1941 Dvivedī wrote to B. D. Caturvedī,

> These days I am involved in writing a book on Kabīrdās. My main endeavour in this is to present as fully as possible the treatment given of him by all earlier scholars and, in light of that, my own ideas of Kabīr. I am labouring hard, but let me see to what extent I will succeed. This time I am trying to write in a language for which you, too, will be obliged to issue me a certificate. It won't be Hindustani, though, but certainly it will not be Sanskrit. If you wish to write on scholarly matters in an easy language, you encounter plenty of obstacles. But see for yourself how far I have succeeded. I hope to complete the draft by July.[9]

This quotation reveals the astonishing speed with which Dvivedī wrote those early books that became landmarks of Hindi scholarship, and, more importantly, it points to a connection of issues established by the author and quite significant for his overarching project of Hindi literature as

---

9 Dvivedī, letter of 14 May 1940, *Hajārīprasād Dvivedī ke patra*, p. 81.

national literature. He is anxious to write in a genuinely readable variant of the idiom that to him is expressive of the uninterrupted tradition of Indian (in reality, mainly north Indian) culture and hence a symbol of national unity, Hindi, which is not named but identified by its distinction from both Hindustani and Sanskrit. This underscores how Kabīr, according to Dvivedī, figures in the tradition of Indian literature. Kabīr is representative of a single continuous stream of tradition neither crucially changed nor diverted by the advent of Muslim culture in India. Kabīr is not alien to the Sanskritic tradition but shares with it the same ground. To Dvivedī, the Sanskritic and the vernacular, the twice-born tradition and the non-twice-born, are integral to the Hindi tradition.[10]

In *Kabīr*, Dvivedī does not abandon the issues that had caught his attention in his earlier books. In fact, in certain regards these exhibit a thrust that is also characteristic of his book on Kabīr. This thrust is on the formation of man and, within that, on the existential transformation that needs to take place to become a Sūrdās, a Tulsīdās, a Kabīr, or, for that matter, an exemplary human being. Such exemplary human beings may be encountered in the medieval tradition. So how does this tradition fit in the history of Indian literature and what is its impact for the India of the twentieth century? If a positive impact can be accorded to it, in which way is the image of man (as drawn on the model of those medieval authors) of any consequence to contemporary Indians or to the world at large? It is in this deepest concern of Dvivedī that his biographical approach is grounded. Moreover, Dvivedī's interest in biography has profound moorings in his own life.

According to Dvivedī, a genius can be born everywhere, not only among the privileged. But being a genius requires more than innate talent. The human being thus endowed is bound to pass an existential turning point in order to come into his own and gain his authentic expression. To attain this, he needs to labour through strife, anxiety, and frustration and eventually has to make an all-decisive leap to realize his true personality. Already Dvivedī's Sūrdās, the blind singer, represents a case in point. Dvivedī is not satisfied with the interpretation that Sūr was either born

---

[10] This view is persuasively put forth in *Hindī sāhitya kī bhūmikā*, first published in 1940 (3. 25-251).

blind or that he turned blind or that his was a spiritual blindness to the mundane. He pleads for Sūr's having deliberately caused himself to be blinded in view of the acme of worldly beauty, represented by a woman whom he would ask to blind him. In this way, in order to turn to eternal fulfilment, he rejects perfection and fulfilment as the world would give them. He introduces his version of Sūr's life by a conscious denunciation of the veracity of existing images of Sūr. Unlike historians who build Sūr's biography on the foundation of historical evidence, he wishes to establish Sūr's 'real biography', *vāstavik jīvanī*. More than in a factual biography (*yathārth jīvanī*) he is interested in the truth behind the facts (4.122). He embarks on his surprising strategy slightly ironically, indicating that he does not claim that his picture is the only possible one. Instead, it is a deliberate construction that commends itself for a powerful symbolic representation of its inherent universal truth (4.122 and 124). In fact, Dvivedī adopted his version of Sūr's blinding from R. Tagore.[11] Man has to pledge his whole existence in order to be able to transform himself and, consequently only to this, to transform the mundane into the eternal (4.124).

In *Hindī sāhitya kī bhūmikā*, Dvivedī does not repeat his bold explanation of Sūrdās's blindness, for here he argues rather differently, namely, in terms of literary sociology (3.114ff.). As far as the Kabīr of the *Bhūmikā* is concerned, it is crucial to the central concept of the book that Hindi literature is integral to what he perceived as the uninterrupted stream of Indian tradition and that, within this stream, bhakti literature is not a reaction against cultural obstacles created by Muslim influence but a broad popular movement (3.71) in which the turning point was set by Rāmānand, the erstwhile orthodox Brahmin, who would establish a new genealogy of saints in which superiority was no longer decided by caste or rank but by the sincerity of bhakti.[12] Already in *Bhūmikā,* Dvivedī links the issue of medieval religious culture to the twentieth-century situation. He contemplates the possibly convincing effect that Kabīr's harsh criticism of the opinionated orthodoxy might have had on its contemporary representatives. But what kind of conviction would Kabīr's

---

11 He points to this himself. His source is Tagore's 'Sūrdāser prārthanā'.

12 In expressing this opinion, Dvivedī sides with Kshiti Mohan Sen; cf. 3.74.

words have caused with them? None that would lead to action, none that would change their attitudes. And what about the opinionated of this century? No change of attitude, no commitment to change, only lip-service to the equality of human beings. Noble thoughts and theorising will not relieve the burden of the marginalised, what is called for is commitment to action (3. 75).

As I said, Dvivedī believes in an existential turning point in the formation of an exemplary character. In his longest, autobiographical letter to B. D. Caturvedī (September 1945) he speaks of the turning point in his own life, his meeting with Tagore.[13] In the same letter he characterizes his gurus, his Jyotiṣa teacher, Pt. Rāmratna Ojhā, Tagore, and B. D. Caturvedī himself. All were 'very generous and very enthusiastic' *(baṛe udār aur baṛe mastmaulā)*. To have *mastī*, an intoxicated passion, was, as is profusely evident in Dvivedī's work and, as has been pointed out by Nāmvar Siṃh, essential to him. Dvivedī even says that life itself has to be taken as a play to which its players need to be fully abandoned, irrespective of loss or gain. But he who plays must be someone who is committed to a task, he must be the servant of that task, and that task invariably will be to form man and to serve mankind.[14] Dvivedī thus posits ideal man, his mentors and ultimately himself in a line with Kabīr whose biography he constructs so persuasively. In so doing, Dvivedī strings Kabīr's sayings on the chain of Kabīr's inner development as he feels it to have evolved. He thus arrives at a biography of a type that runs from imperfection through crisis to perfection. According to Dvivedī and to the now *communis opinio*, Kabīr stood in the Nāthyogic tradition and was nominally a Muslim. Intellectually, he stood on a multiple crossroads (3.324-35). However, to be heir to a multiple tradition, as he was, was not enough: for perfection must be preceded by transformation. For Kabīr, as much as for other Sants, his encounter with Rāmānand (which Dvivedī takes as a fact) opened up a new option of spiritual life. However, having been born a genius, had he not met Rāmānand he would nevertheless have been stifled by rigid social rules and would at best have

---

13 Dvivedī, letter of 19 September 1945, *Hajārīprasād Dvivedī ke patra*, pp. 115-20.

14 Dvivedī, letter of 11 December 1943, Ibid., pp. 104-5.

had the option to lead the life of a lowly yogic sadhu on the margins of society. Rāmānand, in a spontaneous initiation *(sahaj dīkṣā*, 4. 315), imparted to him the understanding *(jñān)* that would enable him to pursue his religious quest within a world that he could henceforth boldly face. To Dvivedī, it was important that Kabīr should have been allowed to apply his genius at the same time to his religious vocation and to worldly life and thus contribute to the transformation of the world from within. For this, Kabīr's encounter with Rāmānand prepared the ground. Rāmānand saved him from becoming a marginalized low-caste mendicant of sorts and revealed to him a religiously-founded dignity beyond caste that, according to Dvivedī's social vision, needed to be put to effect within the world. With Rāmānand, *jñān* is a liberating force which breaks down the confines of dogma and gives access to bhakti. Bhakti as imparted by Rāmānand to his various disciples allowed for numerous ways of individual enactment and superseded dogmatic boundaries. In so emphasising Rāmānand's crucial impact, Dvivedī argues that Rāmānand represented at once the fountain-head of orthodox tradition and the harbinger of new unorthodox options. Kabīr, in the same breath, becomes a link in that process. His ideas and saying do not run counter to the method *(yukti)* of philosophical reasoning or to the *śāstra*s (3.314). In this way, Dvivedī refutes R.C. Śukla's contention that Kabīr was outside the shastric pale of tradition. Dvivedī takes the conversion of Kabīr by Rāmānand as the culminating point of Kabīr's spiritual crisis.

> In every way [Kabīr] felt a peculiar kind of deficiency. The whole world was burning in its various fires. He had met no one to whom he could remain attached. It grieved him that those to whom he disclosed his feelings retorted with stinging remarks; he had met no one whom he might have told his innermost feelings in a mood of comfort, fearlessly. In a mood of distress he looked for something, but he could not find it. His whole mind and soul were consumed by the poison of doubt. His heart was restless; he did not find the kind of lover by the loving contact with whom poison would have been entirely converted into nectar. Exactly at that time he met Rāmānand. It was very good, indeed, that he met the guru, for otherwise he would probably have run into great misery. Who knows if also Kabīr, like others, would not have mistaken the lamp of delusion for his ultimate goal and would

> have precipitated himself into it like a moth. Those fortunate like him who are delivered by the grace of the guru can be counted by the fingers of one hand. When Kabīr obtained the *sadguru* he considered himself fortunate, but a guru's success is not only dependent on the guru's greatness. Also his disciple has to be equally active. Kabīr was exactly that kind of disciple. (4.306)

In profound unifying absorption *(sahaj samādhi),* Kabīr received from Rāmānand the ultimate revelation of loving devotion (4.315). The essence of that revelation was *prem* (-bhaktī). Hence he commanded 'an imperturbable self-confidence' which brought about his famed 'arsonist intoxication, uninhibited carelessness and indifferent truculence' *(Kabīr kī yah ghar-phūṃk mastī, phakkaṛānā lāparvāhī aur nirmam akkhaṛtā unke akhaṇḍ ātmaviśvā*s *kā pariṇām thī.* 4.321).[15] These were the qualities that Dvivedī would come to see as essential for braving the challenge of life. Kabīr was a fighter in an arena where one would have to stake one's head for the gain of love (4. 322). He was a heroic transgressor, uncompromising and the exact opposite of a harmonising reformer or apostle of Hindu-Muslim unity (4. 342).

Dvivedī did not heed particular text-critical caution while allowing the personality of Kabīr to unfold. His main goal was not the accumulation of biographical facts that would stand the test of historical scrutiny, but the creation of the image of man as an individual endowed with freedom and dignity. For the poets he studied, his ideal was that they should have lived as they taught. In the pursuit of this ideal he drew a line from the perfect *bhakta*s, and especially Kabīr, down to Tagore. In a collection of essays entitled 'Mṛtyuṃjay Ravīndra', he uses all the key terms characterising Kabīr to describe Tagore.[16] According to Dvivedī, Tagore was able to raise the most ordinary of men to dignity and greatness, his was intoxicated joyfulness defying death, and his legacy

---

15 Cf. especially Nāmvar Siṃh, *Dūsrī paramparā*, Chapter 3.

16 The date of the original publication of this remains unidentified. Supposedly it was published in or shortly before 1965, for which cf. Dvivedī, letter dated 10 July 1965, *Hajārīprasād Dvivedī ke patra,* p. 194. The volume brings together essays mostly published in *Viśāl Bhārat*.

was the image of man as true, free, self-confident and self-relying (8. 278-80). In Tagore's works he perceives a keynote, which he calls by a name of distinct religious ring, *sahaj bhāv*: the mood of spontaneity and spiritual unity. He defines this in a phrase:

> *manuṣya, manuṣya ko manuṣya kī dṛṣṭī se dekhe, yahī sahaj bhāv hai.*
> 'Man, if you behold man with the eyes of man, then this is *sahaj bhāv*.' (8. 302)

Dvivedī thus merged religious and humanist concerns. However, in his work this merger unfolded gradually over the decades. Kabīr was the seed on which the crystal of Dvivedī's humanism and its vocabulary were to grow. In its ultimate shape it lies before us in *Anāmdā*s *kā pothā urf Raikva-ākhyān*, his last novel (1976). In this, the qualities singled out by Dvivedī come to serve a new purpose. The critic of society and transgressor is ultimately transmuted into a transformer of society. While in *Kabīr*, *prem*, the essence of liberating insight, was the motor of transgressing the world, its restrictions and its opprobrium, it has now taken on a societal, humanist application. This is not achieved in departure from the earlier concept, but by a shift of accent. Love needs to be lived in the world in order to transform and ultimately transcend it. The world is the medium, the otherworldly liberation is man's aim (2. 349-50). The love of life is common to all beings and is their prime concern; this is the realm of the supreme self. So in order to find that which is truly oneself or one's self, one has to follow the call of love. In the vein of the following instruction, Raikva, the young ascetic, is led back to the way of the world and also the world of human love, where he will work for the uplift of the distressed:

> *... tumhārā sva-bhāv prem hai, usī ke mādhyam se tum satya kā sākṣātkār kar sakte ho.*
> '... your nature is love, and only by this you can realize truth.' (2. 370)

Raikva, too, the orphaned ascetic boy suffering the itch of love that he tries to subdue by austerities, needs to pass through a crisis in which he realizes that his doctrinal tenets have failed him. The much-admired repository of ascetic lustre, he is, in fact, empty. Like Kabīr's Rāmānand, it is this time the seer Auṣasti and his wife conduct Raikva through his crisis to the realization of his human nature, which needs to be fulfilled in society but eventually transcend it. All three, Kabīr, Raikva and Dvivedī, are ultimately identical in having been transformed at a critical turning point by a guru, be he Rāmānand, Auṣasti and his wife, or Tagore. Put briefly, under the impact of his own transformation in his encounter with Tagore, Dvivedī came to experience something he surmised to have taken place in Kabīr under the influence of Rāmānand. He also construed related experiences in his fictional writing.

Whereas I have tried to understand Dvivedī's assumptions as partly biographically founded and to see in *Kabīr* the important aspect of a modern social utopia, the recent Dalit approach is different. It has been put forth by Dharmvīr in Chapter 5 of his book on the critics of Kabīr. That chapter is entitled 'Dr Hajārī Prasād Dvivedī: The full eclipse of the Sun' thus expressing the harm done to Kabīr by Dvivedī.[17] According to Dharmvīr, the Brahmin Dvivedī exemplifies in glaring fashion the gulf between shastric and the Dalit cultural traditions. The gulf cannot be bridged by a Brahmin agent. Unable to understand Kabir's message, Dvivedī views his image in the refracting mirror of Brahmin tradition, and this is why Kabīr's work appears difficult to him. He mangles him in order to make him comply with the shastric/puranic tradition. Had he only desisted from claiming him for the Hindu tradition and the Hindu fold, all his problems of understanding Kabīr would have vanished. According to Dharmvīr, Dvivedī is unable to appreciate Kabīr in his own right. He can only appreciate him as a disciple of the Brahmin Rāmānand, who purged him of his low-caste rudeness. Thus Dvivedī's admiration of Kabīr is merely derivative of his brahmanical predilections. Dharmvīr lists five claims that Dvivedī made:

(1) Kabīr's natural expression was rude because he was born in a humble family;
(2) only Rāmānand created in him the sentiment of bhakti;
(3) Kabīr was basically a bhakta and an individualist; the reform of

---

[17] Dharmvīr, *Kabīr ke ālocak*, pp. 73-96.

society was no major concern of his;
(4) Kabīr never thought of organizing a *sampradāy*;
(5) if ever Kabīr wished to reform society, he did not pronounce any sound arguments for this.[18]

In the given context, I will only comment on point (2). Suffice it to say that I, too, see Kabīr neither as a social reformer nor the organizer of a *sampradāy*. That would belie the available historical evidence. It would mean reading modern issues into the past. This is, of course, not to deny the reformist *potential* of Kabīr's work.

Dharmvīr does point, though polemically, to factual problems in Dvivedī's approach, namely, his appropriation of him in the common Hindu tradition, which would imply the shastric one, and the role of Rāmānand in Kabīr's life. It is true that Dvivedī put Kabīr's thought in a wider (to him integral) context of Indian religious thought as it has come down to us in the Sanskritic tradition. He was of the opinion that Muslim influence had not really caused a major change, let alone that paralysing caesura alleged by some authors, in the literary history of India. According to him, the Sufi influence on Kabīr and on other Sants was minimal. As he put it, 'The Sants fall a hundred per cent within the Indian tradition.'[19] While playing down the Muslim contribution, he was eager to establish a shastric-folk-bhakti-continuum. He was not unaware of Kabīr's and other Sants' thinking as being at variance with shastric tradition, but chose to view this as the absence of systematic religion and philosophy in the Sants. However, to him breaking away from inherited traditional systems was no flaw. He liked to see the Sants as commanding the same type of heritage, acquired not by bookish learning but by experience. They were informed by the common Indian tradition, they were avid and critical listeners of the tradition, they were *bahuśrut*.[20] The shastric tradition and the Sants shared a contiguous tradition. Dvivedī does, indeed, grapple with the problem of how to reconcile Kabīr's *nirguṇ* stance with the thinking of Rāmānand, whom he takes as Kabīr's guru and who, in

---

[18] Ibid., p. 87.

[19] *Hindī sāhitya kī bhūmikā*, p. 70.

[20] Ibid., p. 67.

Dvivedī's project of cultural continuity, forms the missing link between the shastric and the Sant sphere and who personifies the capacity of the shastric, caste-bound culture to liberate itself not through the strength of the *śāstra* but the experience of genuine bhakti. Dvivedī invests Rāmānand with a distinct individual personality and a Viśiṣṭādvaita philosophy although, in fact, we are compelled to admit that 'he remains a historical enigma'.[21] Dvivedī takes the discrepancy, partly created by himself, as evidence for Rāmānand's liberal outlook. In him it was not dogma but bhakti that reigned supreme. He would liberate his disciples to come of their own. Rāmānand's and the successive Sants' bhakti as much as the entire medieval bhakti 'movement' figure prominently in Dvivedī's project for he finds the self-healing capacity of India, the recovery of an ailing, ossified Hindu civilisation obsessed with, and dissipating its energy in, pointless, repetitive shastric exercises. The bhakti poets enabled that civilisation to return to the natural and to face the genuine issues of life.[22] That Dvivedī construed Rāmānand out of next to nothing is true. To me, this emphatically pursued construction is founded in his exceptional interest in transforming causes at work in a biography. To him, as I have tried to show, the transforming turning point was invariably connected with a guru-personality (for himself, Tagore; for Kabīr, Rāmānand). Kabīr's transformation liberated him to live bhakti within the world and for the benefit of it. Such a man was the exemplar of Dvivedī's vision of mankind, a utopian vision which from the Dalit perspective can legitimately be considered a failure. However, what he had in mind was not the purging of Kabīr by Rāmānand and his legitimation and usurpation by Brahmin tradition, but the liberation of Indian civilization from dogmatic fetters in the cause of human life in dignity.

---

21 David N. Lorenzen, *Kabir Legends and Ananta-das's* Kabir Parachai, Albany, NY 1991, p. 12; cf. ibid., pp. 8-18, for a review of the historical problems surrounding the relationship of Rāmānand and Kabīr.

22 *Hindī sāhitya: uskī udbhav aur vikās*, 1st ed. 1952 (3. 314-15).

Kabīr and the Nāthpanth

Mariola Offredi

Theories on Kabīr say that he was a highly committed devotee of Viṣṇu, in no way influenced by either Sufism or the Nāths; or that he was influenced by Sufism[1]; or that Kabīr was linked to Nāth doctrines.[2]

---

[1] Tara Chand, *Influence of Islam on Indian Culture*, 2nd ed., Allahabad 1976 [1st ed. 1946].

[2] Hajārīprasād Dvivedī, *Kabīr*, 2nd ed., Delhi 1980 [1st ed. 1964]. Long before Hajārīprasād Dvivedī, Pītāmbardatt Baṛthvāl underlined the debt of the Nirguṇ School to Rāmānand and showed the direct connection of the Nirguṇīs with the Nāths: 'That it has to do something with the Vaishṇava movement, is well known, but that it has a direct connection with the Yoga system of the Nāthas as well, was not so far realised, because of the antagonism displayed by the Kabīr panthīs towards Gorakhnāth and other Yogīs. This antagonism appears to be of a later date than the 16th Century in which the Dādū and the Sādh panths, which do honour Gorakhnāth, were founded. In a paper read before the Sāhitya Parishad of the Kāśī Nāgarī Prachāriṇī Sabhā (Dec. 1930) and subsequently published in its journal (the Nāgarī Prachāriṇī Patrikā, vol. 11, N. 4 Māgha, 1987 V.S.), I showed for the first time that such a connection undoubtedly existed between the two. I am glad that my opinion regarding this connection has been universally accepted by scholars of Hindi .... But this may easily lead one into undervaluing the part played by Rāmānanda in the making of the Nirguṇa School and specially, of the thought of Kabīr ... it was in Rāmānanda that Nāthism and Vaishṇavism discernibly met.' P.D. Barthwal, *Tradition of Indian Mysticism based upon* Nirguna School of Hindi Poetry, New Delhi 1978, 'Preface', pp. XIII-XIV (*The Nirguna School of Hindi Poetry*, Banares 1936). Pītāmbardatt Baṛthvāl had first lectured on the poetry of the Nāthyogīs in December 1930, at the Kāśī Nāgarī Pracāriṇī Sabhā. His lecture was published under the title 'Hindī kāvya meṁ yog-pravāh' in the Sabhā journal (*Nāgarīpracāriṇī Patrikā*, vol.11, No. 4, Māgha, VS 1987, Jan.-Feb. 1931). He himself was aware of the importance of his contribution, declaring that it made 'scholars accept the *bānī* of the Nāthyogīs as an important link in our literary and cultural development' (Pītāmbardatt Bāṛthvāl (ed.), *Gorakh-bānī*, 4th ed., Allahabad 1979 [1st ed. 1942], 'Bhūmikā', p. 11). On the connection between

It has also been argued that Kabīr embraced a combination of these three doctrines.[3]

Hajārīprasād Dvivedī observes that the majority of medieval texts to have furnished scholars with insights into the thought of the yogis and the Nāthpanth were written by Muslim poets. Perhaps these poets, like Kabīr, belonged to a caste of converted Hindus. It is the view of Hajārīprasād Dvivedī that besides the Sants, such as Kabīr, Dādū and Rajjab, notable Sufi poets like Kutuban and Jāysī might be reassessed in this context.[4] Hajārīprasād Dvivedī draws the following conclusions:

1. In the past, most of the castes to which present-day weavers belong did not acknowledge the Brahmins as superior.
2. A caste of householders that had lost its ritual status in the *varṇāśrama*, the Jogī, was widely scattered across northern and eastern India. These people were the Nāthpanthī; they made a living from weaving and spinning, or begging alms in the name of Gorakhnāth and Bhartharī.
3. They believed in the Nirākār ('Formless'), despised the caste system and did not accept the concept of *avatār*.
4. They were regarded by Hindu society as of lowly ritual status or as untouchables.
5. With the arrival of the Muslims, they gradually became converts.
6. Mass conversions to Islam occurred in the Panjab, Uttar Pradesh, Bihar and Bengal.
7. Kabīr was raised in one such newly converted family.[5]

Kabīr was influenced by Buddhist Siddhs, by way of the Nāthpanth, which was regarded as a Shaiva branch of Tantric Buddhism. Social revolution is more apparent in the Siddhs than the Nāthyogīs, for

---

the Siddhs and Kabīr and other Sants of northern India by the way of the Nāthyogīs, also Dharmvīr Bhārtī, *Siddh-sāhitya*, 2nd ed., Allahabad 1968; Charlotte Vaudeville (ed.), *Kabīr Granthāvalī (Dohā)*, Pondichéry 1957, 'Introduction', pp. I-XIII.

[3] Parśurām Caturvedī, *Kabīr-sāhitya kī parakh*, 2nd ed., Allahabad 1964.

[4] Hajārīprasād Dvivedī, *Kabīr*, p. 28.

[5] Ibid., pp. 28-9.

the Siddhs were Tantric Buddhists and openly hostile to Brahmanism. This is illustrated in the following *pad* by Kāṇh:

> Outside the city, oh *ḍombī*, is your home,
> out of fear of being touched the Brahmin flees.
> Come, *ḍombī*, I will stay with you,
> devoid of hate, naked, *kāpālik* Kāṇh [says].
> Upon that sixty-four petal lotus
> alighted, the low-caste *ḍombī* dances.
>
> (Kāṇhpā, *Caryāpad* 10, 'Rāg deśākh')[6]

---

[6] Quoted in Harivaṃś Kochaṛ, *Apabhraṃś-sāhitya*, Delhi n.d. (date of the 'Introduction' [Prākkathan] VS 2013 [AD 1956]), p. 313. Out of the two interpretations (ibid., p. 314) provided by Harivaṃś Kochaṛ—literal and mystic—the translation follows the literal meaning. For a mystic interpretation of the union of Kāṇh with the *ḍombī*, also Nāgendranāth Upādhyāy, *Tāntrik bauddh sādhnā aur sāhitya*, Benares VS 2015 (AD 1958), p. 313. The *ḍombī* is regarded as the *pariśuddhāvadhūtikā nairātmā*, the city as the aggregate of worldly enjoyments. The *avadhūtī* is one of the three conducts or paths (*vṛtti* or *mārg*) of the Tantric practice, the other two being *cāṇḍālī* and *ḍombī* or *baṅgālī*. In *avadhūtī* the adept experiences the dual state, in *cāṇḍālī* the dual-non-dual state, and in *ḍombī* the pure (*pariśuddha*) non-dual state. Hajārīprasād Dvivedī, *Kabīr*, p. 91 (Nāgendranāth Upādhyāy, instead, connects the state of *avadhūtī* with the *ḍombī*. Names vary according to different Tantric texts). *Nairātmā* is both a state and a goddess: it is the state in which the individual self is absorbed, a pure experience of mystic union, an inward encounter with the goddess of the same name. For the expression 'inward encounter' and its analysis, Herbert V. Guenther, *The Tantric View of Life*, Berkeley and London 1972, pp. 72-7. Whatever the mystic meaning, it remains that the *ḍombī* is a woman of the *ḍom* community—formerly a tribe—regarded by strictly orthodox Brahmins as 'unclean' *śūdra*s (J.N. Bhattacharya, *Hindu Caste*s *and Sect*s, Calcutta 1968 [1st ed. 1896]). For a social interpretation of Tantrism, R.S. Sharma, 'Material Milieu of Tantricism', in R.S. Sharma (ed., with the collaboration of Vivekanand Jha), *Indian Society: Historical Probing*s *(In Memory of D.D. Kosambi)*, 2nd ed., Delhi 1977 [1st ed. 1974], pp. 175-89.

In this *pad* we find an explicit description of ritual sexual intercourse, which the Nāthyogīs customarily internalise through yogic practice in the union of Śiva and Śakti, the male and female principles.

The Nāths' rebellious attitude lacks the social force that we find in Kabīr. This may be because the Nāthyogīs preached unworldliness. This is exemplified by their outlook on women. Kabīr—although, of course, condemning lust—believes that men and women are loved by God in equal measure, while Gorakh openly disdains the company of women: 'To sleep beside a woman is to enjoy Yam, one should not even drink water with a woman.' (*Gorakh-bānī*, 'Rāg rāmagrī', *pad* 1).[7] It is also fair to say that this approach may have been prompted by a need to reassert a more specifically Hindu form of Tantrism.

Both Gorakh and Kabīr criticise the sway held by the guardians of orthodox theology. Like Kabīr, Gorakh and the Nāthpanthīs—of both Hindu and Muslim origin—proclaim the futility of sacred texts, which serve to create divisions.

> It is within neither Veda nor the Śāstra, in the Books or the Koran, in books it is not written,
> exceptional yogis know that (Supreme) State, the rest of the world is absorbed in other pursuits.
>
> (Gorakh, *sabdī* 6)[8]

> Qazis and mullahs have studied the Koran, the Brahmins have studied the Veda,
> the *Kāpṛī* (pilgrims) and renouncers have been deceived by the *tīrth*s, they have not obtained the secret of *nirvāṇa*.
>
> (Gorakh, *sabdī* 153)[9]

---

[7] Pītāmbardatt Barṭhvāl, *Gorakh-bānī*.

[8] In Mariola Offredi, *Lo yoga di Gorakh. Tre manoscritti inediti*, Milano 1991. See n. 20.

[9] Ibid.

Hindus meditate in the temple, Muslims in the mosque,
the yogi meditates on the Supreme State, where there is neither temple nor mosque.

(Gorakh, *sabdī* 155)[10]

Hindus say Rām, Muslims [say] Khudā,
yogis say the Invisible (Alakh), where there is neither Rām nor Khudā.

(Gorakh, *sabdī* 156)[11]

Mohammed [is like] silver, Khudā [is like] gold, the *takbīr* ('Allāho akbar') is copper.
Thus says Bābā Ratan Hājī, we (yogis) stay away from them.

(Gorakh, *sabdī* 157)[12]

Kabīr frequently addresses the *avdhū* (*avadhūta* = shaken off, discarded, an ascetic). This might be interpreted as the poet's wish to express his personal beliefs to the *avdhū*; according to Hajārīprasād Dvivedī, however, Kabīr is willing to allow an *avdhū* who fulfils special requirements to become his teacher. This *avdhū* must dissociate himself from the world, including that of the gods. Hajārīprasād Dvivedī notes[13] that Kabīr addresses the *avdhū* in coded language (*sandhā-bhāṣā*) in the following *pad*, which forms an *ulaṭbāṃsī* (paradox).

Avdhū, the *jogī* who is able to solve this *pad* is my teacher. (*ṭek*)
An erect tree without roots, without blossoms, bears fruit,
has neither branches nor leaves, [yet] fills the whole sky.

---

[10] Ibid.

[11] Ibid.

[12] Ibid. This *sabdī* is by a Muslim Nāthpanth follower, for he bears the epithet 'Hājī', 'one who has been to Mecca'; Ratannāth, the founder of a branch of Nāthpanth, is revered by Muslims. George Weston Briggs, *Gorakhnāth and the Kānphaṭa Yogīs*, Delhi 1989 [1st ed. 1938], p. 66; P.D. Barthwal, *Tradition of Indian Mysticism*, p. 287.

[13] Hajārīprasād Dvivedī, *Kabīr*, p. 38.

Without feet it dances, without instruments or tongue it sings,
the singer is without form, [but] the perfect teacher (*satguru*) can disclose him.
The bird's quest, the fish's path,[14] says Kabīr, after much thought,
infinite [and] eternal is the Supreme Being (*puruṣottam*),
I devote myself to that God (*mūrti*).

(Śyāmsundardās (ed.), *Kabīr granthāvalī*,[15] 'Rāg rāmkalī', *pad* 165)

Like other *pad*s by Kabīr, *pad* 165 is firmly embedded in the Nāthpanth tradition. It may be regarded as a response to that tradition. This response takes the form of a paradoxical question which seems to have been devised as a counter to a *pad* which has been attributed to Gorakh, and which is far more complex than the *pad* by Kabīr quoted above.

The liana of *tattva* (Supreme Reality; the true nature of the human soul, identical to the all-pervading supreme spirit), Gorakhnāth knows, oh *Avdhū*,
it has neither branches nor roots, blossoms or shade, it grows without water. (*ṭek*)
Within the grove-body is your garden, oh *Avdhū*, [in it] the *sadguru* has planted this liana, the [vital] breath waters it and reaps a fine crop.
Its root is just like the moon (= the root is in the *sahasrāra*, the 'thousand-spoked' dwelling of Śiva, located on the top of the head), oh *Avdhū*, its leaves are just like the sun (located in the *mūlādhāra cakra*, the lower plexus, at the base of the spinal column; in other words, the liana grows in reverse, from top to bottom).
Its fruits are just like the *pūrṇimā* moon (full moon—because it is full of nectar and located in the 'thousand-spoked'; the moon is a sign of gnosis and immortality), familiar only to those with knowledge (*sujān* = *jñānvān*).

---

[14] The bird's path in the sky and that of the fish in the sea cannot be identified, as they are known only to the bird and the fish who experience them. The path to Supreme Reality is comparable to these.

[15] Śyāmsundardās, *Kabīr granthāvalī*, 9th ed., Varanasi 1964 [1st ed. 1928].

When the liana catches fire (= the fire of *māyā*), oh *Avdhū*, its flames reach the sky.
As the liana burns, its branches and buds toss (= the more worldly desire grows, the more man is entrapped in *māyā*).
The more one tries to cut this liana, the more its buds grow (they cannot be destroyed), [but] if it is watered (with the nectar cascading from the moon located in the 'thousand-spoked') it withers.
By the grace of Machindra, the ascetic Gorakh says, it remains eternally new.

(*Gorakh-bānī*, 'Rāg rāmagrī', *pad* 17)

In the above *pad*, of which Gorakh is believed to be the author, the image of the rootless liana is comparable to Kabīr's tree without roots, yet it is far more complex. First, the same image is used in relation to two antithetical elements—Supreme Reality and *māyā*. Second, this liana is described as being upside down, and has clear links with the yogic practice of breathing control by which the *kuṇḍalinī* is made to rise from the bottom to the top of the body.

Kabīr's *pad* may well be a response to that of Gorakh, but whilst emulating its paradoxical style, it rejects the value given to yogic practice by Gorakh and the Nāthpanth in the pursuit of the Supreme State. Kabīr refutes the validity of Haṭhayoga elsewhere:

Sant, if the thread [of concentration] breaks, the *samādhi* (*gagan* = *gaganvās*, *śūnyasamādhi*) is destroyed,
this doubt remains inside me night and day, no one can explain it to me. (*ṭek*)
There is neither *brahmāṇḍ* nor *piṇḍ*, the five elements are not there,
there is neither *iṛā* nor *piṅglā* and *suṣumnā*, where are all these constituents (*guṇ*) absorbed?
There is neither home nor place or maker.
The soul (*jovanhār* = spectator) is beyond [them] and remains with him always, all these elements are absorbed there (= into the Supreme State).
It breaks and it joins together, it joins together and breaks once more, and is destroyed,
he who was master now becomes the servant (after encountering Supreme Reality, the ego—which, in yogic practice, continues to be

master—loses its ego function, and becomes a servant), no one believes this (the ego disputes the absence of the ego function).
Kabīr says [that] with this thread (of the sense of service) the sky (= *samādhi*) will not be destroyed,
what use are teaching and study to someone who is not absorbed into the [Supreme] State?

(Śyāmsundardās (ed.), *Kabīr granthāvalī*, 'Rāg gauṛī', *pad* 32)

On another occasion, Kabīr says that without love for Rām, yogic practice is worthless:

Void dies, *ajap* dies, *anhad* dies,
love for Rām does not die, says Kabīr.

शून्य मरै अजप मरै अनहद हू मरि जाय।
राम सनेही न मरै कह कबीर समुझाय।।

(*Kabīr-vāṇī*, 256, in Hajārīprasād Dvivedī, *Kabīr*, p. 357)[16]

An analysis of the *pad* in which Kabīr acknowledges Gorakh as the true *avdhū* aids our understanding of the poet's views on the *avdhū*. Kabīr regards Gorakh as the person who has gained true knowledge of Rām. Once again, Kabīr adopts coded language, and at least some of the *pad* is an *ulaṭbāṃsī*:

Avdhū, Gorakhnāth had recognised the liana of the virtues of Rām (*Rām gun belṛī*),
it has neither form nor shadow, it grows without water. (*ṭek*)
The two tips of the liana touch the earth and sky,

[16] The collection *Kabīr-vāṇī* (Hajārīprasād Dvivedī, *Kabīr*, pp. 233-357) consists of 256 *pads*. The first hundred—a selection from the collection edited by Kṣitimohan Sen—correspond to those translated into English by Tagore (*One Hundred Poems of Kabir*, 1923). According to Vaudeville, Kṣitimohan Sen's collection is largely based on the oral traditions of wandering *sādhus*. Charlotte Vaudeville, *Kabīr Granthāvalī (Dohā)*, 'Introduction', p. II.

when the *sahaj*'s liana starts to blossom, it is covered with branches and buds.
The *sadguru* has sent the elephant-mind to that liana,
the five sisters (= the five senses), breaking away [from sensual objects] with the [vital] breath began to water the garden.
Cut down, the liana becomes covered with buds, if watered, it withers,
says Kabīr, few are the *yogī*s who know *sahaj*.

(Śyāmsundardās (ed.), *Kabīr granthāvalī*, 'Rāg rāmkalī', *pad* 163)

In adopting the coded style of the Siddhs and the Nāthpanth to describe the yogi who might become his teacher, Kabīr slips to some extent into their tradition, revealing that he is not totally against their beliefs; unquestionably, he is hostile to yogis who daub themselves with ashes or perform severe or whimsical ascetic practices. It should also be noted that Gorakh himself objected to public displays of asceticism and the use of intoxicating substances and the consumption of meat popular in certain sects.

Clogs make your feet slip, oh *Avdhū*, irons destroy the body,
those who go naked or silent, those who live on milk have not attained yoga.

(Gorakh, *sabdī* 62)[17]

He is a yogi, he speaks ill of others, consumes wine, meat and hemp,
[thanks to him] 7,100 generations go to hell, the Lord Gorakh states the truth.

(Gorakh, *sabdī* 134)[18]

It should also be pointed out, however, that Gorakh, in Kabīr's eyes, is above all the person who recognised the liana of Rām's virtues.

Many other aspects may be regarded as a re-working by Kabīr of Nāthpanthī views. For instance, Kabīr's particularly vehement claims of the futility of pilgrimages to holy places may be interpreted as a response

---

[17] In Offredi, *Lo yoga di Gorakh*.

[18] Ibid.

to, or a re-working of, the Nāthpanthī notion of the interiorisation of external practices.

On the one hand, then, Kabīr draws upon the Nāthpanth, whilst introducing distinguishing features of his own. Above all, Kabīr appears to be involved in an ongoing debate with the Nāthpanth, who was influenced by him and his religious beliefs. The problem lies in the fact that Nāthpanthī texts are of a later date than Kabīr's, making it feasible that they were altered or revised on the basis of religious beliefs which by that time had become widespread.[19] This is especially true of the *Sabdī* and the *pad*s ascribed to Gorakh (and other Nāthpanthīs). The *Sabdī* are short poems (two line aphorisms) which, handed down orally by wandering yogis, were subject to change over the course of time; the *pad*s are ceremonial hymns which were sung in the presence, and with the participation, of adepts belonging to the various sub-sects, and as such were also liable to change with the passing of time. Conversely, more

[19] This is also the opinion of Hajārīprasād Dvivedī, who writes: 'It is difficult to say how old the *pad*s attributed to Gorakhnāth available to us are. Among these *pad*s, several have been found as works attributed to Dādūdayāl, several to Kabīr and several to Nānak. Some *pad*s have assumed the form of popular sayings, some that of *jogīṛā* songs, and some have caught on the folk in the form of wisdom acquired by experience.' Hajārīprasād Dvivedī, *Nāth-sampradāy*, 2nd rev. ed., Varanasi n.d. (date of the 'Introduction' [Nivedan], 1966; 1st ed. 1950), p. 222. The oldest surviving manuscripts of the works attributed to Gorakh were written in a period when ideals and practice of bhakti had become widespread. The views of bhakti even influenced commentators of Patañjali's *Yoga-sūtra*. Vijñāna Bhikṣu (sixteenth century) mentions the 'grace of God' in his *Yoga-sāra-saṅgraha*, while another commentator, Nīlakaṇṭha, maintains that God 'helps the yogin like a lover'. Surendranath Dasgupta, *Yoga as Philosophy and Religion*, London 1924, p. 89; Mircea Eliade, *Tecniche dello Yoga* (Italian translation of *Techniques du Yoga*, Paris 1948), Turin 1984, p. 88. On yoga theism and its subsequent modifications, also Surendranath Dasgupta, *A History of Indian Philosophy*, Delhi 1991 [1st ed. 1922], 5 vols., vol. I, pp. 222-35, 258-9.

rigorously theoretical texts (such as *Gorakh bodh* and *Gyān tilak*) are more strictly Nāthpanthī.[20]

Although surviving Nāthpanth texts were written later than those of Kabīr, in terms of style they are more cluttered with technical terms, and lack Kabīr's freshness. As an example, let us compare the description of yogic practice in one of Kabīr's *pads* ('Rāg gauṛī', *pad* 69) with a *pad* by Gorakh ('Rāg rāmagrī', *pad* 10). I also give another *pad* by Gorakh ('Rāg rāmagrī', *pad* 1), containing a list of days in the month that are sacred to Hindus. Although Kabīr's text includes Nāthpanthī technical terms, they are less numerous, and at the same time his work has greater mystical and emotive force. The number of technical terms in Gorakh's *pad* is notably larger, and we even find a tedious catalogue of analogies between exterior and interior worship, including a list of internalized votive offerings; and it is totally lacking in mystical and emotive force.

Kabīr, 'Rāg gauṛī', *pad* 69

> *Avdhū*, the *jogī* is isolated from the world.
>
> He practices *mudrā*, *iṛā* and *piṅglā* (*nirati surati*), *sīṃgī* and *nād* (thus reaching the *brahmarandhra*), [where] the stream [of nectar] flows [ceaselessly]. (*ṭek*)
>
> He dwells in heaven (*gagan* = *brahmarandhra*) and, absorbed in meditation, pays no heed to the world.

[20] Italian translation of the *Gorakh bodh*, *Gyān tilak* and the *Sabdī* in Offredi, *Lo yoga di Gorakh*. The text of the three manuscripts is also given. The manuscripts, different from those edited by Pītāmbardatt Barṭhvāl in *Gorakh-bānī*, are the following: *Gorakh bodh*, folios 51-63 of codex 11583, Jodhpur collection, *ad quem* date VS 1693 (AD 1636); *Gyān tilak*, folios 215-17 of codex 12380, Jodhpur collection, *ad quem* date VS 1724 (AD 1667); *Sabdī*, folios 415-25 of codex 14716, Jodhpur collection, *ad quem* date VS 1826 / AD 1769. Since only the codices are dated, the manuscripts may be of an earlier date. The manuscripts of the *Gorakh bodh* and the *Gyān tilak* are the oldest manuscripts of these texts hitherto published, while that of the *Sabdī* is definitely more recent than the text published by Pītāmbardatt Barṭhvāl. The manuscripts edited by Pītāmbardatt Barṭhvāl are dated, respectively, c. VS 1715 (AD 1658) c. VS 1743 (AD 1686), VS 1715 (AD 1658).

> Having ascended into heaven (*ākāś* = sky, Voidness) he remains immobile, he drinks the sweet juice [of ambrosia].
> On the outside, the *jogī* [wears] the *kanthā* (patched cloth worn by ascetics), in his heart he sees (...)
> with 21,600 threads (= *nāṛī*) (= with body and mind) immobile, he puts the thread in the [needle's] eye (= he is immersed in Brahman with all his body and mind).
> [When he] burns his body in the fire of Brahman (= purifying his body in the Brahman-light) he awakens in the *trikuṭī* (= he experiences Brahman).
> Kabīr says, the Lord of yoga is he who, attaining the *sahaj* [state], fixes his mind on Voidness.
> (Śyāmsundardās (ed.), *Kabīr granthāvalī*, 'Rāg gauṛī', *pad* 69)

Gorakh, 'Rāg rāmagrī', *pad* 10

> Oh, my will (*mansā* = *icchā*), bind (= control, close) your activity, breath (*pavan puruṣ*) is created (= the union between mind and breathing has become possible),
> (with the union of mind and breathing, that is, by breath control) the *jogī*, having awoken, has become focused on the spirit (*adhyātma* = identity of the soul with the supreme spirit according to Vedānta), he must enter the city-body. (*ṭek*)
> In the six-petal lotus (*svādhiṣṭhāna cakra*) the 21,600 breaths are the *jap* of breathing, in the *nāṛī* -*iṛā piṅglā suṣumnā*- breath flows by day and by night.
> The six-petal lotus (*svādhiṣṭhāna*) and the sixteen-petal lotus (*viśuddha cakra*) are in that current, there dwells the soul (*brahmacārī*),
> the nine rivers (the entire *nāṛī* system) are the water sprinkler [that waters] the soul (*haṃs*) with its breath (*pavan*), enabling it to thrive.
> On the bank of the Ganges (*iṛā*), *Avdhū*, there grows the water melon (which is the knowledge [*jñān*] that brings coolness), this should be sold once again,
> carry upwards the downward flowing current (the current of ambrosia or breath), unite sun and moon.
> Moon and sun both vanish from the sky (*gagan* = *brahmarandhra*) (that is, *suṣumnā* predominates), a terrible darkness has fallen,

when the five soldiers (= the five senses) have fallen asleep, the doors appear in the wall (in other words, when the senses are distracted from their objects, the door leading to spiritual life opens).
The body is the *kanthā*, the mind is the *jogī*, the *satguru* revealed (this secret) to me,
Gorakhnāth says, keep this secret safe, there are thieves in the city.
(*Gorakh-bānī*, 'Rāg rāmagrī', *pad* 10)

Gorakh, 'Rāg rāmagrī', *pad* 1

Spending the night in intimacy and in sleep, the world flows in the objects of the senses,
with arms upraised, Gorakh summons: do not lose the primary source (semen), oh my brothers. (*ṭek*)
(For a yogi) concentrating the mind and body within Voidness is a celebration of *amāvas* (the last day of the dark fortnight of a lunar month, the night of the new moon) and *paṛivā* (the first day of the lunar fortnight), Voidness is the Tuesday votive offering,
the Brahmin who ponders on *daśmī* (the tenth day of a lunar fortnight) bases himself on the Veda, [but for a yogi, to celebrate *daśmī*] is to banish sins (of the body through *yam* and *niyam*, etc.).
Paṛivā [for a yogi, is identical with] bliss, at the *dvitīyā*, making *darśan* of the moon [is identical with] keeping the five senses from their objects.
The votive offering-rules of *aṣṭamī*, *caturdaśī*, *ekādaśī* [are for a yogi] not to allow his body to be touched by a woman.
Externally, in the evening you must sleep, but inside you must remain awake, at daybreak you must keep watch,
when two of the three *pahar*s of the night pass by, during the third *pahar*, Time-Death lies in wait (= Time-Death devours the man who is fast asleep, even in the moments just before sunrise [*brahm-muhūrt*] and for this reason a yogi stays awake at *brahm-muhūrt*).[21]
To sleep beside a woman is to enjoy Yam, one should not even drink water with a woman.

---

[21] 'Devalnāth says: during the first *pahar*, everyone stays awake, during the second *pahar*, the bhogī stays awake; during the third *pahar*, the robber stays awake, during the fourth *pahar*, the jogī.' Quoted in Pītāmbardatt Barṭhvāl, *Gorakh-bānī*, p. 86.

> In this way you will become immortal, oh Machindra, Gorakh says these words.
>
> (*Gorakh-bānī*, 'Rāg rāmagrī', *pad* 1)

Despite differences, however, it is undeniable that a link exists between Kabīr and the Nāthpanth, and it can be perceived in the fact that they both adopt the form of the Vedānta known as Bhedābheda or Dvaitādvaita, according to which Supreme Reality is both transcendent and immanent.[22]

---

[22] Pītāmbardatt Barṭhvāl is critical of Farquhar's opinion that in Kabīr the approach is to the Bhedābheda doctrine of Nimbārka (eleventh century?). J.N. Farquhar, *An Outline of the Religious Literature of India*, Delhi 1984 [1st ed. 1920], p. 326 n. According to Pītāmbardatt Barṭhvāl, at least three trends can be seen in the Nirguṇ School, Advaita, Bhedābheda and Viśiṣṭādvaita: 'The first trend is headed by Kabīr himself (...). In fact all *isms* or *vādas* can be deduced from his writings. But he identifies himself with none and transcends every one of them. To form a proper estimate of the views of Kabīr, subtle as they are, we must view the whole that he has given us; and when we have done this we entertain no doubts as to his thorough monistic outlook.' However, (pp. 194-251), he asks, 'Was Kabīr an eclectic? .... the question cannot be answered in a categorical "yes" or "no".' P.D. Barthwal, *Traditions of Indian Mysticism*, pp. 32, 35, 195. As a matter of fact, the same expression *nirguṇ* bhakti is a contradiction in terms, as there can be no devotion without an object of devotion, i.e. someone or something other than the devotee. Thus, *nirguṇ* bhakti cannot be connected with monism or non-dualism. It should be noted that, against the Advaita or Kevalādvaita doctrine of Śaṅkara (AD 788-820), Nimbārka accepts the theory of *saguṇa* Brahman, both transcendent and immanent, both almighty and merciful. He stresses the need of an intimate relation of love and friendship between God and man, emphasises inner spiritual experience against external ritualism, and maintains that renunciation is not required for spiritual freedom: salvation may be reached either by the renouncer and the householder unselfishly performing his duties. Scholars also hold different opinions about the ideal of Nāthism. The Tantric texts stress abolition of duality, consisting in the *sahaj* state in which subject and object concide. Mircea Eliade, *Tecniche dello yoga*, p. 174. Again, '... the Nātha ideal is analogous to what we find in the Āgamic systems of non-dualistic thought in ancient and medieval India. This ideal is described in one word as *Sāmarasya*, which implies obliteration of traces of all kind of existing differences, not by a process of *transcendence* as in Sānkhya, or of *subl[im]ation* as in Vedāntic

Māyāvāda, but by a positive process of what may be described as *mutual interpenetration.*' Gopinath Kaviraj, 'A Prefatory Note' to Akshaya Kumar Banerjea, *Philosophy of Gorakhnath*, Gorakhpur Temple, Gorakhpur n.d., pp. XXV-XXVI. It should be noted, however, that the author of the book holds a different opinion, and describes Gorakhnāth's philosophy as Dvaitādvaita-vilakṣaṇa-vāda and Pakṣapāta-vinirmukta-vāda (ibid., pp. IV and 55), defining the Absolute as impersonal as well as personal, transcendent as well as immanent (ibid., p. 61). The same concept of *sāmarasya* leads Surendranath Dasgupta to a different interpretation of Gorakh's teachings. 'The concept of *sama-rasa* is homogeneity. A thing which appears as different from another thing, but is in reality or essence the same, is said to be *sama-rasa* with the first one. It is also a way in which the *bhedābheda* theory of the reality and the appearance is explained.' Basing himself on the *Siddha-siddhānta-paddhati*, a Sanskrit work attributed to Gorakh, he comes to the conclusion, 'We find that there is a curious combination of Haṭha-yoga, the control of the nerve plexuses, the idea of the individual and the world as having the same reality, though they appear as different .... It also holds a type of *bhedābheda* theory and is distinctly opposed to monistic interpretation of the Upaniṣads as introduced by Śaṅkara.' Surendranath Dasgupta, *A History of Indian Philosophy*, Vol. V, p. 59.

Kabīr's Secrets for Householders: Truths and Rumours among Rajasthani Nāths

Daniel Gold

The ambivalence of Kabīr toward the popular Nāth traditions he knew has certainly been noted by scholars. Most seem to agree at least that the Kabīrian corpus shares an esoteric vocabulary with Nāth texts, but gives the jargon a different turn and sometimes mocks the external pretensions of Nāth yogis.[1] Less well known, however, is the ambivalence toward the figure of Kabīr found in popular Nāth traditions that evolved in the centuries after him; indeed, some of these traditions have returned Kabīr's equivocal compliment to them in ways that are left-handed in more than one sense. Thus, even though people in contemporary Nāth communities may hold Kabīr in high regard, they may not always do so for reasons that the rest of us find so exalted. Here I will talk about the significance of Kabīr in one of the more vital of these communities, the householder Nāths of Rajasthan. Living largely as reasonably prosperous peasants, but born into a caste with a yogic heritage, Rajasthani householder Nāths participate vigorously in a tradition of *nirguṇ bhajans* in which the figure of Kabīr looms prominently among other Sants. Kabīr, for them, was certainly a knower of esoteric secrets; moreover, as a married Sant rather than an ascetic, celibate yogi, the secrets he knew seemed particularly appropriate for them as householders. Just what these secrets were, however—indeed, the value of the very tradition of Sants represented by

---

[1] See Charlotte Vaudeville, *Kabīr,* Oxford 1974, p. 89, 144 and Daniel Gold, *The Lord as Guru: Hindi Sants in North Indian Tradition,* New York 1987, p. 204. Nāgendra Nāth Upādhyāya, in his extensive *Nāth aur sant sāhitya,* Varanasi 1965, tends to treat Nāths and Kabīr's Sants together, minimizing distinctions between the two, but his chapters 10 and 11 do present differences in their yogic practices. For a translated verse of Kabīr that seems to attack Nāth hypocrisy, see Linda Hess and Shukdev Singh, *The Bījak of Kabir,* San Francisco 1983, p. 76, and their qualifying note, p. 183.

Kabīr—was contested by different segments of the householder Nāth world I came to know.

Unlike many of the Nāth and Jogī castes of the Gangetic plain, which are often found near the lowest ranks of rural society, the householder Nāths of southeastern Rajasthan with whom I worked are a middle peasant group.[2] They usually have their own land to farm and share commensal relationships with other clean peasant castes. This relatively high status derives in good part from the Nāths' reputed magical power, which impressed royalty as well as commoners. In particular, the Nāths were said to have the ability to save villages from locusts. (They did not kill the locusts, but instead drove them to another village.) Every prudent village had to have its own Nāth, and local *ṭhākur*s tried to attract Nāths through grants of land. Householder Nāths in our area thus developed as a sparsely diffused community, with many villages each having a few families descended from the originally invited Nāth magician.[3]

The roles of the village Nāths in rural religious life are in fact most diverse. In addition to saving the village from locusts, they are called on to help in face of collective danger like a long drought or the threat of hail. Many also serve as *pujārī*s at particular Shaiva shrines, the rights to which pass down in families. The esoteric lore the Nāths have inherited, moreover, makes many of them popular as curers, particularly of children, and—importantly—tends to give them leadership roles in the esoteric cults that remain active among the peasantry. A few know the Nāth epics of Gopī Cand and Bharthari, performing them regularly at harvest time as well as at occasional sponsored performances. And almost all the male Nāths participate, at least to some extent, in *jāgaraṇ*s in which they excel.

It is in their participation in *bhajan* parties that Nāths most obviously and universally identify with a version of Sant tradition. Most

---

[2] This paper draws on fieldwork done in 1993 in villages around Kekri in Ajmer district.

[3] The exception to this were large communities found around major Nāth shrines, of which one is described on pp. 70-6 of my 'Nath Yogis as Established Alternatives: Householders and Ascetics Today', *Journal of Asian and African Studies*, vol. 34, No. 1, 1999, pp. 68-88.

of the Nāths in the area were conversant with a repertoire of hymns that they called *nirguṇ bhajan*s; these they saw as separate from *saguṇ bhajan*s, usually oriented toward Krishna, which were sung by other groups. The Nāths' *nirguṇ bhajan*s were clearly similar in theme and vocabulary to the Sant songs I had earlier heard sung by Rādhāsoāmīs and others. There were songs dedicated to warnings and to guru devotion, as well as to esoteric secrets in a familiar Sant jargon. And amid the signatures of many local figures I had never heard of before—Kanhī Rām Gūjar, say, or Bhavānī Nāth—there were also some familiar ones: Dhannā Jāṭ, Raidās, Gorakh, and very frequently Kabīr. Indeed it was the similarities of the village Nāths' song tradition with some of those I already knew that first interested me in them—but not just the similarities, the differences too. For despite the familiar topics and some familiar names, the Nāths not only sometimes gave the songs—as I would learn—interpretations diverging radically from those I would have anticipated, but also sang them in a very different way. I was at that time more used to hearing Sant songs sung rather decorously, with a commentary by a guru if one was around. The Nāths, however, sang them lustily, with lots of music, percussion and repetition, with a chillum frequently being passed around; rounds of singing were regularly followed by group discussions of the songs' significance—not the pronouncements of a guru, but what they called 'knowledge-gossip': *gyān carcā*.

It soon seemed pretty obvious to me that an ecstatic participation in devotional songfests was, for the majority of Nāths, an important component of personal religion. For some it was also a crucial element of socio-religious identity. A number of Nāths travelled widely in the area, invited to *bhajan* parties sponsored by devotees from diverse peasant castes. Some Nāths were known as talented singers, others as insightful interpreters, still others as knowledgeable in the texts. A few would sometimes travel for weeks or even months at a time, from one songfest to another, maybe returning home with money given to them as offering. Yet, the *nirguṇ bhajan* tradition, while central to the religious life of many householder Nāths, was not understood as an exclusively Nāth affair. People from other castes also participated, and the songs, although often bearing the names of Gorakh and other Nāths, just as often bore the names of non-Nāth singers of narrower and wider renown, whom the Nāths referred to loosely as Sants. The greatest of these, with by far the largest number of signature lines, was unarguably Kabīr.

Where, then, does Kabīr stand in this Sant tradition? In 1993 I recorded and had transcribed a number of long Nāth *bhajan* sessions, and in looking through these transcriptions recently with an eye for Kabīr's significance, I started by seeing if I could find any special features of the songs actually attributed to him. No striking characteristics particularly hit me in the eye—Kabīr's name was attached to all kinds of songs, devotional and esoteric—and on reflection such a search did not seem a fruitful way to proceed. In the popular corpus, signatures often seemed promiscuously used, and while they might indicate lineage for more recent singers, it didn't make sense to take them all that seriously for the great Kabīr. To try to ascertain Kabīr's significance for the Nāths, I ended up looking beyond the transcribed songs to my broader field notes. There I noticed the way in which Kabīr really was regarded by the Nāths as a great person—given a status nearly equal to Gorakh, from whom they trace their spiritual origin. 'Gorakh is the first person made, but Kabīr is important for his literature (*śairī*) and has as much knowledge as Gorakh',[4] said one of my most knowledgeable imformants. This general perspective—that Kabīr is almost as great as Gorakh—is one that seems to be widely shared.

One of the sessions I recorded was a *Gorakh Kabīr saṃvād*—a conversation between the two figures.[5] It had been performed with a commentary by a locally celebrated singer named Gokul Nāth, who echoed the perspective of my last quoted informant. 'Gorakh and Kabīr are one', Gokul Nāth exclaims at one point in his performance, 'Don't recognize any difference [between them]'.[6] The equality of the two is further suggested in one of the more vivid descriptions of their meetings.

---

[4] Unless otherwise noted in the text, speech given as direct quotations is cited directly from my fieldnotes, which consist largely of English paraphrases of Hindi voices.

[5] On Sant *saṃvād*s in general see David Lorenzen, *Praises to a Formless God*, Albany, NY 1996.

[6] *Gorakh Kabīr ek hai, koī mat jānoṁ bhed* (my transcription *Gorakh Kabīr saṃvād*, part 1, p. 29); recorded at Sāpuṇḍā (Ṭonk), May 1993.

Gorakh is doing penance on Girnar while Kabīr takes incarnation in Kashi. As Kabīr's fame spreads, Gorakh hears of him as a 'very learned Sant' (*bahut vidvān sant*) and wants to meet him. Meanwhile, in Kashi, corresponding events happen with Kabīr. He hears of Gorakh as 'a yogi among yogis', and the two, with their disciples, set out to meet each other—Gorakh's party in the orange of renunciates and carrying an orange banner; Kabīr's in householders' white and carrying a white banner. As they meet on the road, they recognize each other immediately. Soon, however, Gorakh reveals his relative superiority: he performs a yogic miracle, flying through the air, and ends up doing most of the teaching.[7] Still, Gokul Nāth insists, Kabīr also 'told secrets' brought with him from Kashi. Even though Kabīr may not have been quite as great as Gorakh, he and his corps of Sants in white also had something special of their own to offer—something connected, I think, with the white banner they carried, an emblem here of their non-renunciate status.

Gokul Nāth's description of the meeting of Gorakh and Kabīr makes it clear that the two cannot be considered in isolation, but as teachers among their disciples, leaders of large groups, respectively, of renunciate yogis and possibly married Sants. The description presents a graphic parallel to the composition of the local corpus of *nirguṇ bhajan*s: the corpus is clearly dominated by the names of Gorakh and Kabīr, but these stand among a wide array of others—including, in my transcriptions especially, several Nāths who were actually present and singing. Continuing enthusiastically to participate in the tradition and sometimes consciously to add to it, avid singers can see themselves as part of a greater group who knew the secrets of the *nirguṇ bhajan*s, a combined party of Sants and Nāths. And as Gorakh is the primal Nāth, so Kabīr is the primal Sant. Understanding the significance of Kabīr for householder Nāths, then, means examining more carefully the role of the Sants' *nirguṇ bhajan* tradition in Nāth socioreligious identity, what it means for the Nāths that a vital element of their tradition overlaps in an important way with that of the Sants. And in their relationship to the Sants' *nirguṇ bhajan*s, I think, householder Nāths are more than a little conflicted.

[7] From my transcription, part 2, pp. 14-19.

On the one hand the Nāths see themselves as prior to all the Sants, as their elders and teachers. Repeatedly, I heard them affirm that poet-singers from other castes were 'their disciples' and that 'all the *nirguṇī* knowledge came from the Nāths'. Although such statements were presented—perhaps with some justification—as historical claims, they in fact offer a fair representation of the current sociological status of householder Nāths in rural Rajasthan: they are indeed religious leaders among the lower and middle castes from whom those they identified as Sant singers typically came. Recognizing the peasant caste milieu in which their *nirguṇ bhajan* tradition developed, the Nāths seek acknowledgement of their own religious rank within it.

On the other hand, the particular secrets of the *nirguṇ bhajan*s that Nāths shared with the Sants can give them their own edge over religious groups with whom they feel competitive: Shaivite Brahmins and Nāth ascetics who otherwise tend to be held in greater esteem. For in the rural Nāth context the lusty singing of devotional songs is primarily a practice of married people from peasant castes. Since the practitioners of a more Sanskritized orthodox Shaiva ritual tradition don't come from peasant castes, and rough Nāth ascetics aren't married, they do not participate in *bhajan* singing and are not privy to secrets in the *bhajan*s. Command of the *bhajan*s is thus a competence that distinguishes householder Nāths from these perceived competitors.

Against Shaiva priests, the Nāths vie as *pujārī*s. Even though the Nāths in the area are oriented in their more esoteric practices toward Hiṅglāj Mātā, whose shrine lies in Baluchistan, their public stance is Shaiva, and they sometimes serve at Shaiva shrines. In both their clientele and their manner of service, however, they differ from the orthodox Brahmin priests more typically associated with such work. In general, their clients come from the lower fringes of the social order. In our area, the shrines served by Nāths are most often sponsored by Mīṇās, a caste with tribal origins. The service at the shrines may appear similar to simple high caste ritual, but it is done without brahmanic Sanskrit flourishes. Even though the most important of the Nāth ritual formulas are called *gāyatrī*s, in emulation of the Sanskrit mantra *par excellence*, they usually sound like rough and potent Hindi spells.

With their ritual function recalling a capacity for effective magic, individual Nāths are sometimes revered by members of less-than-Sanskritized castes as beneficent gurus. When I asked what this kind of guru-disciple relationship entailed, the reference was to the *dasnāmī pūjā*, an esoteric funereal cult in which the Nāths were leaders. I was told that when 'an ordinary Nāth' is treated as a guru 'by a Mīṇā or someone it means that he has told them the ten names [of the *dasnāmī* funereal cult] and gives general instructions about respect for Nāths and sadhus'. Nāths serve middle peasants and below, then, as both exoteric ritual priests and esoteric teachers.

In both their Shakta esoteric and Shaiva exoteric functions, moreover, Nāths draw significantly on *nirguṇ bhajan*s: the secret Hiṅglāj Mā *pūjā* of the funereal cult was the climax to a long, all-night *bhajan* session; while more public *bhajan* sessions featuring Nāths can also be taken as Shiva worship, and are frequently punctuated by 'Jai Śaṅkar Bhagvān'. The singing of *nirguṇ bhajan*s, then, along with the performance of ritual and mantra, are an important part of what the Nāths as religious specialists provide their clients. And if their rituals and mantras aren't quite up to par with those of the Brahmins—who will also deal with the lower classes for a fee—their *bhajan*s are something that the Brahmins, as a group, don't have at all.

The householder Nāths' *bhajan*s are something for which Nāth ascetics have little use. The two groups in fact have a relationship that often appears somewhat strained. There is little doubt that the caste of Nāth householders is descended from Nāth ascetics who, as the caste members themselves euphemistically say, took 'female disciples'. Interaction between the two persists and the ascetics continue to recruit from the outside. But these interrelationships aren't very extensive—considerably less so than that recently described by Véronique Bouillier in her excellent ethnology of a Nāth community in Nepal.[8] And any respect that the householders may have for the ascetics is not reciprocated. One case I remember involves a householder Nāth who used to pay regular visits to a local Nāth ascetic. He offered to introduce me to him, taking

[8] Véronique Bouillier, *Ascètes et rois: Un monastère de Kanphata Yogis au Népal*, Paris 1997, especially Chapter 6.

with him a recording of the *Gorakh Kabīr saṃvād* discussed above, which he thought was most admirable. The resident ascetic, however, together with his visiting comrade, showed little interest. When I visited alone later, the two made light of the tape—not particularly because it concerned Kabīr, but because it was a *nirguṇ bhajan* performance. 'That's something the householders do', they told me, 'not us; we do real *bhajan*', meaning meditation practice.[9]

The *nirguṇ bhajan* tradition, then, is generally held in disdain by the religious specialists—vaunting either a high caste or a celibate, ascetic lifestyle—with whom householder Nāths most often find themselves in tension. But the *bhajan* tradition is an integral part of the religious life that most Nāths share with other householder peasants of an esoteric religious bent. And many of the most avid of these people do not content themselves with just singing *bhajans*; they also participate in the secret cults in which the Nāths played leading roles. Of these cults there are two, one much more secret than the other.

The more widespread is the *dasnāmī* funereal cult, mentioned earlier, which was talked about openly. Only initiates are permitted to attend the ceremonies, but most people participating in the cult have few qualms about admitting their membership, and some were ready to describe the ritual to us in detail.[10] Whenever a member of the cult dies someone else had to take their place and the cult tends to perpetuate itself in families, and all the Nāth families we knew were seriously involved in it. But even though the Nāths with whom we talked were open about many matters, they respected that cult's strictures about secrecy enough not to let us simply observe. For once people had witnessed the ritual, it had to be done for them at their death; if not, trouble could ensue for

---

[9] This particular incident is described more fully in my 'Nath Yogis as Established Alternatives', p. 77, an article that examines more closely the relationship between householder and ascetic Nāths in Rajasthan.

[10] Some of this detail is given in Daniel Gold and Ann Grodzins Gold, 'The Fate of the Householder Nath', *History of Religions*, vol. 24, No. 2, 1984, pp. 113-32. The ritual seems to be a somewhat simpler variant of one presented by Bouillier in an exclusively Nāth context (*Ascètes et rois*, pp. 153-7).

everyone involved. The ritual's secrecy here is seen to stem from a practical occult danger.

Beyond the *dasnāmī* funereal cult is the *bīsnāmī* cult, which entails a sexual ritual that must be kept secret at least in part because of conventional social strictures. Since people in the cult are not supposed to admit membership in it, let alone talk about it, it is hard to find out just what the ritual entails. Two of my closest Nāth associates—including one of my main research assistants—were most likely members. When asked directly about the *bīsnāmī*s, of course, they would usually say something like: 'I can't tell you, I don't have the information.' But they tended to avoid looking me in the eye when they said this; they also often dropped hints, did in fact give out some information, and got genuinely angry when other people denigrated the cult. 'You shouldn't say bad things about the *bīsnāmī panth*', I noted my research assistant retorting sharply to another Nāth, 'it will cause your destruction'. I am thus hesitant myself to repeat here the salacious rumors I have heard about the *bīsnāmī*s. Encounters with my two associates, however, plainly suggested that there was some kind of woman swapping involved. 'You have to go as a pair (*joṛā*)', my assistant told me as he discreetly inquired if I would be interested in joining (I was in the field those days with my wife). On a different occasion, but also talking about pairs, the other emphasized that in *bīsnāmī* 'what's mine is yours and what's yours is mine'. He smiled broadly.[11]

Needless to say, the *bīsnāmī panth* is a subject of controversy. Most people, including many Nāths, are scandalized by it: 'There are so many *jāti*s in it', said one older householder Nāth, well-versed in many of his community's traditions, 'and they have sense-enjoyment with one another.' Others, also including many Nāths, feel differently. In fact, most of the handful of Nāths in the area understood to have exceptional esoteric authority are also reputed to be involved in the cult. My research assistant

---

[11] For a fuller description of what seems to be the same cult (there called the *kuṇḍā panth*), see Dominique-Sila Khan, *Conversions and Shifting Identities: Ramdev Pir and the Ismailis in Rajasthan,* Delhi 1997, p. 131. Khan also describes the funereal '*daśa panth*' which she speaks of as a 'milder' form of the *kuṇḍā panth* (ibid., p. 132).

affirmed that the *bīsnāmī*s 'had a lot of respect among Nāths' and that they shouldn't be maligned. The other went so far as to say that the cult was the twelfth-and-a-half *panth* of the traditional twelve *panth*s of the Nāths, explaining: 'In the Nāth community there is another way. It's Shiva's way; the union of Shiva and Shakti takes place in it. This is the *bīsnāmī panth*. The great way of the Nāths is this one.'[12]

If the great secrets of the Nāths are to be found in sexual practice, and the *nirguṇ bhajan*s reveal great secrets, it makes sense that sexual secrets too will be revealed in the *bhajan*s. And in fact, many people involved in *bīsnāmī* practice are avid *bhajan* singers and sometimes do interpret the songs in light of the cult. I can remember being flabbergasted at the sexual explicitness of one of the very first interpretations of a *nirguṇ bhajan* I heard in the village. It was given by an old and respected ironworker known for his esoteric knowledge, at the time the main local leader of the funereal cult. I thought then that his interpretation might have been some idiosyncratic view of his own, or that he was teasing us. But I later heard other, similar interpretations. I have noted at least one such interpretation by my research assistant of what seemed a rather innocent and conventional Sant turn of phrase: *had kā jīv base behad meṁ*, which I would innocently read to mean: 'the limited soul settles into the limitless.'[13] But I was told that here *behad*, the 'limitless', refers to a woman and the line could be interpreted in a sexually explicit way.

Examining the song more closely, I saw how my assistant might have come to his interpretation:

Whoever asks about the land of liberation
I'll clearly explain him the truth.
Listen to my words: pay close attention, brother sadhu. (refrain)

---

[12] This statement seemed so striking at the time that I noted the words in Hindi: *Nāthoṁ ke samāj meṁ ek aur mārg hai; is ko śiv mārg kahte haiṁ; is meṁ śiv śakti kā milan hotā hai. Yah bīsnāmī panth hai. Nathoṁ meṁ baṛā mārg yāhī hai.*

[13] From transcription of Jāgaraṇ Gaṇeṣ Bāg part 2, p. 53 (recorded at Sāvar [Kekri], April 1997).

Leisure, the piquant, communion, the goodlooking—
four liberations I declare;
The limited soul settles into the limitless
It merges into truth. (1)

Imagine the mortal world as the light of the sun
The light of truth is untouched by destruction—
A sign of the self's liberation. (2)

Earth, sky, air, water: the constructions of *māyā*'s pavilion—
The Lord's land is beyond them.
*Sant*s and enraptured ones go there. (3)

The sadhu who's reached there and all the *siddha*s know the secret
They've forgotten their confusion.
Jīvā Rām's found the complete, unapproachable place,
the unshakeable world of rapture! (4)

Victory to Lord Satguru![14]

While the refrain seems like unremarkable Sant poetry, the four liberations—*mukti*s—with which the first verse begins are unusual. Not only is the plural form itself uncommon (as final release, *mukti* is normally singular) the liberations enumerated seem curious. While one could easily conceive of a singer speaking of a set of spiritual states as *mukti*s' the four terms given here are not frequent descriptions of internal states, and all can have sensuous overtones. These I attempt to preserve in

---

[14] जो कोई पूछे देश मुक्ति का, साफ़ कहूं सत ब्याना
साधू भाई सुणों शब्द धर ध्याना हां हां जी (टेक)
समय सालोंगा संयोजा सुरूपी रे चारों मुक्ति बताणां हां हां रे जी,
हद का जीव बसे बेहद म, सत में जाई समाना (१)
मृत्यु लोक का कर अनुमाना रे, जैसे प्रकाश रवि भाना, हां हां जी
सत्य प्रकाश नाश से न्यारा, आतरम मुक्ति निसाना (२)
धरनी गगन और पवना पानी रे, ये तो माया मण्डप रचाणा हां हां जी,
हां इनसे आगे रे देश सायब का, पूगें सन्त मस्ताना (३)
पुग्योड़ा साध सभी सिद्धा जाण भेद ऊ जी, भरम भुलाणां हां हां जी,
जीवा राम अगम पद पूरण, हे अटल भौम मस्ताना (४)
सतगुरु भगवान की जय।

my less than conclusive translations: *samaya*, 'time'—which I have rendered as 'leisure'; *sāloṅgā*—probably a Rajasthani form of *salonā* (from *lūṁ* Raj. *lauṁ*, 'salt'), 'piquant, charming'; *saṁyojā*—'union' (used of a couple); *surūpī*—'good looking'. These four somewhat provocative 'liberations' could then prompt a *bīsnāmī* hearer to find a sexually explicit meaning in the union of 'limited' and 'limitless' in the rest of the verse. While we cannot say just how an initiated listener might sustain such a line of interpretation throughout the song, possibilities can be conceived, and the first line of the second verse ('imagine the mortal world as the light of the sun') really does seem to make most sense when interpreted from a tantric perspective that looks to material means. The clincher, however, is in the signature. My assistant identified Jīvā Rām as a Gūjar from near Jodhpur who had been a guru to my other suspected *bīsnāmī* associate. Knowing the origins of the song, he interpreted it accordingly.

This is not to say that all the songs were always explained to me in sexually explicit terms. And in the public group discussions interspersed among the singing, I did not notice this dimensions explicitly addressed. I do, however, remember wondering about the point of several extensive discussions of Shiva and Shakti, and which of the two referred to a particular member of a pair of terms. There, too, no doubt, things could sometimes be understood at a variety of levels, with different people in attendance grasping truths according to their own experience. I think that the singers who were also *bīsnāmī*s are in fact open to reading—and 'writing'—a wide range of experience into the songs, both explicitly sexual and internally yogic. One might imagine how Jivā Rām, or his predecessor, adapted a more conventional Sant song about 'the land of liberation' to fit more aptly his own experience. There seems to be a parallel here with Baul tradition, where similar songs are also normally created and interpreted within a broad tantric spectrum.[15]

And who is to know just when *bīsnāmī* meanings were deliberately written into the songs or just read into them by *bisnāmi* enthusiasts? As

---

[15] For a popularly accessible account of the Baul tradition, with translations, see Bhaskar Bhattacharyya, Nik Douglas, and Penny Slinger, *The Path of the Mystic Lover: Baul Songs of Passion and Ecstasy,* Rochester, Vt. 1993.

with my assistant interpreting Jivā Rām's song, people knew what else singers from the villages in the region had been up to besides composing and performing. And weren't local Sants, like Kabīr, married men from ordinary castes looking for spiritual truth where they could find it? The whole *nirguṇ bhajan* tradition of the Sants, Kabīr and his successors could, then, when appropriate, be interpreted from an all-inclusive tantric perspective.

The term Sant, for *bīsnāmī* members, can thus have some special, somewhat questionable connotations. As elsewhere in North India, the term is used in specific reference to singers of *nirguṇ bhajan*s as well as more generally to especially qualified, possibly married, religious virtuosi. But for those involved in the *bīsnāmī* cult, the most spiritually qualified non-celibate *nirguṇ* singers would also be *bīsnāmī*s, to which the term Sant can then be taken to refer. Speaking of a well-travelled householder Nāth reputed to be a *bīsnāmī* leader, my research assistant told me of two ashrams he stays in, both with Sant in their name. This, in his mind, specifically suggested a *bīsnāmī* affiliation. In his circles, it is the *bīsnāmī* secrets that were the special preserve of the greatest Sants—including, presumably, Kabīr.

The *bīsnāmī* view, however, was that of a religiously elitist minority. The majority of villagers hold to what scholars, too, would consider the more historically probable case: that Kabīr and most other Sants preached an internal religion and their esoteric vocabulary referred first of all to inward yogic states. This would put Kabīr and the Sants over *against* the adherents of *bīsnāmī* practice, an alternative to them that may in fact at times have stood as an historical counter-tradition. According to Komal Kothari, in southern Rajasthan many of the reformist movements—including the Kabīr-panthīs—worked specifically among lower classes involved in *bīsnāmī* practice, if not particularly among householder Nāths.[16] From this perspective, Kabīr's secrets would then refer to those of the higher esoteric truths in contrast to a local sexual ritual that many thought was degraded. The secrets brought from Kashi would thus be reformist truths re-established from outside by a sectarian tradition that included many renunciates.

---

[16] Personal communication, 31 July 1993, Jodhpur.

For all the householder Nāths, then, Kabīr and the Sants presented the Nāths' own *nirguṇ* truths in ways particularly apt for people who were married, a state seen to have advantages of its own. Specifically citing Kabīr as an example, a Jaipur Kālbeliyā guru stressed the greatness of the householder stage of life and thus of his own situation: 'With us you can split your ears and still live as householders.' It was good to be a Nāth and married, too, he seems to be saying, and Kabīr can help us understand why. For those Nāths who saw the religious superiority of their householder status over celibate ascetics as the ability to participate freely in a tantric sexual cult, Kabīr and the Sants could represent that freedom. For the rest, Kabīr could represent the pinnacle of an internal religion in which householders might excel at least as well as renunciates. In either case Kabīr's secrets remain valuable and very important; here, as in many non-brahmanic traditions throughout north India, Kabīr stands for a supremely high truth beyond official orthodoxy, however that truth, and that orthodoxy, are conceived.

Kabīr in Literature by and for Muslims

Peter Gaeffke

The oldest reference to Kabīr in the Muslim literature of India is found in the *'A'in-i Akbarī* by Abū'l Faẓl where Kabīr is mentioned in at least two passages, always with the *epitheton ornans muwaḥḥid* (monotheist). The passages occur in the context of possible burial places of Kabīr near Darbhanga and at Konarak. Understandably, the friend of Akbar and co-founder of the Dīn-i Ilāhī was interested to find traces of monotheism among Hindus.

The next reference to Kabīr in Muslim writings occurs in the *Dābistān-i maẕāhib* by Muḥasan Fānī (1615-75), who was born in Kashmir under Jahāngīr and died when Aurangzeb ruled. He was a judge in Allahabad, appointed by Shāh Jahān, and was obviously patronized by Dārā Shikūh. Therefore his book shows the interest of Muslims of Shikūh's circle in non-Muslim religions. This interest was ignited by Qādarī Sufis who were the teachers of Shikūh and who spread a very open interpretation of the *waḥdadu'l-wujūd* theory of Ibn 'Arabī in India. They must have enthused Muḥasan Fānī with the idea that God could be found in all religions, not only in Islam. In this environment he wrote about Jews, Christians, Buddhists and also about *vairāgī*s. The only person mentioned in this category is Kabīr. Fānī's information must have come from oral tradition. He tells about the birth of Kabīr in a weaver family, his unhappiness with Islam and Hinduism, and how Kabīr found Rāmānanda as his teacher. Then there is the story how he proves to Brahmins that their belief in the power of Ganga water is an illusion and that flowers are too precious to be sacrificed before images. Finally, he says, as Abū'l Faẓl said before him, that Hindus and Muslim quarreled in what manner his dead body should be disposed of. So, except at his birth and at his death, there is no relation of Kabīr to the Muslim community mentioned. He is put in this book between Vaiṣṇavas and Nānak. There is only his anti-idol position and his opposition to brahmanical ritual.

When Aurangzeb rose to power and Dārā Shikūh was pushed aside, Muḥasan Fānī lost his position and retired to Kashmir. His book became a scandal among Muslims. When it was shown to William Jones, he read it but suppressed it because of the many heretical statements in it. In the times of Jones, it was not advisable to discuss Kabīr in Muslim circles. However, we have evidence that the knowledge of Kabīr, the monotheist, lived on among some Muslims.

In the circle of Jones's successors in Calcutta, Rām Mohan Rāy in his Vedānta writings brought up Kabīr's name. In the introduction to his Upaniṣad translations, Rām Mohan Rāy speaks about an Indian tradition of monotheistic religious poets, and mentions Kabīr, Dādū Dayāl and Nānak. The question is from where Rām Mohan Rāy had gotten this information. We know that his family had a close relationship to the Muslim rulers of Murshidabad and that under the influence of Muslims, he wrote his first major work the *Tuḥfatu'l-muwaḥḥidīn* which like the *Dābistān-i mazāhib* is a collection of beliefs. In it is a reference to the Indian tradition of monotheists. The *'Ain-i Akbarī* and *Dābistān-i mazāhib* allow us to assume that among a continuous number of Muslims from Akbar until Rām Mohan Rāy the tradition to call the Sant poets *muwaḥḥidīn* lived on. Rām Mohan Rāy wrote for Hindus and the British. The Muslim world of this time, in general, was not interested in Kabīr even when he was presented as a monotheist among the polytheists. The reason is that Urdu poets in the eighteenth century were too busy to develop the criteria for the Golden Times of Urdu literature and, therefore, completely overlooked the developments of Urdu in the Dekkan. Due to the same preferences, writers of other linguistic idioms, such as *sadhukkaṛī,* remained outside of the field of interest not only for the poets but also for the composers of *tazkira*. In Mīr Tākī Mīr's *tazkira* and the famous nineteenth-century *Āb-i ḥayāt* by Āzād, Kabīr is absent.

In this situation a change occurred when Urdu scholars had to defend their territory against claims by scholars of Hindi literature. The latter had defined Hindi as reaching from the Jaina literature in old Rajasthani in the twelfth century to the so-called *premkathā* in Avadhī of the fifteenth and sixteenth centuries. They were also claiming geographical breadth by including the Sant literature and even Hinduwī of the Dekkan as part of the Hindi tradition. The movement against this involved also the question of the age of origin, an issue of major importance in the period of historicism, for assigning weight and rank. It was spearheaded by an Urdu scholar who did not come from the heartland of classical Urdu, i. e., the great Muslim centers of northern India, but from the Dekkan. There the name *qadīm urdū* was coined first and also promoted by 'Abdu'l-Ḥaqq in the journal of the same name. 'Abdu'l-Ḥaqq, the founder of the Anjuman-i Taraqqī-yi Urdū, fought for the extension of the age of Urdu beyond the magic year of 1709 when Walī appeared in Delhi and *Rekhtā/Urdū* started to become the fashion of the day.

'Abdu'l-Ḥaqq's primary aim was the inclusion of Dakkinī literature in the history of Urdu literature. He was only partly successful in this. Even today, Urdu poets and scholars of classical Urdu feel uncomfortable when they hear Dakkinī Urdu recited and avoid serious study of the poets of this pre-classical period. However, the pressure of Hindi that grew enormously in the twentieth century, did not leave the writers of the history of Urdu literature any choice but to expand their studies beyond classical Urdu.

This is the climate in which Kabīr became a focus of interest again among scholars of Urdu. But again, it were not Muslims well trained in classical Urdu but a Brahmin who wrote the first and until now only book on Kabīr in Urdu. This was Manoharlāl Zutshī, who, coming from a Brahmin family from Kashmir, was born in Faizabad in 1876 and was educated at Canning College at Lucknow. Later on he became Principal of the Allahabad Training College, Registrar of the Benares University, Under-Secretary and Assistant Director of Education, and after 1921 he was Principal of the Jubilee College. He died in 1944.

He has written a book in Urdu entitled *Kabīr Ṣāḥab*. It consists of two parts: (1) 'Hindu *mazhab*' and (2) 'Kabīr'. The book was published in 1930 by the Hindustānī Akādamī, which was founded by Gāndhī in Allahabad and worked for Hindu-Muslim understanding and friendship. The book would have been forgotten by now had not the events around the Babri Mosque in Faizabad in 1989 instigated those who still believed in the bond between Indian Muslims and Hindus to rescue the book from oblivion. In 1994 the Khudā Bakhsh Library in Patna republished the orginal part on Kabīr with the title *Kabīr Ṣāḥab*.

Manoharlāl Zutshī's presentation of Kabīr follows a simple arrangement. He speaks first about the life of Kabīr in which he uses sources available in his time. Then he writes about his teachings and religious instruction (*talqīn*). These and the following chapters consist only of quotations from Kabīr presented in Nāgarī followed by a paraphrase in Urdu. The chapters have the following headings: 1. *tauḥīd;* 2. *bhakti* and *prem;* 3. *mazhab kī numā'ish* (ritualism in religion); 4. rebirth; 5. the mix of Hindus and Muslims; 6. *mutafarriq* (separation, i.e., a pessimistic view of the world). A short assessment of Kabīr's poetry follows and then a sketch of the Kabīr-panth. There is a bibliography at the end of the book.

At that time, such a study of Kabīr was not possible for a Muslim. Manoharlāl Zutshī had a background that allowed him to use the *Kabīr bacanāvalī* edited by Ayodhyāsiṃha Upādhāyaya; the *Kabīr-granthāvalī*, edited by Śyāmsundar Dās; and the poems of Kabīr in the *Hindī navratna*, edited by Gaṇeśbihārī Miśra, Śyāmbihārī Miśra, and Śukdevbihārī Miśra. One of these books was published by the Nāgarī Pracāriṇī Sabhā, an overtly anti-Urdu organisation. The fact that a Brahmin was writing in Urdu is not surprising given the status of Urdu at this time. The fact that he wrote on Kabīr, in a publication accessible to Muslims, had one primary reason, namely, the importance that Kabīr attached to *tauḥīd* and devotion. At the end of the well-documented presentation of Kabīr's life, Zutshī writes that he wanted to give actual information about a person such as Kabīr but not stories about his miracles. He wanted to let his readers know about his cultural and metaphysical teachings and his opposition to pride and heresy; and that Kabīr spread justice and truth and wished to unite Hindus and Muslims. Hindus and Muslims love him, so Manoharlāl Zutshī says, because of the openness of his nature and the breadth of his views.

As for the topic of rebirth, Manoharlāl Zutshī had greater difficulties to put it before his Muslim audience. However, especially in Ismā'īlī circles, rebirth was not a completely foreign idea. But it is doubtful whether Manoharlāl Zutshī relied on this very specialized knowledge in this matter. However, every Muslim in India could be supposed to know that for Hindus this was a pillar of their religion.

So we see here not an inclusion of Kabīr in the Muslim tradition but an emphasis on the common beliefs and recognition of the differences. This was a courageous statement from an Urdu writer at this time. The orginal position of some Muslims that Kabīr is a monotheist is nowhere expanded and he has become a bridge between Hindus and Muslims.

Manoharlāl Zutshī, together with the people connected with the Hindustānī Akādamī, still believed in the possibility of a common culture of Hindus and Muslims and produced Kabīr as evidence for it. The political developments at that time spoke another language: Iqbāl's speech about Pakistan at the meeting of the Muslim League in Lahore and the hardening position of Jinnāḥ was not yet taken seriously by a Hindu whose Indian culture was Urdu culture.

After Independence, the situation changed again: Pakistan had to construct its own history. In 1971, the Panjab University of Lahore started to publish a comprehensive *Tārīkh-i adabiyāt i musalmān-i pākistān o hind* in twenty volumes in Urdu. Here we meet again the territorial claims of 'Abdu'l-Ḥaqq. In the now widely expanded knowledge about pre-classical Urdu, Kabīr finds a place.

The contribution on Kabīr is by A. D. Nasīm in vol. VI of this work. Kabīr appears between Khwāja Ashraf Jahāngīr Samānān (d. 1405) and Shaikh 'Abdu'l-Qadūs Gangohī (d. 1528). We read: Bhagat Kabīr, as generally accepted, had Muslim parents who could read and write. And since he was a *bhagat*, who was aware of the fact that the lower classes of the population accepted bhakti when it was presented in their languages, he used for his poetry a language closer to the colloquial of his time. This poetry which contains vedantic thought, calmed the minds of the people. Nasīm describes Kabīr's poetry as pure and sweet and adds that today it is still alive. The five samples he gives from Kabīr's poetry are all contained in Manoharlāl Zutshī's book; however, one *dohā* has different readings. Nasīm wrote this contribution by quoting the authority of 'Abdu'l-Ḥaqq who, as he says, had included Kabīr in *Qadīm urdū*.

In Karachi, absolutely on his own, Jamīl Jālebīl, who came from a family of journalists in Delhi, but migrated to Pakistan in 1947, wrote *Tārīkh-i adab-i urdū*, whose first volume was published in 1974. Jamīl Jālebīl is an accomplished linguist and had proven this in his edition of *Padam Rāo o Kadam Rāo* in which he carefully analysed the origin of the vocabulary of this work of the Bahmani period. He was also intimately familiar with the Dahlawī, Gujarī and Dakkinī languages and the literature preserved in these idioms. Jamīl Jālebīl does not make the monotheism of Kabīr the starting point of his assessment, but that he was the greatest poet of the bhakti movement and disgusted with the differences in religion, country and caste in India. Only after this, Jamīl Jālebīl says he was against image worship and polytheism and that the spread of monotheism was his profession. Love was for Kabīr the means to reach God and through it the *ātmā* finds peace (*śānti*). Jamīl Jālebīl then continues with an explanation of Kabīr's concept of God.

Again Jamīl Jālebīl returns to the unifying power of Kabīr who portrayed people in such a way that one was reading the Veda and another the Koran. Purity of love is the simple essence of man, if it is not there, the being is no more human. This is brought forth with such deeply felt heart-rending emotion that it even today vibrates in the heart. And the magic of Kabīr's poems is of purity, intimacy and warmth of love.

After this, the linguist takes over, for Jamīl Jālebīl says that although Kabīr lived in the east (of India), he used a language that could be understood by everybody outside the Panjab. It contains Persian, Arabic and Turkish words, albeit in colloquial forms, and then the author concludes by listing the replacement of Arabic sounds by familiar Indian consonants.

Jamīl Jālebīl's samples exceed the collection in Zutshī, most probably because Jamīl Jālebīl was familiar with the Kabīr poems in the *Adī Granth* which at this time was available in Urdu script.

So from an interest of marginal Muslims searching for a bridge to Indian religion, Kabīr became part of Urdu literature not primarily because of his monotheism but for his voice of devotion, which touches the heart of anybody in northern India. This reception was facilitated by the widely held opinion that 'bhakti is a lyrical version of Vedānta' (Zutshī, p. 32).

Bibliography

Abū'l Faẓl 'Allāmī, *'A'īn-i Akbarī*, ed. by H. Blochmann (Bibliotheca Indica vol. 58), Calcutta 1877.

Āzād, Muḥammad Ḥusain, *Āb-i ḥayāt*, Lahore 1967.

Fānī, Muḥasan, *Dābistān-i maẕāhib*, Lakhnau 1881; trs. by David Shea and Anthony Troyer, repr. Lahore 1973.

Gul, Ḥasan Wāqar, *Urdū sawāniḥ nigārī āzādī ke ba'd*, Karachi 1997.

Ḥaqq, 'Abd'ul, *Qadīm urdū*, Karachi 1961.

Jālebīl, Jamīl, *Tārīkh-i adab-i urdū*, vol.1, Karachi 1971.

Kabīr, *Bacanāvalī*, ed. by Ayodhyāsiṃha Upādhyāya, Allahabad 1917.

Kabīr, *Granthāvalī*, ed. by Śyāmsundar Dās, Benares VS 1985.

Mīr Tāqī Mīr, *Nikātu'sh-shu'arā* [in Persian, 1752]. (Contains 103 Urdu poets; Kabīr is not among them.)

Miśra, Gaṇeśbihārī, Śyāmbihārī Miśra, Śukdevbihārī Miśra (eds.), *Hindī navratna*, Benares 1910-11.

Panjab University, *Tārīkh-i adabiyāt-i musalmān-i pākistān o hind*, Lahore 1971 ff.

Robertson, Bruce C., *Raja Rammohan Ray: The Father of Modern India*, Delhi 1995.

Walī, Muḥammad, *Dīwān*, Lahore 1965.

Sāqib Shāhābu'd-Dīn, *Bābā-yi urdū maulwī 'Abdu'l-Ḥaqq: ḥayāt aur 'ilmī khidmāt*, Karachi 1985.

Zutshī, Manoharlāl, *Kabīr Ṣāḥab*, Allahabad 1930, second print: Patna 1994.

Kabīr and Mystic Poetry in Urdu

Sadiqur Rahman Kidwai

A child of a Brahman widow floating on a lotus leaf in a lake, rescued and adopted by a childless Muslim weaver couple and named Kabīr—this popular legend says a lot about what Kabīr has come to signify. Despite the mystery that surrounds him and the innumerable questions regarding the authenticity of all that has come down to us about Kabīr, this legend, like the other legends about him, points towards historical and social realities of our society. It is also a metaphorical description of the powerful common urge to subvert the social reality. This at times results in conflicts, violent as well as passive. Underneath it also lies the idealism of the *bhakta*s, Sufis and other saints that has survived and modified the history of tensions in Indian society. Religion, caste, gender, social legitimacy and status based on birth are issues at the core of most conflicts. The *bhakta*s' idealism also aims at a reconciliation of tensions created by these conflicting elements to which Sufis and saints, as also reformists of modern times, have devoted all their energies. High ideas have always been appearing in literature, folk songs and popular stories, but society has broadly remained unchanged and social organisation based on the interest of powerful groups, supported and cemented by religious sanctions for centuries, has not been easy to break.

Kabīr in his time symbolized the natural aversion of the oppressed classes to the established system of society and the search of an ideal alternative that would be free from those strains. He expressed his astonishment at the prevailing inequalities, showed irreverence to the clergy and all forms of worship and gave a call to all to abandon the system if they could not destroy it. His Rām bhakti is a metaphor that linked the traditional belief system of Indian society to the humanism based on day to day experience of life and concrete realities of his time. Thus his preferences for the common language and mode of expression reflected the objective of reaching out to the largest number of people, especially the oppressed class to which he belonged. From the very early days of his life, he rejected the traditional system of education, averse to what transmitted by it to impressionable minds. Thus we find a coherent and complete system in Kabīr's life and thought which is common among most Sufis and *bhakta*s.

Kabīr stands out among them as a saint-poet because of his power of expression, flexibility and assimilative and communicative qualities that are unique. His poetry is full of metaphors and symbols borrowed from the ordinary life of peasants and craftsmen. His lively and vibrant voice, when adapted to music, could move large crowds, reach wide areas and transcend time. His humanism is aimed at the reform of society, but like all mystics he addresses the individual. The *guru-śiṣya* and *pīr-murīd* relationship had to be a one-to-one relationship. Person-to-person contact and concern with individual character and situation is most important for Sufis as well as *bhakta*s. This is crucial because the time-honoured oral tradition, without which the poetics of Indian literature cannot be understood, would not have survived in the absence of a receptive crowd. Coming together of individuals in a crowd means commonality of purpose, yet each individual receives the message in his own way and relates it to the context of his own circumstance. It is with the beauty of Sufi poetry that the listener instantly establishes natural affinity. The rapport established by mystic poets such as Kabīr through their brilliant communicative skills enhances the appeal of their message built up over a period of time through legends, stories and songs. It is not by chance that all mystics have been great communicators. In fact, communication with the masses had a primacy in the whole system of mysticism.

Islamic mysticism does not depart from the basic tenets of religion. The Sufi claims to represent the true spirit of Islam. He traces the origin of his system of thought to the Koran and the *ḥadīṣ̤*. He never rejects the *sharī'a* but calls upon to even go beyond it. According to him, while form as prescribed by the *sharī'a* is essential, it is not enough as it is the bare prescribed minimum. As for the substance of religion, for him it is much more than formal adherence to prescribed tenets. Also the Sufi stresses the importance of attaining the true path to God through personal endeavor. For him to observe the *sharī'a* is one thing and to imbibe the spirit of religion, another. Sufis stress the supremacy of personal experience over the mere observance of formal rules. They traced their origin from the earlier days of Islam and their obedience to Muḥammad and his companions, especially 'Alī, as the models of selfless devotion. The influence of the Sufis became strong when the Islamic state came into being. The requirement of state craft, the logic of the expansion of empire and the desire to hold power encouraged those in command of society to interpret religion and *sharī'a* according to their objectives. It was against the hegemony of these affluent and oppressive regimes that the Sufis raised their voice.

The concept of God as we find it in Urdu Sufi poetry is similar to that of Kabīr. *Waḥdat al-wujūd* or 'unity of existence', according to which the ultimate reality exists in every particle of the universe, is the most common concept. Thus God resides in all human beings. To them, treating all fellow human beings with respect and tolerating even those who differ is the way to find ultimate reality or to commune with God. Mujib quotes Mu'īn ud Dīn Chishtī as saying, 'Whoever wishes to be secure against the tribulations of the Day should perform that act of obedience that which no act is better in the eyes of God.'[1] Then people asked, 'What act of obedience is this?' He replied, 'To answer the call of those in distress, to fulfill the needs of the helpless, to feed the hungry.' He also said, 'If anyone has these three qualities, you may know that God holds him to be His friend: First, a generosity like the generosity of the river, secondly, a benevolence like the benevolence of the sun and thirdly a hospitality like the hospitality of the earth.' Mujib also convincingly argues that '[t]he outlook of the Sufis was broad enough for them to recognise without inhibition and reservations the possibility of there being many paths to God. God has a different secret, a different mystery, a different relationship with each person.'[2]

The Muslim mystical concepts of *waḥdat al-wujūd* and *waḥdat ash-shuhūd* have great affinity with Hindu mystic concepts. Sufism has borrowed much from monastic tradition and yoga but total renunciation of the world is not a part of Islam, though renunciation of worldly comforts in the path of the truth and rising above the self is a highly regarded religious virtue. Service of fellow human beings is considered the service

[1] Muhammad Mujib. *The Indian Muslims*. Montreal 1967, p. 146.

[2] Ibid., p. 148.

of God. Sufis are supposed to live in the society but keep themselves away from ordinary indulgences. Living in the seclusion of *khānqāh*s, they must however be available to ordinary people.

The development of Urdu was a long process, but its poetry bloomed on the Indian literary scene a little after Kabīr. No direct influence of Kabīr on Urdu poets is attributed. But cultural and linguistic links bring them together in many ways. Mysticism had deep roots in Indo-Iranian society and much of poetry is influenced by mysticism. Urdu absorbed much of its poetic tradition from Persian poetry. The most popular genre in Persian and Urdu is the *ghazal* and the structure of the *dohā* has much in common with verse in Urdu *ghazal*. Brevity, rhyme, rhythm, interwoven with metaphors, similes, symbols and lines which could be memorized easily are some of the qualities common between the *dohās* of Kabīr and the couplets of *ghazal*s. Another feature of Urdu is the adoption of Western and Central Asian legends through the influence of Persian. Urdu mystic poetry was full of names used as metaphors like Manṣūr, Moses and the Sinai, Lailā and Majnūn, and Shīrīn and Farhad. Sarmad, who settled in India and was beheaded by Aurangzeb because of his proximity to his brother Dārā Shikūh, is often glorified by mystics. They can be considered as parallel of Kabīr's Rām bhakti because they are used for symbolising the same message of love and devotion. Dissidence and rebellion against the clergy and the ruling elite and the willingness to accept the consequent persecutions are eulogized as gestures of devoted love.

Mystic poetry is usually sung at the gatherings around the mausoleums of Sufis. Qawwalī is the popular form in which Urdu and Persian verses from *ghazal*s and *rubā'ī*s are frequently juxtaposed with *dohā*s that are most often taken from Kabīr. Thus the channel of communication between Sufis and the common folk has continued to flow for centuries after their deaths. In fact, Sufism set the tone of classical Urdu *ghazal* that survives long after the age of Sufism. Even progressive poets of modern times from Majāz to Faiz̤ have taken the advantage of mystic metaphors. Their verses have been freely recited in large gatherings during the freedom struggle and also against post-Independence regimes of India and Pakistan. Thus the mystic poetic tradition stretched much beyond the specific situation in which it first appeared. Indo-Persian influence is found in all the languages of northern India, but Urdu is distinct as it reflects the completion of the process of assimilation as far as language and literature are concerned.

Undoubtedly the assimilation of fresh and foreign elements is a process that passes through the phases of rejection and acceptance. After having passed through the test of times, whatever remains becomes the ethos of an age. Kabīr's role in Indian history is most important because, like Amīr Khusrau, he came to represent a pseudonymous tradition within Indian literary and social history. He is credited with building up this ethos when forces of conflict were active. Thus despite the distance in time, Kabīr is not obsolete. He keeps pace with history. At the level of thought and expression the unorthodox attitude of Kabīr highlighted issues that are relevant even today and are commonly found in Urdu poetry. Mutual tolerance, respect and accommodation of others are the essential requirements for any pluralistic society to survive. Even global survival depends on the harmony among diverse elements. But the forces of negation have always been active and the world has been structured according to the design based on their interest. It is here that Kabīr and the likes of him appear as rebellious, irreverent and often blasphemous according to the standards set by dominant classes. The relevance of mystics like Kabīr can be seen in the fact that during the times of general political and social upheaval their verses and sayings provide inner strength to the people to challenge the system.

The time of Kabīr overlaps with the early phase of development of the Urdu language in northern India and also the appearance of literature in the Deccan. Historically Khusrau preceded Kabīr by more than two hundred years. Like the Kabīr tradition, also the Hindawi poetry in the name of Khusrau is largely inauthentic. It has been rendered in music and from region to region has undergone changes according to the linguistic habits of the speakers and singers. As a Persian poet he is held in great esteem both in Iran and India. What Khusrau called *zabān-i-Dihlī* was a form of language which was developing from the local dialect spoken around western Uttar Pradesh and Delhi in the thirteenth century. The same language was called Hindi or Hindawi. However, according to whatever has come down to us through oral tradition, Khusrau's Delhi dialect and Kabīr's eastern Uttar Pradesh dialect have great affinity. So much so that the receivers of the message of both the poets form a common group. Khusrau and Kabīr are sung by the same group of singers in the gatherings of the same audience. Similarly, Urdu poetry too reached the same audience in its time.

Urdu poetry started flourishing from the later sixteenth century and reached its height in the eighteenth and nineteenth centuries. The poets of this period are supposed to represent the classical period. Most important among them are Walī, Mīr, Saudā, Dard, Naẕīr and Ghālib. During this period, mastery of Persian along with local languages was considered essential by the elite. In Kabīr's time, Sufi poetry in Persian had pride of place. Along with Khusrau, Iranian poets like Rūmī, Sa'dī and Ḥāfiẓ were popular in India. Sufi poetry of Urdu had drawn much from Persian that was most widely used language of India and central Asia at that time. Sufism is the common world view of the poets of this time till Ghālib appears on the scene. While accepting Sufism, he also questions its beliefs.

ہستی ہے نہ کچھ عدم ہے غالبؔ
پھر کیا ہے تو اے نہیں ہے

When there is no being, no non-being, O Ghālib,
Then what are you, you 'nothingness?'[3]

جب کہ تجھ بن نہیں کوئی موجود
پھر یہ ہنگامہ اے خدا کیا ہے

When there is nothing but You,
Then why all this fuss, O Lord.[4]

---

[3] Asadullāh Khān Ghālib, *Diwān-i Ghālib*. New Delhi 1997, p. 170. All translations from the Urdu are by Sadeem Kidwai.

[4] Ibid., p. 144.

Ghazal, the most popular genre of Urdu poetry, suits Sufism because of its beautiful ambiguity. The ultimate truth, the creator of the commanding force behind all that is seen in the universe is perceived and explained through metaphors and similes. The undefinable, unknown and unidentifiable has to be brought to a perceivable arena and this is possible through easily intelligible words. But ambiguity has its own romance. The object of love has to be one that evokes emotions to the extreme. The qualities of the worldly beloved (man or woman) in flesh and blood are magnified in such a way that they can be sublimated and applied to someone who is too remote to reach. The relationship between the lover and the beloved is through pure unobstructed and selfless love, and, to achieve union with the beloved, the lover has to devote himself to a state where his very existence melts into the object of his love. The verses of the *ghazal* allow a vast space to the receiver. The object of the all-consuming love may be anyone from a human being to God.

However, the situation of the Urdu poet is different from that of Kabīr. In Kabīr's time, the Sultanate was in decline and the Mughal rule was not far. When the great Urdu poets emerged on the scene, the Mughal monarchy was in decline; colonial intervention and regional powers were gaining strength. However, monarchy as a political system had strong roots. Urdu poets lived in a general period of strife and uncertainty. The seats of power and the courts of kings and nobles were under great stress due to persistent political turmoil. Kabīr spoke in a language not spoken or favoured by the court. Kabīr addresses himself to the ordinary folk who are agile and dynamic. The language of the Urdu poets had 'classical' roots and the audience consisted of those who had lost the agility and dynamism that characterised them at the peak of Mughal rule. Thus the impermanence of life in this world is not an abstract idea but a real life experience. The rationale of the renunciation of the worldly life emerged from their own situation. No regime could survive the onslaught from all directions. In Urdu poetry we find recurrence of certain themes: that the world is an illusion; pain and pleasure are both unreal and passing phases; the worldly status and distinctions are also illusory, therefore all men, to whichever caste, class or religion they may belong, are equal because God resides in each one of them. Service of humanity is service of God.

Like Kabīr, the Urdu poet when expressing dissatisfaction with established forms of religion shorn of its true spirit does not hesitate to become irreverent. About clergy Saudā says:

عمامے کو اتار کے پڑھیو نماز شیخ
سجدے سے ورنہ سر کو اٹھایا نہ جائے گا

Cast off what you carry on your head, o pious one!
Or else who will you lift it, once you prostrate yourself.[5]

Acquisition of knowledge through traditional education is equally demolished by all mystics. Their stress on the transformation of the inner world cannot be achieved by mere reading or remembering of books by heart. One has to look at the wide world for the real knowledge.

Thus the dichotomy between the mind dependent on conventional knowledge and the heart free from all worldly compulsions is also a common theme:

وہ عجب گھڑی تھی کہ جس گھڑی لیا درس نسخۂ عشق سوں
کہ کتاب عقل کی طاق پر جو دھری تھی سو وہ دھری رہی

What a fateful moment it was when I decided to learn
from the treatise of love,
Now the tome of wisdom on the shelf stays untouched.[6]

سب کتابوں کے کھل گئے معنی
جب سے دیکھی نظیرؔ دل کی کتاب

I finally unravelled all that I had read
When I, Naẕīr, read what was in my heart.[7]

---

[5] Rashīd Hasan Khān (ed.). *Intikhāb-i Saudā*. New Delhi 1993, p. 350.
[6] Sirāj Aurangabādī. *Kulliyāt- i Sirāj*. 2nd ed. New Delhi 1998, p. 667.

Similarly the wisdom that represents reason is undependable as it is vulnerable to all profane temptations. It is therefore set against 'madness' that represents rejection of the ways of the world though it is laughed at by ordinary worldly people. The mad 'outsider' is the most exalted figure in Urdu poetry. Mīr says:

باولے سے جب تلک بجتے تھے سب کرتے تھے پیار
عقل کی باتیں کیاں ، کیا ہم سے نادانی ہوئی

They loved me when I babbled like an idiot,
What a fool I was to start talking sense.[8]

And for places of worship like mosques and temples and even the Ka'ba, he says:

کس کا کعبہ ، کیسا قبلہ ، کون حرم ہے ، کیا احرام
کوچے کے اس کے باشندوں نے سب کو یہیں سے سلام کیا

Whose is the Ka'ba, which is the right direction,
Which is the sacred space, how do you dress?
Those who live around him greet all –
As they are, no matter from where they be.[9]

His faith in the supremacy of spirit over form carries him to a stage where all manners of worship become equally good or bad.

---

[7] Rashīd Hasan Khān (ed.). *Intikhāb-i Naẓīr Akbarābādī*. New Delhi 1992, p. 215.

[8] Mīr Ṭāqī Mīr. *Kulliyāt-i Mīr*, vol. 1. Allahabad 1972, p. 395.

[9] Ibid, p. 21.

اس کے فروغِ حسن سے جھمکے ہے سب میں نور
شمعِ حرم ہو یا کہ دیا سومنات کا

His dazzling light flashed from everywhere,
Be it the lamp at the Ka'ba, or the one at Somnath.[10]

Even though the Urdu poet does reject his religion like Kabīr does, his mystic worldview brings him close to Kabīr. Urdu poets share with Kabīr their revulsion at the clergy as the worldly interests of mullahs and pandits clouded the message they claimed to convey. Mullahs overstress the importance of form over spirit. What remains is how one appears, not how he really is. Like Kabīr, the Urdu poets express their anguish through satire. They are both fond of making fun of everything that is associated with the clergy.

The Urdu poet in other ways is very different from Kabīr for he generally does not flout the established norms of poetic language and expression. However, within the available space his individual creative talent does make significant departures and leaves an overall impact on Urdu aesthetics. Thus despite the rigidity of the *ghazal* form, poets like Walī, Mīr, Dard, Ghālib and in the later period Iqbāl and many others, have added to the richness of the tradition. In fact, for great minds these rigidities posed a challenge to their mastery over the craft as well as their creative resource in which they eminently succeed. Thus the Sufi content in Urdu poetry, particularly the *ghazal*, has come down through the ages as one of our most cherished heritage. Urdu poetry is known for its soft, delicate, ornate and elegant style.

Even a poet like Naẓīr, who has taken unusual liberties with the tradition, is not totally out of tune if seen in the overall scenario of Urdu poetry. But perhaps he is the only Urdu poet who comes close to Kabīr in his treatment of language and choice of themes. His resource is more in the settings of Agra of his times and the culture of urban folk while other Urdu poets mostly looked inwards and dwelt on abstract perception. Thus Urdu Sufi poetry, despite the basic mystic spirit that it had in common

---

[10] Ibid., p. 257.

with Kabīr, has its own distinct character. Kabīr's style is raw, rough and vigorous. Urdu poetry is chiseled, polished and melodious. Kabīr shocks, the Urdu poet seduces. But despite such differences, their verses survive not only in the written text preserved in libraries but in the open environment. They have their own dynamism and have grown with the culture and the consciousness of the people. The fact that many of them remain unauthenticated and have constantly been altered by the people is, in fact, a tribute because they have through their words become one with history.

A Contemporary Legacy of Kabīr: A Hindu Sufi Branch and its Relation with the Kabīr-Panth

Thomas Dahnhardt

Various examples testify to the liveliness of Kabīr's legacy over the past centuries up to the present day. This paper draws attention to a curious case of interreligious relationship that began to unfold at the turn of this century, involving Hindus and Muslims. In particular, we are concerned here with an intersection of the spiritual tradition of the Kabīr-panth, with the teachings of a Sufi *ṭarīqa*. The latter was known for its strictly orthodox interpretation of Sunni Islam in accordance with the ways of the prophet Muḥammad, viz., the indigenous Mujaddidiyya branch of the Central-Asian Naqshbandiyya the name of which is derived from Shaikh Aḥmad Sirhindī (1564-1624) hailed by his followers as the 'renewer of the second millennium' of Islam (*mujaddid alf-i ṡānī*). The confluence of elements from these two directions resulting in a distinguished spiritual discipline since the last decade of the nineteenth century, has led to the gradual formation of a new Sant *paramparā* that in many ways amalgamates into the wider framework of the north Indian *nirguṇa* bhakti tradition, albeit in a modern environment. The natural and spontaneous way in which it was able to attract a considerable following into the folds of the *satsaṅg*, from where they continue to spread their supposedly simple and straightforward teachings, suggests the extent to which such a message still appeals to many contemporary Indians, independent of their social origins or religious affiliation.

But let us take a closer look at the circumstances involved in this case. An exhaustive analysis of the internal and external reasons that determined the passage of the esoteric heritage of the Naqshbandiyya Mujaddidiyya into a particular Hindu environment would involve a study that lies beyond the scope of this paper. We shall, however, try to single out some of the circumstances that led a recognized authority of that generally rather conservative Sufi order, set in the urban and rural environments of the Doāb, to initiate a young Hindu of the local Kāyasth community into the discipline and methodology of the *ṭarīqa*, even if this is complicated by the scarcity of reliable sources. By sifting the information contained in the numerous hagiographic accounts, it will be understood that the initiative for taking such a bold step lay primarily with Shāh Faẓl Aḥmad K͟hān (1838-1907), a locally respected *shaik͟h* and *'ālim* originally belonging to a small village close to the *qaṣba* of Kaimganj in Farrukhabad district. His spiritual genealogy goes back to Shaik͟h Aḥmad Sirhindī through the order's renowned eighteenth-century authority at Delhi, Shaik͟h Mīrzā Maẓhar Jān-i Jānān (d. 1781) who himself appears to have counted a number of Hindus among his disciples.

Moreover, it was from Shāh Abūl Ḥasan Zaid Fārūqī, the recently (1993) deceased head of the Mujaddidī convent in the old city of Delhi which developed around the sepulchre of Shaik͟h Mīrzā Maẓhar, that I first learnt about the existence of this particular group of Hindu devotees. I was told that they used to pay regular visits to the tombs of the *ṭarīqa*'s revered ancestors in order to derive spiritual benefits from prolonged meditation sessions at that place. Although Abūl Ḥasan himself denied having Hindus under his tutorship, a possibly compromising statement, his open attitude towards these visitors, who were allowed unrestricted access to the precincts of the *k͟hānaqāh* and the tombs of the lineage's forefathers, provides a strong indication of contact between the two spiritual families in question.

All this stands in stark contrast with the alleged hostile attitude toward Hindus that some modern scholars have attributed to Shaik͟h Aḥmad and his followers, a claim that has gained some currency since the period of growing nationalist feelings among India's educated urban Muslim class in the 1920s.

As became evident from the study of some mid-nineteenth-century manuscripts and letters in possession of a Mujaddidī Shaik͟h of Bhopal, a descendant in the line of Shāh Faẓl Aḥmad K͟hān, it was one of the *ṭarīqa*'s earlier masters, Sayyid Maulānā Abūl Ḥasan Naṣīrābādī (d. 1856), a leading Mujaddidī authority in the Awadh region holding the title of *quṭb al-zamān* or 'pole of his time', who explicitly entrusted one of his disciples with the task of recruiting Hindus as disciples. In a letter written shortly before his death, he states:

> By the grace of God, through your most intimate essence a new world will be illuminated. Some from among the *ahl-i hunūd* [Hindus] will come to enjoy your company, and since they possess the required qualities, do not refuse them the incomparable treasure of our spiritual heritage....[1]

In another letter, he adds while referring to the same point:

> ... this matter will constitute the proof of your being a 'pole of right guidance' (*qutb al-irshād*); ... if your spiritual energy (*tawajjuh-i khāṣṣ*) will reach the infidels and those who have departed from the right path (*kuffar wa fāsiq-i rāh-i mustaqīm)*, they will attain to the perfection of faith (*kāmil-i īmān*)....[2]

This task, which was left unaccomplished by the Maulānā's immediate successor, was eventually fulfilled by Shāh Fazl Aḥmad Khān. In winter 1891-2, he met Rāmcandra Saksenā, a young Hindu student from an impoverished Kāyasth family that had lost its ancient zamindari privileges in the area around the *qaṣba* of Bhogaon (dist. Mainpuri, U.P.) in the aftermath of the 1857-8 uprising, and started giving him his spiritual attention. It was, however, only four years later, in 1896, that Rāmcandra was granted full initiation into the order by making his vow of allegiance to the Muslim *pīr* (*bai'at*) thus receiving the secret *zikr*.

From that moment onwards till the death of the Shaikh in 1907, Rāmcandra kept receiving instructions and spiritual guidance (*hidāyat*) in the *ṭarīqa Mujaddidiyya*. Some time later, this master-disciple relationship culminated in the conferment of full licence and the rank of deputyship (*kullī ijāzat o khilāfat, ācārya padvī*) that entitled Rāmcandra to perpetuate the initiatory chain (*silsila*) in the predominantly Hindu environment independent of his disciples and family members.

---

[1] Makātib-i Sayyid Shāh Abū 'l-Hasan, letter no. 1 (manuscript letter collection in possession of Shah Manzur Ahmad Khan at Bhopal, M. P.). Cf. also *Damīma-i ḥālāt-i māshaikh-i Naqshabandiyya Mujaddidiyya*, Aligarh: Matba' Aḥmadī, 1943, p. 11.

[2] Makātib-i Sayyid Shāh Abū'l-Hasan, letter no. 3; *Damīma*..., p. 11.

The figure of Shāh Faẓl Aḥmad Khān emerges thus as representing a significant stage in the particular development of this Mujaddidī branch after Mīrzā Jān-i Jānān and Sayyid Abūl Ḥasan Nāṣīrābādī, for it was his interpretation of the attitudes assumed by his predecessors that paved the way for an inclusion of Hindus into this supposedly puritanical Sunni order. It comes, therefore, as no surprise that later Hindu hagiographies praise him as the revered *Ḥuẓūr Mahārāj*. The importance of his role becomes clear from the following paragraph by one of the Shāh's more sober biographers:

> Possibly, *Ḥuẓūr Mahārāj* was the first authority of the Naqshbandi *silsila* who has divulged the secret spiritual science (*gupta ādhyātmik vidyā*) pertaining to the saints of Islam without discrimination of any sort. Although he himself adhered to the Islamic faith he was completely free from religious bias. He never indulged in any controversy regarding different religions nor did he ever reprimand anybody for his religious affiliation. Whenever he came across any sort of criticism of any religion, he felt extremely displeased and consequently tried to avoid the company of such persons. His saying was that in every man the spiritual component (*ṭarz-i rūḥāniyat*) is one and alike, while the manners of social life (*ṭarz-i mu'āsharat*) are multiple. He paid equal respect to all sacred traditions and used to repeat that spiritual life begins essentially beyond the limits of institutional boundaries pronouncing himself against any exterior noise and battle....[3]

We learn from other sources that Shāh Faẓl Aḥmad Khān's first and foremost Hindu disciple at some stage was ready to convert to Islam, but was prevented by his master from doing so. This anecdote is illustrated in the sources in the following fashion:

> One day, a fellow Muslim disciple asserted in the presence of Rāmcandra that no spiritual progress could be achieved on the Naqshbandī spiritual path (*sulūk*) without adhering to the tenets set out by the Islamic Law. The *Mahātmājī* replied that in this case he was

[3] Bāl Kumār Khare, *Mahān Sūfī Sant Hazrat Shāh Fazl Ahmad Khān: unkā dharmik evam sampradāyik ekatā*, Varanasi 1982, p. 85.

> ready to embrace Islam. When learning about that conversation, [Shāh Faẓl Aḥmad Khān's] eyes turned red in anger and he immediately left the scene. A short while later, on his return, he asked Rāncandra: What sort of reprobate told you this? Having calmed down, he then explained that the sort of knowledge he was concerned with does not depend on any particular religious observance (*mazhab*) since pure spirituality lies far beyond the religious sphere....[4]

The attitude thus described recalls closely the feelings and ideas expressed by the *nirguṇa* Sants since Kabīr and Guru Nānak. And, perhaps not too surprisingly at this stage, it is reported that one of the most frequently recited verses by the Shaikh on such occasions is one attributed to Kabīr:

> *Jāti na pūchai sādhu kī, pūcha lījiye jñāna* /
> *kāma karo talavāra se, parī rahān do miyāna* //
>
> Do not ask about the caste of a sadhu, ask for his knowledge,
> Accomplish your task with the sword, leave the sheath where it is.

All this leads to the assumption that Shāh Faẓl Aḥmad Khān's radical drift away from the *sharī'a* oriented outlay of the discipline, followed by the Naqshbandī Mujaddidī authorities ever since Shaikh Aḥmad Sirhindī, goes far beyond the cautious approach adopted by the Shāh's predecessors. At first sight, one may be tempted to argue that the impact that modern Western ideas left on the mentality of the educated Indian middle class by the end of the nineteenth century could be held responsible for the change in attitude of these authorities. But although the importance of this factor should not be outrightly rejected as altogether insignificant, in view of the particularly Indian circumstances, I was convinced that other reasons too were involved here.

In fact, as I discovered while digging out other documents preserved with the family of Rāmcandra's descendants, both Shāh Faẓl Aḥmad Khān and Rāmcandra Saksenā had for a long time been in the company of a locally revered Hindu saint affiliated to some Dharmdāsī branch of the Kabīr-panth, a certain Svāmī Brahmānanda who lived on the

[4] Ibid., p. 34.

banks of the Ganges at Fatehgarh and whose age, the popular legend goes, was well over a hundred years. Although the texts do not comment about the nature of the relationship that existed between the Kabīr-panthī Svāmī and the Mujaddidī Shaikh, it became clear that the two met regularly during the period from 1867 to 1996, either at the Svāmī's simple shelter on the river or, later on, at the Shaikh's residence at a *madrasa* in nearby Farrukhabad. Shāh Faẓl Aḥmad Khān's frequent use of verses currently attributed to Kabīr is, however, strongly indicative of the influence of the latter. Equally revealing was the discovery that Rāmcandra's family kept alive a long-standing tradition of maintaining intimate ties with authorities of the above-mentioned *panth*, which were outwardly reflected in the pious atmosphere of Rām-bhakti practised in his mother's family. Since his early childhood, Rāmcandra had been entrusted by his father to the tutorship of Svāmī Brahmānanda, who provided the boy with the fundamental notions of the Hindu dharma. When he was almost fourteen, his Svāmī initiated him formally into the Sant *paramparā*. His instructions in the doctrines of the Kabīr-panth were to prove essential for the elaborations made by Rāmcandra in the later stages of his life and were brought to conclusion by the Svāmī's granting him unlimited authority to initiate and instruct new members of the order in the knowledge of the *sampradāya*.

Thus equipped with the authority of both a Hindu and an Islamic esoteric tradition, Rāmcandra, after the death of his two masters in the first decade of the twentieth century, began to act as an independent authority, at first hesitantly and with some reservations, but gradually gaining in confidence and proposing his own synthesized version of the two disciplines.

In the late 1920s, after Rāmcandra's retirement from government employment in the local district tax office, his *satsaṅg* expanded from an initially intimate group into a fairly large audience of followers and devotees eager to listen to the simple speeches delivered by their *guru mahārāj* and to catch his glance, reputedly charged with a powerful current of spiritual energy.

Obviously, this sort of cross-cultural experiment that attracted members of both communities from among the local population, did not escape the attention of the orthodox establishment. The hagiographical accounts abound in stories about how both Rāmcandra and his Muslim *pīr* were publicly harassed by Farrukhabad's enraged mob led by a group of influential local Brahmins and *'ulamā*, some of whom we are told in the typical hagiographical imagery, later repented—a few even decided to join the ranks of Rāmcandra's and the *pīr*'s disciples. It is nevertheless understood that at some stage the situation assumed quite unbearable proportions at least in the case of Shāh Faẓl Aḥmad Khān, since the biographers (Muslim) report that the frequent disturbances by angry traditionalists forced him to return to the more secluded environment of his native village.

In the years prior to his death in 1931, Rāmcandra, anxious to preserve his lifework for posterity, compiled a series of works that condense his thought and his teachings in a unique blend of Sufi and Tantric Kabīr-panthī theories and methods. These form the textual base on which this Sant discipline rests till today and constitute the core around which the *sampradāya* established by him and his master developed among his successors. Hence, they furnish us with the most important source for an analysis of the lines and modalities along which it developed.

The bulk of these texts was originally written in a fluent Urdu style that betrays the early education of this Kāyasth according to the pattern prevalent in the olden days when fluency in both Urdu and Persian were part of the standard requirements for members of this caste that enabled them to exercise their traditional role as clerks and scribes in the Mughal administration. However, most of these works were later rewritten or translated into Hindi, partly by the master himself and partly by his only son, Jag Mohan Nārāyaṇ, to enable a wider circulation among Rāmcandra's mainly Hindu disciples less acquainted with Urdu, especially in the post-Independence period. Interestingly, this process was accompanied by an absorption of the discipline's Islamic component into a Hindu context, since much of the original Sufi vocabulary expressed in Arabic and Persian was now rendered in a Sanskritized version more faithful to the Kabīr-panthī component with its largely Tantric terminology.

One of these works, *Tattva prabodhanī* ('The awakening of the subtle centres'), reveals that Rāmcandra perceived as his main task simplifying the discipline in a natural process to counteract the decreasing spiritual capacities of humanity in the course of history. In his view, this was to be achieved through a cautious but continuous externalization of the ancient esoteric doctrines in order to guarantee their utility for the people of every era while at the same time ensuring their survival for generations to come. A key element in this development consists, in the author's opinion, in a renewed approach towards the 'science of the subtle centres', referred to alternatively as *'ilm-i laṭā'if* or *cakra-vidyā*, a cornerstone of the Tantric tradition and the old Nāth-*sampradāya* as well as that of the *ṭarīqa Mujaddidiyya*. Assuming that this could form a common or at least compatible base, he perceived the possibility that it could therefore ideally act as the vital link between the two traditions. In the introductory chapter of this work which, as the title suggests, deals extensively with this topic, Rāmcandra affirms:

> After careful investigation, the great spiritual authorities of both traditions [Hindu and Muslim] have perpetuated this science over the centuries in order to preserve the treasure of its perfectioning realization; in ancient times this did not require a detailed explanation regarding the colour, name, shape, property and sound vibration of each of these subtle centres; due to the innate virtues of their disciples, they did not feel the need to leave any written testimony or to engage in any further discussion of their knowledge, but transmitted it through direct experience; if ever necessary, they integrated this by the means of subtle hints that are hardly intelligible in our times....[5]

According to the author, this pattern was current in India during the Vedic and post-Vedic period and remained valid long after, and he continues:

> In the Upaniṣad, the entire transmission of knowledge occurred through subtle hints (*ishāra*) expressed in the form of question and answer between disciple and master. The oral teachings of Janāb Kabīr

---

[5] Rāmcandra Saksenā, *Tattva prabodhanī*, Fatehgarh 1971, pp. 23-4 (1st Hindi ed. Fatehgarh 1941).

> Ṣāḥib, Nānak Ṣāḥib, Dādū Ṣāḥib and Tulsī Ṣāḥib Hathrāsī still follow to a large extent this pattern....[6]

This last paragraph hints at an element of continuity which Rāmcandra perceives as connecting the ancient tradition of the Veda preserved by Brahmin orthodoxy with the medieval Sants right down to Tulsī Hathrāsī (1763-1843) who flourished in the region around Agra. But later Rāmcandra discloses some important information regarding the perception of the tradition into which he inserts himself as the last link in a long chain:

> Thereafter, the process of disclosing through explicit descriptions and major details the hitherto hidden secrets [of the doctrine] has been undertaken by the blessed personalities of Janāb Alīmaqām Rāy Ṣāḥib Śāligrām Sant, Janāb Devī Ṣāḥib Sant Murādābādī and Paṇḍit Brahmaśaṅkarjī Ṣāḥib. But the way Mahāriṣi Śivbratlāl—may the *Paramātma* grant him the fruits of his efforts!—has taken up the challenge of unfolding it in an extremely rich and detailed way explaining its sacred and hidden secrets (*muqaddas o poshīda bhed*) without any hindrance in front of the entire world, has so far remained unmatched.[7]

The author's tribute to these nineteenth- and twentieth-century Sants provides evidence for the sources that are likely to have inspired Rāmcandra in the development of his own *satsaṅg*. The evidence indicates that these are oriented along the lines of other, perhaps similar contemporary devotional currents and are helpful in understanding the immediate context that qualifies his role as a modern *sant*. The first name mentioned is that of Rāy Śāligrām alias *Ḥuzūr Mahārāj* (1828-98) who was the successor of Śiv Dayāl Siṅgh (Soāmījī, 1818-78) as the head of the Rādhāsoāmī community at Agra. A Kāyasth by birth like Rāmcandra, he organized the *satsaṅg* founded by his predecessor building up an efficient administration of its affairs, setting up rules and regulations for the devotional practices and editing and publishing the records of the oral

---

[6] Ibid., p. 24.

[7] Ibid., p. 24.

teachings delivered by his *satguru* thus providing a solid doctrinal and institutional framework for the growing number of adherents to the community.

His name goes along with that of Paṇḍit Brahmaśaṅkar Miśra (1861-1907), reverentially called 'Maharāj Ṣāḥib' by his followers, who represents the third link in the Agra line of the Rādhāsoāmīs. A Brahmin from Banaras employed as a high-ranking government official, he joined the *satsaṅg* at Agra in 1885 and was one of its leading figures thirteen years later, following the death of *Ḥuẓūr Mahārāj*. His *samādhi-sthān*, erected in the precincts of his former residence at Banaras near Kabīr-Caurā, became the site of an annual *bhaṇḍārā* for his followers. Mahāriṣi Śivbratlāl (1860-1940), to whom Rāmcandra appears to have been particularly indebted, was a disciple of Rāy Śāligrām, who established his own *satsaṅg* at Gopiganj near Banaras in 1922.[8] A contemporary of Rāmcandra described by Caturvedī as 'a very able and intelligent person', he was the author of a number of Urdu works about different doctrinal aspects and also comprising biographies of numerous earlier Sants besides an extensive commentary on Kabīr's *Bījak*. However, his teachings occasionally disagree with those of the masters of the mainstream Rādhasoāmī *satsaṅg*s at Agra and Beas (Panjab).

Although Rāmcandra's teachings differ from those of all the personalities listed above, both from the point of view of methodology and some important doctrinal points, the former apparently drew inspiration from Śivbratlāl's works in using brief tales to illustrate the teachings of some famous and popular Sants.

Finally, the only name mentioned by Rāmcandra in relation to the last stage of display of the spiritual doctrine which is not directly related to the Rādhasoāmīs is Bābā Devī Ṣāḥib Murādābādī (1841-1919), considered by Caturvedī as the first promulgator of the *santmat-satsaṅg* adaptation of the older Sant tradition.[9] Although his connection with Rāmcandra is not clear, he seems to bear some relation with the earlier mentioned Sant Tulsī Ṣāḥib Hathrāsī, even if the two never met.

[8] See Paraśurām Caturvedī, *Uttar bhārat kī sant paramparā*, Allahabad 1964 (1st ed. VS 2007), p. 801.

[9] Ibid., pp. 811-18.

Curiously, all four Sants listed by Rāmcandra take us back to Sant Tulsī Ṣāḥib. This somewhat enigmatic figure, according to some sources, was the spiritual tutor of the founder of the Rādhasoāmī tradition. He apparently represents the principal link between the medieval Sant tradition and its revival in the eighteenth century, which embraces most of the modern Sants. His main work, the *Ghaṭ Rāmāyan*, intended as a sort of esoteric comment on the eponymous epos, consists largely of instructive dialogues between the author and a certain Phūl Dās, a *panthī* in the Dharmdāsī line going back to Kabīr. According to Mark Juergensmeyer who has studied the Rādhasoāmī tradition, in style and content this composition follows so closely the *Anurāg-sāgar* ('Ocean of Love'), a doctrinal text current with the Dharmadāsīs who attribute its authorship to Kabīr himself, that it can be safely assumed that Tulsī used it as a model for his own composition.

Unfortunately, to date no reliable information regarding possible links or affiliations of this Marathi saint to one of the institutionalized *panth*s is available that could perhaps confirm the continuity in the transmission of this spiritual heritage. Also the connection between the later representatives of the revived Sant tradition, whose teachings evidently bear signs of a previous Sant-matrix, with Tulsī Sant Hathrāsī or any other authority of a regular *paramparā* remains as mysterious as that of their predecessors in the medieval period. In this sense, the limited information I could gather from the sources available to me regarding Rāmcandra's master Svāmī Brahmānand's affiliation to the Kabīr-panth does not represent an exception but puts him in line with the often observed pattern that has these saints appear suddenly on the scene almost out of nowhere and without a traceable genealogy.

But there is a fundamental difference. Unlike most of his Sant predecessors, the *paramparā* initiated by Rāmcandra does have direct affiliation with a Sufi *silsila* that furnished its leaders with the necessary background for the elaboration of a true spiritual synthesis between the subcontinent's most widely diffused sacred traditions. This provides us concrete proof of the often theorized encounter between Islamic and Hindu spirituality within the folds of the Sants' teachings and thereby pleads for further investigations aimed at discovering traces of similar links to other lineages or spiritual communities (e.g. the Rādhasoāmīs).

Rāmcandra continued to teach some of the old Sant themes having adapted them to the time in which he lived (e.g. no caste barriers, in favour of remarriage of widows, against ritualized idol-worship and the priestly monopoly held over it by the Bṛahmins, etc.). And in the process of the activation of the subtle centres he forged the Mujaddidī and the Tantric Kabīr-panthī teachings into a new practically oriented discipline (*abhyā*s) by integrating both. By including the total of ten (5 plus 5) subtle centres (*laṭā'if*, pl. of *laṭīfa*) into the threefold cosmological hierarchy laid out by the Dharmadāsīs, Rāmcandra seems to favour the silent invocation (*zikr-i khafī*) of a chosen formula (these can differ but the equal validity of both Hindu and Islamic formulas or syllables is stressed). This process of invocation follows a progressive pattern of increasing interiorization of the method, the efficacy of which is said to be based on the subtle sound vibration (*surati*) contained in the intimate essence (*zāt*, *bīja*) of the formulas, words, terms or syllables employed during the ritual of their repeated rhythmical recitation (*zikr*, *japa*).

The use of the entire range of invocations comprised by this practical discipline (*abhyāsa*) is supposed to culminate after having gone though a series of contemplations or visualizations (*murāqabāt*, *samādhiyān*) in an unlimited vision of the Supreme Principle (*al-Ḥaqq*, *Zāt-i pāk*, *Paramātma*) in the purely transcendent sphere of the *Satya-loka* or *Maqām-i Ḥaqq*.

Much stress is laid thereby on the responsibility held by the spiritual guide. His effusion of grace (*kṛpā dhārā*, *dayā* or *faiẓ*) lifts the neophyte's inner states (*ḥālāt*) in a sort of sudden attraction (*jazba*, *sahaja ākarṣan śakti*) to the higher spheres of self in the spiritual dominion (*'ālam-i rūḥāniyya*), beyond the boundaries of the ego-tied soul corrupted by all sorts of vices and weaknesses (*fanā-i nafs*). Because of the relative ease which allows the follower of this discipline under the guidance of the perfect master (*pīr-i kāmil*) to experience since the very beginning of his spiritual career such sublime degrees of inner beatitude as are usually reserved for the more advanced stages of the path, this *sampradāya* is called by our Mujaddidī-Kabīr-panthīs either *sahaja-yoga* (the 'natural, spontaneous or easy yoga') or *ānanda-yoga* (the 'yoga of beatitude').

According to Rāmcandra and his successors, their discipline integrates the preliminary level of yoga represented by *haṭha-yoga*, which remains concerned with the reintegration of the inferior, gross elements of the phenomenal world achieved through the unfolding of the subtle centres situated between the bottom of the back and the heart-region, into the more intellectual perspective of *rāja-yoga*, the royal discipline that contemplates the possibilities inshrined in the heart-region *(hṛdaya-cakra, maqām-i dil*). This, according to Rāmcandra, is in consonance with the Mujaddidī wisdom regarding the five subtleties located inside the human breast (*maqām-i sīnā*) which need to be reactivated or awakened through the repeated invocation of the sacred Name (*ism-i ẕāt o muqaddas*), directed gradually on each of these in order to accomplish their reintegration into, or union with, their celestial principles or archetypes associated with the cerebral region in the human skull.

Through this conception based on the science of the subtle centres, the ancient knowledge of India's sages is claimed to have remained accessible and alive well into the twentieth century to the benefit of both religious groups. In this sense, it appears to be no contradiction but rather a confirmation of the Sant line of ideas that parts of it have been preserved and perpetuated for centuries by the country's Muslim elite. Thus, Rāmcandra, the householder yogi from Fatehgarh, constructs a fascinating image of an integral path that is apt to lead those who follow it steadily under the supervision of the spiritual master towards the peaks of esoteric wisdom, weaving into each other the threads offered to him by virtue of his double initiation in imitation of the spirit of his famous fifteenth-century predecessor at Banaras, Kabīr the weaver.

Problems of Authenticity in the Kabīr Texts Transmitted Orally in Rajasthan Today[1]

Bahadur Singh

In 1995 and 1996 I was in Rajasthan recording Mīrā and Kabīr texts as they are recited today during devotional sittings called *satsaṅg*s. While these devotional sittings were indeed held at my request, in every other regard they were entirely normal, with no change whatever in their traditional sequences or procedures. Let me add too that the recordings, three hundred of Kabīr alone, were made in the north, west and south of Rajasthan, in villages and hutments there; unfortunately, I could not cover the east. Of course, even the three hundred I could record are but a small fraction of what is really there in this remarkable oral tradition; remarkable also because almost none of them are to be found in the *Bījak* or the *Granthāvalī*.[2] Again, of the very popular twenty songs of Kabīr in oral tradition recorded by Lorenzen, only two are found in my recordings.[3]

The themes in my recordings are the ones of the printed texts, namely the greatness of the *guru* (*gurumahimā*), the importance of the *haribhajan* or singing in praise of the absolute, the transitory nature of everything in the world, and the *nirgun* categories like the *cakra*s, *ulaṭbāṁsī*s, etc.

As to the formal composition of my recordings, the *helī* is very common, and in these, Kabīr addresses Dharmīdās. What is worth noting is that in the *Bījak* and the *Granthāvalī* there are no *helī*s at all. Again, the *Bījak* and the *Granthāvalī* contain no instances of the *maṅgal*, a composition frequently occurring in my collection, and sung early in the morning to describe the marriage of *surati* and *śabd*. Further, the *sākhī* is a dominant type in the Kabīr published texts, yet only a small number of

---

[1] This paper is based on a project founded by the Deutsche Forschungsgemeinschaft whose support I gratefully acknowledge.

[2] *Kabīr Bījak*, ed. Śukdev Siṃh, Allahabad 1972; *Kabīr-granthāvalī*, ed. Śyāmsundardās, Banaras 1978.

[3] David N. Lorenzen, *Praises to a Formless God*, New York 1996.

these are to be found in the Rajasthani oral transmission, and of them only a few are to be found in the published texts. Let me add one more difference: social protest, generally accepted to be typical of Kabīr, and typical also of the *Bījak*, is found only in a few texts recorded by me, and in these the protest is quite mild.

My purpose in describing, briefly, the variegated distribution of the texts was to give an idea of the situation in Rajasthan, a situation not really known in Kabīr research. But now let me turn to the problem of authenticity and begin with two passages:

...tahāṃ gagana ghāṃma nahīṃ chāṃhīṃ
tahāṃ canda sūra nahīṃ jāī
tahāṃ kāla kāyā nahīṃ bhāī
tahāṃ raiṃṇiṃ divasa nahīṃ chāyā
tahāṁ bāva baraṃṇa nahīṃ māyā
tahāṃ udai asta nahīṃ hoī
tahāṃ marai na jīvai koī
tahāṃ naṃhīṃ pāṭha purāṃṇāṃ
tahāṁ agāṃma nigāṃma nahīṃ jānā...[4]

There is no sky there, nor heat nor shade. No moon, no sun reaches there. O brother, there is no time, no human body (*kāyā*) there. Night and day do not exist there. There is no wind there, no colour, no illusion. There is no rising or setting [of heavenly bodies] there, nobody dies or lives there. There are no exegetical texts there and no Vedas ...

vāṃ nahīṃ dukha sukha saṃc jhuṭha nahīṃ
pāpa punna nahīṃ pasārā
candara sūra devasa nahīṃ rajanī
binā jota ujiārā
gyāna dhyāna japa tapa nahīṃ sādhana
veda kurāna nahīṃ bāṇī
pāṃca tanta guṇa tinūṃ nāhiṃ
surata sabada vāṃ nāhīṃ

[4] Winand M. Callewaert and Bart Op de Beeck (eds.), *Nirguṇ-bhakti-sāgar, Devotional Hindī Literature*, vol. I, New Delhi 1991, p. 230.

> There is no happiness or suffering there, no truth, no lie, no evil, no merit is present there. No moon, no sun, no day, no night, there is light there without a source of light. There is no knowledge, no meditation, no prayer, no austerities are there. The Vedas, the Koran and the word do not exist there. The five *tattva*s, the three *guṇa*s, *surati* and *śabd* are not there.

I have deliberately left out the signature verse, the *mudrikā*, for what I wish to point out is that in this world of non-dualities, of overcoming dualities, the language is inevitably the same and we have no criteria to prove that the first quotation is Dādū's or the second attributed to Kabīr by Sohan Lāl (village Rattāsar, Sūratgaṛh) who sang it for me: it could be the other way round just as well.

Let us take further examples, showing how similar the metaphorical language of Sant poetry is:

> *yahu sansāra saiṃbala ke suka jyūṃ*
> *tā pari tūṃ jini phūlai.*[5]

> This world is like the silk-cotton [flower] to a parrot; don't get inflated with joy over it.

> *yahu saṃsāra dekhi jini bhūlai*
> *sabahīṃ saiṃbali phūl.*[6]

> Gazing at this world, don't get deceived, everything [in it] is but a silk-cotton [flower].

> *ā saṃsāra phūla samala kau, sūo dekha lubhāyo*
> *mārī cāṃca nikala gaī rūī sira dhuni kai pichtāyo.*

> This world is a silk-cotton flower; seeing it the parrot got enticed. It pecked at it, but what came out was cotton, and [the parrot] beat its head in repentance.

---

[5] Ibid., p. 204.

[6] Ibid., p. 218.

My quotations are from Dādū and Kabīr; the last one, ascribed to Kabīr, is again from my recordings. Considering the common metaphor and the substantial uniformity of the language, whether written or oral, would we be able to identify the authors if we did not have the *mudrikā* ? I am afraid we have again no criteria to reach an objective conclusion.

Let me continue with another, even more extreme, example:

prītama jāni lehu mana māhīṃ
apnai sukha kau saba jaga bāṃdhyau, kou kāhū kau nāhīṃ
sukh maiṃ āī sabai mili baiṭhata, rahata cahūṃ disi ghere
vipati parī tab saba saṅga chāṃṛe, kou na āvai nere
ghara kī nāri bahuta hita jāsauṃ, rahati sadā saṅga lāgī
jā chana hansa tajī yaha kāyā, preta preta kahi bhāgī
yā bidhi kau byaupāra banyau jaga, tāsauṃ neha lagāyau
sūrdāsa bhagvanta-bhajana binu nāhaka janama gaṃvāyau.[7]

prītama jāni lehu mana māhī
apne sukha siu hī jagu phāṃdhio ko kāhū ko nāhī
sukha mai āni bahutu mili baiṭhata rahata cahūṃ disi gherai
bipati pari sabha hī saṅgu chādita kou na āvata nerai
ghara kī nārī bahutu hitu jā siu sadā rāhata saṅga lāgī
jaba hī hansa tajī iha kāia preta preta kari bhāgī
ih bidhi ko biuhāru banio hai jā siu nehu lagāio
anta bāra nānaka binu hari jī kou kāmi na āio.[8]

O loved one, keep [this] in mind: the whole world is tied up in pursuit of happiness, nobody is your's [your true friend]. In prosperity, all come to you, sit in your company, surrounding you in all four directions. In adversity, all abandon you, nobody comes near you. Your wife, whom you love so much, continues to remain at your side. [Yet] the moment [your] life-breath leaves this [your] body, she runs away, crying out: "A ghost! A ghost!". This is the customary behaviour of the world, and you have gone and fallen for it. Sūrdās

[7] *Sūrsāgar*, ed. by N.D.Vājpeyī, Kāśī Nāgarī Pracāriṇī Sabhā edition, 2 vols. Varanasi 1958, vol. I, p. 26.

[8] *Sri Guru Granth Sahib*, part I, ed. by Winand M. Callewaert, Delhi 1996, p. 634.

> says: You have wasted your life, for you have not sung in praise of *bhagvant*.

The first passage is taken from the *Sūrsāgar*, the second from the *Gurū Granth*. Of the *Gurū Granth* version let me translate only the *mudrikā*:

> Nānak says, at the last moment of your life, nobody but Harī will come to your help.

Certainly, tradition says that the passage with Nānak's *mudrikā* is a composition of Tegh Bahādur's, for it forms part of *mahalā*. Tegh Bahādur lived 125 years after Sūrdās; but in spite of that, we cannot say with certainty that it was not Tegh Bahādur or a devotee of his who simply took over a Sūrdās *pad* that he found exceptional, or a devotee of Sūrdās took it from Tegh Bahādur and substituted the *mudrikā* of Sūrdās. I could continue with a series of further examples revealing the basic problem we have: the language and the ideas of our texts are so similar that we just cannot talk of authentic Kabīr texts, in the case of oral transmission at least.

We do have, of course, a few cases where there can be no doubt as to authenticity. Let me give three examples.

> *tan kā aṇjan samjhau bhāī...*
> *jīv musāfir jiske māṃhīṃ letā vāsā hai*
> ....
> *apnī ṭikaṭ ko mat nā khoie, ṭem jarāsā hai*
> ....
> *ek laiṇ amarāpurī jāvai, dūjī laiṇ maiṃ jampurī āvai*
> *dās kabīr ye jugat saiṃ batāvai...* (1)

> Look upon the body as an engine... in which the soul is a passenger..., don't lose your ticket, the time [you have] is very short... One track leads to Amarāpurī, the city of the Immortal, the other track leads to Jampurī, the city of the god of death. Humble Kabīr explains this with skilful words....

To the devout, this too is a genuine text of Kabīr's, who was able to foresee things to come, as Bhikharamji Sharma told me, most hurt because I dared to doubt that these could be Kabīr's own words.

guru rāmānanda dīnī mhānai amara jaṛī...
aṇi jaṛī tau mīrābāī tariyā... (2)

Guru Rāmānand gave me the herb of immortality...
and by this very herb Mīrābāī crossed [the ocean of life].

kahai kabīro kai suṇa jatī gorakha
katarā parusa nai katarī nārī...
....
kahai gorakha kai suna re kabīrā
ek purusa bījī sab nārī... (3)

Kabīr says, 'Listen, Gorakh, you who are an ascetic: How many *puruṣ*s are there, how many *nārī*s are there...?'... Gorakh says: 'Listen Kabīr : there is only one *puruṣ* and all others are *nārī*s...'

It seems rather strange that Kabīr is the one asking questions; but since the text is said to be Kabīr's, we have to assume that Kabīr is putting Gorakhnāth to the test. Or is it in reality a text of the Gorakhnāth community? In historical terms, the Gorakh-Kabīr debate is only a legend. Kabīr could not have known Mīrā, nor was he a contemporary of Gorakhnāth. But all this is again a rare bit of historical comfort. In the huge majority of texts, at any rate those orally transmitted, there can be no proof of authenticity or inauthenticity.

Let me now look at the question of authenticity from an entirely different point of view. The historical point of view I just mentioned has no meaning for the Kabīr devotees; to them Kabīr was a seer and therefore he could foresee things, he could, quite naturally, have spoken with Mīrā or with Gorakhnāth. The main criteria of authenticity for the Kabīr devotees is that the message is profound. In this regard, let me quote Winand Callewaert's view, which I very much share:

> There are two ways to approach the songs of medieval saints. One is to merely derive devotion from reading or singing these songs, and then it does not matter whether the songs are really of the particular saint or whether they were created in the tradition.[9]

It seems to me that this aspect of cultural anthropology is of great value and deserves the attention it has not yet received. What is important is also this: the singers mostly belong to the so-called low castes, but are held in high esteem precisely because they sing Kabīr and other Sant poets. It is also a most moving experience to see the joy and spiritual contentment of the singers and the audience.

Let me conclude with a *vāṇī* sung by Śri Birjāpurī Mahāraj, a blind *sādhu* of Shivdānpurā of Hanumāngaṛh District; I have recorded a few songs recited by him. When I asked him how he knew that a vā*nī* was really Kabīr's own, he said: '*Je vāṇī rau arth gūṛh hwai jaṇā to vā Kabīrsā rī nitar vāṃrī nakal*'—'If a *vāṇī* has a deep meaning, then of course it is Kabīr's; if not it is only an imitation.' Here is his song:

āpa hī dāraṃdāra gurujī āpa ḥī sabada khilāṛī O
gigana maṇḍala maiṃ tambū tāṇyā dharaṇa galicā ḍārī O
gigana maṇḍala gā tambū baṇāyā
cāṃda suraja to musāla baṇāī, tārāṃ gī phulvāṛī O
duniyā thārī hai phulvāṛī, the bāṛī gā māḷī O
peda peda nai pāṇī the siṃcau, āpa karo rakhvāḷī O
cit-caupara gā khela maṇdyā hai, do pāsā jaga sārī O
jingā jīva jīta ghara āvai, vo nara sabada khilāṛī O
sata gā cīra vikhama gī jholī, jina gī to surata aṭārī O
jina para satguru rājī hovai, ungā mulaka bhikhārī O
amara desa nai kiyā piyaṇā, gyāna ghoṛai asvārī O
kahai kabīra suṇau bhāī sādho, abkāḷai jīta hamārī O
āpa hī dāramdāra gurujī āpa hī sabada khilāṛī O

The gist of the *vāṇī* is this, and its meaning is really deep (*gūṛh*), for not everything is clear:

---

[9] Callewaert and Op de Beeck (eds.), *Nirguṇ-bhakti-sāgar*, vol. I, p. 10.

> O revered *guru*, you alone are [our] refuge, you alone have mastery over words. The sky is [your] tent, the earth is [your] carpet, sun and moon are [the tent's] torches, the stars are a flower garden. The world is your flower garden, and you are the gardener. You water every single tree and protect it.
> The whole world is playing the game of dice of the *citta* (*citta-caupaṛ*), and he who returns home victorious has mastery over words. Truth is his ascetic cloak, hardships are his bag, his abode is *surati*. To him, whom the *satguru* regards with favour, the world is a beggar. Now I begin the march to the country of immortality, my steed is knowledge. Kabīr says... this time (sc. otherwise than till now) victory will be mine.

Homespun Threads of Dignity and Protest: Songs of Kabīr in Rural Rajasthan

Nancy M. Martin

Woven into the fabric of the devotional traditions in India is a critique of social hierarchies, inseparable from their fundamental affirmation of religious experience as the sole criteria for spiritual authority. Many of the leading figures in these movements are themselves members of very low castes and/or women, and whether low or high in the ranks of caste and gender, many speak out against social distinctions—God sees no difference between Brāhmaṇ and Śūdra, man or woman; indeed, the lowest may be highest.[1]

The challenges of these movements to the existing social and religious structures have been radical, with the Vīraśaivas in the south under the leadership of Basavaṇṇa and Allama Prabhu, even going so far as to set up an alternative egalitarian community (although the wider society did not tolerate it for long).[2] Yet this latter example is the exception rather than the rule, and many movements restricted equality to the religious realm as they became institutionalized (sliding into an implicit support of social hierarchy once again) or reproduced that

---

[1] In the words of Nammāḷvār (translated by A.K. Ramanujan and resonating with the Christian 'Sermon on the Mount'), we must:

> ... go down, far down
> to the lowliest outcastes
> of outcastes
> if they are the intimate henchmen
> of our lord
> ... then even the slaves of their slaves
> are our masters.

A. K. Ramanujan, trans., *Hymns for the Drowning: Poems for Viṣṇu by Nammāḷvār*, New Delhi, London, New York 1993 (1981), p. 60.

[2] A. K. Ramanujan, trans. and introduction, *Speaking of Śiva*, New Delhi, London, New York 1973.

hierarchy in understandings of human-divine relations. Some leaders of tribal and Dalit liberation struggles have claimed inspiration from the stories of the saints' lives and the biting critiques of their devotional songs, and *panth*s have formed around some, such as Kabīr and Raidās (as David Lorenzen and Joseph Schaller have detailed).[3] Yet a wider revolutionary impulse seems lacking. This absence has generated considerable scholarly debate, with some scholars like Ranajit Guha asserting that bhakti functions in precisely the opposite way as 'an ideology of subordination *par excellence*'.[4]

Theologically, however, the songs and stories of these saints may be playing a quite different role *within* low-caste communities *outside* the institutional structures of *panth*s and *sampradāya*s. The theology we find articulated in narrative and song by Meghvāl performers in rural western Rajasthan, for example, is not revolutionary, but rather speaks of loving God in the midst of struggle and pain. It is a theology of survival, of dignity and self-respect, which privileges the wisdom and religious authority that are particularly the province of the poor and disenfranchised. I would argue that this constitutes a kind of Hindu liberation spirituality, paralleling in many ways the theological reflections of poor or oppressed communities in other regions and religions, particularly within Christianity.

This liberation spirituality is a type of theological reflection engaged in both by and for the 'poor' broadly defined, reflecting their understanding of the nature of God and of the religious life. Herein we find a critique of social and religious hierarchies, but also an affirmation of true religious authority as derived from lived experience and an assertion that knowing and loving God grows within the radical living practice of religion. Moreover, reflection focuses primarily on the struggle to affirm dignity and (re-)claim one's true identity as beloved of God and

---

[3] David Lorenzen, 'The Kabīr Panth and Social Protest', in: Karine Schomer and W. H. McLeod (eds.), *The Sants: Studies in a Devotional Tradition of India*, Delhi 1987; Joseph Schaller, 'Sanskritization, Caste Uplift, and Social Dissidence in the Sant Ravidas Panth', in: David Lorenzen (ed.), *Bhakti Religion in North India: Community Identity and Political Action*, Albany, NY 1995.

[4] Ranajit Guha, 'Dominance without Hegemony and its Historiography', in: Ranajit Guha (ed.) *Subaltern Studies V*, Delhi 1992, p. 259.

to know a loving God while living under inhuman conditions. Indeed, these reflections are marked by a deep and nuanced sense of joy, hope, and faith, tested and tempered in the fire of suffering.[5]

Within this type of theological reflection, we also find the poor and disenfranchised laying claim to religious practices and narratives as their own, interpreting their relevance for their own lives, and retelling the stories in the idioms of their own experience. An example from the Hindu context would be the Meghvāl epic song recounting Mīrābāī's life '*Mīrā janma patrī*' in which this spirited saintly queen beats her servants (as a woman of her social status might) when they try to persuade her to put on wedding finery, but she also asks to be allowed to live in a hut and continue to weave her royal husband's clothes when he rejects her, as if she, too, were a weaver woman. Such a telling stands in stark contrast to the story of Mīrā told in the *Amar Citra Kathā* comicbook series—an upper-caste appropriation of her story that leaves Mira as a swooning devotee who never acts except under the express direction of a male, whether human or divine.[6]

---

[5] In the Christian context, such reflections are also marked by a call for justice encompassed within the wider horizon of God's completely unconditional and abundant love. Gustavo Gutiérrez's *Theology of Liberation* (Maryknoll, NY 1973) is a foundational work and his later book *We Drink from Our Own Wells: The Spiritual Journey of a People* (Maryknoll, NY 1984) explores more deeply the spirituality of the poor, as does *On Job: God-talk and the Suffering of the Innocent* (Maryknoll, NY 1987), the latter through a very different reading of this biblical story. For a survey of women's liberation theologies (including White Feminist, Womanist, and Mujerista perspectives), see Linda Moody's *Women Encounter God*, Maryknoll, NY 1996.

[6] See my '*Mīrā Janma Patrī*: A Tale of Resistance and Appropriation', in: N.K. Singhi and Rajendra Joshi (eds.), *Religion, Ritual and Royalty*, Jaipur 1999, and John Stratton Hawley, 'The Saints Subdued: Domestic Virtue and National Integration in *Amar Chitra Katha*', in: Lawrence A. Babb and Susan S. Wadley (eds.), *Media and the Transformation of Religion in South Asia*, Philadelphia 1995. A parallel to this type of appropriation by the poor from the Christian context may be found in the Solentiname paintings depicting Jesus's arrest and death as a Nicaraguan peasant at the hands of Somoza's soldiers. See Ernesto Cardenal, *The Gospel of Solentiname*, Maryknoll, NY 1979.

A primary site where this type of Hindu liberation spirituality is articulated is in the songs of the saints of devotional Hinduism and the stories told about them among low-caste people. There are many songs attributed to each saint and extensive narrative traditions. These different songs and stories potentially offer support for a wide array of theological and social positions. Which songs people choose to sing and which stories they tell in the names of the saints is the key. To begin to explore low-caste religious perspectives, scholars have analysed textual material attributed to saints who are themselves low-caste, such as Kabīr, using sometimes unstated criteria for selecting the particular songs analysed from the wider corpus. Because in most cases we do not know which songs were actually composed by the individual saint in question, however, it is essential that we also examine what actual low-caste people in India today are singing for themselves in the name of the saints. In doing so, we can hear the voices of the poor themselves and begin to elucidate the role the poet-saints play in low-caste people's articulation of their experience of God and the bhakti path.

With respect to Kabīr, David Lorenzen and Edward O. Henry have already begun this work.[7] The '*nirguṇ bhajans*' of Kabīr translated and analysed by Henry were sung by mendicant Jogīs in the Bhojpuri-speaking region of eastern Uttar Pradesh and western Bihar, and Lorenzen identified and analysed Kabīr's most popular *bhajan*s as sung among Kabīr-panthī *sādhu*s and *bhagat*s in the Banaras region. Both scholars noted a consistency of themes between the textual traditions and the oral material they examined but also a softening of the social and religious critique in comparison to the *Bījak*. Recurrent themes within the songs collected by both included the impermanence of the things of this life, the immanent approach of death, and the importance of inner religiosity rather than external forms of religious practice.[8] Henry further identifies a noticeable lack of specificity regarding the nature of God and little development of concepts like *karma* or *mokṣa* (although several of the

[7] David Lorenzen, *Praises to a Formless God*, Albany 1996, pp. 205-23; Edward O. Henry, *Chant the Names of God*, San Diego 1988, pp. 160-89.

[8] Lorenzen, *Praises to a Formless God*, p. 207; Henry, *Chant the Names of God*, pp. 183-5.

songs reported by Lorenzen do contain references to *karma*). In addition Henry notes an emphasis on detachment, coupled with the affirmation of *bhajan* singing as a form of liberative religious practice.

What are we to make of this softening of social and religious criticism and increased emphasis on the transitoriness of life and the need for detachment? Is it merely the watering down of Kabīr so that challenge becomes part comfort and part complicity with an oppressive social and religious world? Or is it something more—a theology of empowerment by and for the 'poor' broadly defined, reflecting their life experiences and perspectives, and articulating their suffering, resistance, dignity and wisdom?

To explore this latter possibility further, considerably more study of the Kabir of oral traditions, particularly among low-caste groups outside the formal structures of the Kabīr-panth, is needed. I have begun such a study among selected Meghvāl singers in western Rajasthan where Kabir is extremely popular. The Meghvāls are a very low Hindu caste traditionally associated with leather working and weaving, who have a long history of severe caste oppression. The singers among them perform primarily at *jāgaraṇ*s or all-night devotional singing sessions—the principle form of regular religious gathering at the village level—during which they sing the songs of a great variety of Hindu (and also Muslim) saints.[9]

The religious world in which the Meghvāls live is marked by abundance and overlapping and fluid boundaries. None of the singers with whom I worked had any formal affiliation with any of the more organised Vaiṣṇava, Śaiva, or *nirguṇ panth*s and *sampradāya*s that form a part of this religious milieu, but their fellow caste members were affiliated with the Kabīr-panth, Dādū-panth, Rāmānandīs and related Vaiṣṇava sects, Nāths, or Dasnāmīs. Tantric practices also enter into the religious mix as does devotion to deified heroic figures like Rāmdev (a very popular

[9] For a more detailed discussion of the musical performance traditions of these Meghvāl singers, see my 'Kabīr and Mīrābāī in Folk Traditions of Western Rajasthan: Meghwāl and Mānganiyār Repertoires', in: Mariola Offredi (ed.), *The Banyan Tree: Essays on Early Literature in New Indo-Aryan Languages*, Delhi 2000, where I first presented their Kabīr (and Mīrā) repertoires.

regional folk deity with both Hindu and Muslim followers to whom the Meghvāls, including the singers, are particularly devoted). Forms of Sunni, Sufi, Twelver Shia, and Ismā'īlī traditions of Islam are also woven into the religious fabric of village Rajasthan, and Hindu saints and Muslim *pīr*s are revered by Hindus and Muslims alike (although there *are* trends toward oppositional definitions of Hindu and Muslim identity in the current political climate). The singers move easily through this world of religious multiplicity, and their audiences often include people with very different religious leanings.

These Meghvāl singers in western Rajasthan sing songs of Kabīr. But which Kabīr is he, and what theological insights and religious guidance might be found in his songs, interwoven with resistance and social critique?[10] The voice we hear is radically different in tone from that found in the Kabīr-panthī *Bījak*, paralleling the observations of Henry and Lorenzen. The sharp critiques aimed at Hindu and Muslim religious leaders and high caste Brāhmaṇs with their false sense of purity and pride are absent, as is the harsh and berating language of challenge designed to jar the listener out of his or her complacency or delusion. Yet we also do not find the Vaiṣṇava tendencies identified by Linda Hess in the 'western' traditions of the Sikh *Ādi Granth* and Rajasthani manuscript traditions of the Dādū-panth—i.e., Vaiṣṇava terms in reference to God tied to personal devotion expressed in the vocabulary of love with devotee as parent, child, servant, or lover of God.[11]

The Kabīr of the Meghvāl oral traditions of western Rajasthan appears not so much as a fiery preacher full of condemnation or as a tormented lover in a stormy relationship, but instead, as a weaver of dignity and protest. Rather than being direct, his social and religious critique is embedded in what is praised and what devalued. He is still addressing others (a fundamental characteristic of Kabīr), but his words are directed to ordinary people and *sādhus*, both encouraging and

[10] For purposes of our discussion here, although I will use material from the repertoires of other Meghvāl singers as well, I will draw heavily on songs sung by an unusually gifted Meghvāl singer Padmaram whose repertoire includes thirty songs attributed to Kabīr.

[11] Linda Hess, 'The Three Kabīr Collections: A Comparative Study', in: Schomer and McLeod (eds.), *The Sants*, pp. 111-42.

challenging them. He cajoles and goads people into acting responsibly and respectfully toward self and others, and into claiming their own dignity and place as full human beings in the world. The images used are quintessential Kabīr—the bullock tied to the oil press, the thirsty fish, death's imminent approach, etc.—but it is the choice of particular images and the way they are used that defines the character of this particular 'Kabīr' and the theology embedded within the songs attributed to him here.

As we examine the words of the songs performed, we find this Meghvāl Kabīr heralding Death's approach, even as Kabīr does elsewhere. The human birth each listener has been given is precious, containing the seed for liberation, and Kabīr calls each person to take control of and responsibility for this life. The potential for liberation is a mark of basic humanity and a ground for self-respect and dignity, and this theme is strong among the Kabīr songs sung by the Meghvāls. The things so often valued in this world—youth, wealth, the love of family, lovers, friends—are all passing, and we ultimately have no control over them. It does not matter whether we are powerful and wealthy or poor and powerless. Not even the love of family and friends can provide us with an ultimate sense of meaning or source of security. The only truly meaningful pursuit in life and source of liberation from endless meaningless rebirth is the search for and remembrance of God. And the only truly important and absolutely necessary human relationship is that between disciple and guru (with the caveat that God may take even this role).

Yet embodiment is affirmed by the Kabīr of the Meghvāl singers. We all have bodies by virtue of birth. They have been crafted over time by a master artisan and thus provide a ground for self-respect, though not for pride. Body and soul together form the ladder to heaven, to relationship with God. Senseless pursuits can weaken them or shameful actions sully them, so we must take care to keep them clean. When necessary, they must be washed by God, the *satguru* Dhobī. In successive songs God is described as a washerman, weaver, potter, and spinning woman. Humans and God are both seen to mirror each other—in their embodiment (both male and female), in their fundamental involvement with the embodied world, and in their creative and maintaining activity. Such imagery is marked by parity rather than hierarchy.

The intimate connection between body and soul and also between individual and community is articulated in another song which speaks of a *haṃs* who does not try to escape the forest's burning. Highly flammable bamboo had taken root among the trees and ignited the fragrant sandalwood and other trees. The *haṃs* could fly away as all the other birds do, but it remains—true to the tree in whose branches it had played and on whose fruit it had feasted. Undaunted by the fires of suffering, it acts with integrity and commitment, and suddenly milk rains down from the sky to extinguish the flames. Soul and body move through this world as one, and there is no true life for the individual apart from the body or apart from relationships, both with fellow humans and with God.

Listening carefully to these Meghvāl Kabīr songs, we also hear a veiled but definite critique in repeated assertions that the only real possession is knowledge, and those who think they know are not the ones who possess it. This is not the directly confrontational 'rough rhetoric' of the *Bījak,* but the carefully crafted language of resistance of the powerless. True knowledge can only be understood by those who speak the same 'language', who know the unspeakable experience. Its meaning is hidden from those from 'another country' in the east who do not share this language.[12] Understanding belongs only to Kabīr, the guru, and by implication those who sing Kabīr's songs—those whose inner knowledge

[12] Elsewhere, the east is the land from which Kabīr and his difficult language come. Is it possible that this counter-claim may be made against other 'Kabīrs'? Some of the songs also reflect Kabīr-panthī influence. One song suggests (as Kabīr-panthīs affirm) that Kabīr is an incarnation of the divine (and perhaps more broadly that this distinction between human and divine may ultimately be transcended by any human). In another song Kabīr speaks of a *sādhu* who meditates in the sky and in a third of a mysterious cosmic man (Alakh Puruṣ) who lies sleeping in space. Kabīr cries, 'Tell me the hidden meaning!'—Brahmā, Viṣṇu, and Śiva serve him, Alakh offers *āratī* while Nirañjan fans him, and Kabīr says to concentrate only on this man (not, by implication, on his attendants). Lorenzen explains that Nirañjan often refers to a lessor creator God in Kabīr-panthī literature rather than the Formless Absolute (Lorenzen, *Praises to a Formless God*, p. 217.)

yields true power over life and death, and the coming and going of *saṃsāric* existence. The others, Kabīr suggests, are in the dark, and the blind cannot give directions to the blind.

Further, what we need in this life we already possess within, and shall not find outside. The treasure lies tied up in our own garments, yet we are always looking elsewhere rather than untying the knot and examining its contents. We walk carelessly over diamonds, even as we search for illusive rubies. Having acquired the bad habit of always wanting more, we become mired in the sticky sweetness of our excesses, as a fly does in honey. We search in the wrong places for appropriate things—like fish completely surrounded by water but dying of thirst, or the musk deer searching among the grasses for the scent whose source lies in his own navel. If this is so, then all already possess the greatest treasure within, and there is no hierarchy of privilege in an ultimate sense, only a shared delusion or realization.

Yet this inner reality is also expansive and transcends time and space. The Meghvāl Kabīr asks us to ponder who we were in the time before all that is, and he speaks of a place in the vault of the sky beyond or before distinction—where no mountains exist, no winds blow, no rivers flow; where there is no hunger or thirst; where no gods or goddesses reside; and where no religious rituals take place and no meditation is done. Such songs speak also of abundance—a paradise where there are no unmet needs or requirements. In so doing, Kabīr voices a rejection of the existing order and invokes a world where the rules and hierarchies of this *saṃsāric* realm do not hold. This 'country', this alternate reality, is claimed by the singers and their audience as their own.

Kabīr invites the hearers to draw water from the upside down well in the sky without a pot and without a rope, if only they know how, and all are welcomed to join in this surprising or strange game of reversals. The upside down language of *ulaṭbāṁsī* is designed to subvert our normal ways of thinking by inverting all types of relationships.[13] James Scott discusses examples of similar 'world-upside-down' phenomena in other times and places in detail, suggesting that while they may provide an imaginative safety valve for social frustrations, they also clearly challenge

[13] Linda Hess, *The Bījak of Kabīr*, San Francisco 1983, pp. 135-61.

and threaten the existing norms.[14] Kabīr's upside down language is not *merely* social critique—it has clear religious import with respect to our habitual ways of thinking and acting—but it does provide for the articulation of veiled resistance and protest.

The religious path advocated here by Kabīr is definitely not one of consolation for those who must suffer in this world. There is no mention of enduring to be reborn to a better life or any indication that the oppressors will get what they deserve next time around. The concept of *karma* is invoked within the songs, described as a gourd that the thief cannot force into hiding beneath the water's surface, but past *karma* is not offered as a justification for suffering or low birth. Rather, concern is focused on one's present actions and their cost with respect to one's realization and experience of God in *this* life.[15] Individual responsibility is the key in this regard. Rather than talking of *karma* in relation to life's difficulties, the songs more often speak of a problematic fate seemingly guiding this life and of the freely bestowed blessings of God. When fate or fortune is tied to previous lives, it is given as the reason for having received the boon of a human birth and thus the possibility of liberation. This is a hope-filled view of this life—one informed by knowledge of God's care for human beings—out of the midst of suffering.

The greatest danger, Kabīr says, is that we will fritter away our lives in an endless treadmill of work or blind searching—wandering directionless like an ox, neither looking within nor remembering and singing the praises of God. The path is narrow and hard, and so many fail to see it. Nor can it be followed with anything less than complete commitment—partially crushed sesame seeds are useless, though either whole or pressed to oil they have great value. Those who choose it must be like the heroic warrior who holds his ground even though his body may be hacked to pieces and the woman who faces death fearlessly on her husband's funeral pyre as a *satī*. Such is the courage that is required and perhaps also the suffering that must be endured on this path. As a barren

---

[14] James C. Scott, *Domination and the Arts of Resistance*, New Haven 1990, pp. 166-72.

[15] This is also true of the reference to *karma* in the song reported by Lorenzen, *Praises to a Formless God*, p. 212.

woman desires a child, so must we desire God. Our concentration must be as single-minded as that of a parrot devouring sweet fruit, and we must learn to recognise and leave behind bitter fruit, keeping ourselves apart. Should we fail in our discernment, we will burn even as the bitter vine does when the heat comes, and Māyā will deceive us even as she has the *ṛṣi*s and gods.

Kabīr urges us forward to victory like the drummer on the battlefield. His are words of encouragement, calling those who sing and listen to commitment, courage, and discipline—riches of the heart which have nothing to do with external possessions or inherited position and inner qualities over which one may have control even if one cannot control outward aspects of one's existence.

Many other images from the everyday life of the singers are woven through these songs. Death's approach is revealed in the empty stalls of the market place, an abandoned game of *caupaṛ*, the bellows and anvil of the ironsmith lying unused as the embers cool. In another context, while we live, this world is a marketplace where the wise make a fourfold profit and the fools lose what they have, or a garden that attracts parrots only to disappoint them with the inedible fruit of its silk-cotton trees. The *man* (heart-mind) is a clay pot, the body the butter churn—from the churning of concentration one may get rich ghee or watery buttermilk, though the whole world feeds the cow with the grass of love and keeps on drawing milk. Yogic meditation is described in terms of the purifying and transformative fire of the kiln. A nomad's 'matchbox' of stone and iron become a metaphor for how to meet God who dwells in the body like fire in the stone—we must become like the iron striker to kindle the relationship with this indwelling God, acting with concentration, discipline, and desire.

Images associated with marriage and the bride leaving home also enter the songs. Once the elaborate marriage rituals have begun, there is no turning back, even as the movement toward union with God must be single-mindedly pursued and cannot be reversed once truly initiated. When the ceremony is over, the groom comes to fetch the bride to take her to his home in a ceremony called the *gaunā*. This ritual of heart-wrenching separation becomes a language to speak alternately of death and the renunciation necessary for union with God.[16] None are spared this leave-taking, no matter how young and innocent, though the entreaties of the young bride's mother to the approaching stranger who will take her away are echoed in many hearts. Rām's orders are clear. Ultimately, Kabīr says, we must all go to this *sasurāl* (to these 'in-laws'), and each must go alone, whether it be to God or to death.

These latter images come from traditions of women's songs and explore the experiences and relationships of women. The impending separation is between daughter and her family and friends rather than between lovers. These are not images of women who are 'ill' for love in their longing but rather of heroic and utterly single-minded women, bound to the familiar yet stepping out into the unknown, or of innocents coming of age.[17] Nowhere in these Meghvāl repertoires of Kabīr are women portrayed as temptresses or dangers to religious pursuit (though other 'Kabīrs' speak in this way), but rather they are courageous models of the religious life. The image of the virtuous wife fearlessly ascending her husband's funeral pyre is invoked in this way. While there is no critique of gender hierarchies, the institution of marriage, or the ideal of *satī* here, there is an assertion of a kind of equality between the sexes, with both female and male images for God and for the heroic devotee.

Moreover, the bond of human and divine is no sentimental love, and the language of love that marks much devotional literature—and some songs attributed to Kabīr found elsewhere—is largely absent from these songs (though very much a part of the Mīrā songs performed by the same singers). Here, the images of everyday life and of folk song traditions are transformed into a language for articulating devotion even as the tropes of classical and folk love songs have been in other times and places.[18] This

---

[16] Henry has also noted the use of the *gaunā* in this latter sense in the Jogī songs he recorded, though not in the former. Henry, *Chant the Names of God*, pp. 174-5.

[17] See John Stratton Hawley, 'Krishna and the Gender of Longing', in: Joseph Runzo and Nancy M. Martin (eds.), *Love, Sex and Gender in the World Religions*, Oxford 2000.

[18] A.K. Ramanujan, *Hymns for the Drowning*. In his afterword Ramanujan discusses in detail the transformation of classical love imagery into the language of devotion.

Kabīr speaks of true love as marked by the utter concentration and trust of the acrobat and the unshakable conviction (rather than longing) of the particular bird that drinks only the first drops of rain, refusing any substitute, or embodied by the moth that is irresistibly drawn to the flame. Love's union is such a fiery merging, not a sentimental emotional encounter.

This is also not a world where Hindu and Muslim are adversaries, as they are in many verses of the *Bījak*. The emphasis in the songs is not on outward forms of religious practice, even to negate them, and there are very few specific references to Hindu and Muslim beliefs and practices. Instead this Kabīr advocates singing the praises of God and remembering the name of Rām, and stresses the inner religious life. One song does invoke specifically Muslim imagery to speak of this interior life: there is a Maulvī within the heart-mind (*man*), Kabīr says, and a mosque which lies in the mouth, where 'Adam' is saying *namāz*. He counsels us to listen to this inner Maulvī—an implicit critique of an outer Maulvī perhaps, but also an internalization and thus affirmation of these Muslim images.[19] This particular song also speaks out against the value of the Vedas, Śāstras, Gītā, and other holy books, but the contrast is not with Islam but between book learning and inner realization, with the latter being affirmed. The knowledge of such sacred texts was traditionally forbidden and inaccessible to people of the lowest castes, and it is this knowledge that is being soundly rejected. Other Hindu practices are questioned in other songs in ways reminiscent of other 'Kabīrs'—bathing in Kāśi or Mathurā and meditation, for example—but the emphasis is on the unnecessariness of such outward actions and on a state that is in some sense beyond such actions and distinctions.

Clearly God is God to this Kabīr and for these people, and both Hindus and Muslims have recognised this in rural western Rajasthan and articulate its truth not through critique but through affirmation and overlapping imagery. In one song Rām is praised equally as God of all the gods and Pīr of all the *pīr*s. Kabīr himself does appear to be thoroughly

[19] Similar verses can be found attributed to Pīr Shams and Guru Nānak, as Dominique Sila Khan has noted in *Conversions and Shifting Identities*, Delhi 1997, pp. 236-7.

identified as a Hindu, with several songs mentioning his encounter with Rāmānand and the final signature lines of the songs generally address 'brother *sādhus*' or Kabīr's disciple Dharmdās. This is a wide Hindu fold, however, one in which God is addressed as Rām but also by the *nirguṇ* appellations, Alakh and Nirañjan, and the names of Kṛṣṇa, Śyām and Govind. This religious 'country' of Kabīr and the singers reflects abundance rather than the either/or of competition, and distinctions fade away in the reality of a oneness that precedes all.

Although our sample of Meghvāl performance repertoires is limited, clear theological insights emerge here in the songs of Kabīr. To complete our understanding of Kabīr's role in the articulation of low-caste understandings of the nature of God and the devotional path, however, we also need to explore any narrative traditions *about* Kabīr that might be performed in this low-caste world. A number of such extended songs exist about Mīrābāī, but I know of only one in western Rajasthan connected to Kabīr.[20] Although at this time I do not know its caste origins or who the primary carriers of this tradition are, the song recounts the incident in which Kabīr's wife Loi agrees to prostitute herself to a local merchant who has been eyeing her, in order to get provisions for Kabīr to offer hospitality to visiting holy men.[21] When Kabīr insists that she tell him how she managed to obtain what was needed, she reveals her bargain, and he offers to carry her to the merchant himself so that her feet will not get

---

[20] There are a number of such traditions about Mīrābāī, with *Mīrā janma patrī* being sung primarily among Meghvāls, and *Kumbhā Rāṇā rī bāt* being sung for them by Turi Bhāts in the Sirohi region.

[21] Reported to me by Manohar Lalas and Komal Kothari from their field experience. I have recorded a portion of the song sung by a Mānganiyār singer who performs for Viṣṇoī patrons, but he did not know the complete text. Although I know of no other full songs about Kabīr's life, the *dohās* sung by the Mānganiyārs and sometimes also by Meghvāl singers before the performance of the songs of Kabīr and other saints also contain a wealth of material about Kabīr and invite more detailed study of this additional well of oral tradition about this saint. I have also heard the words of Kabīr's songs threaded together with legendary material about him in the spoken teaching of a Kālbeliyā Jogī guru. For further details, see 'Kabīr and Mīrābāī in Folk Traditions of Western Rajasthan', in: Offredi (ed.), *The Banyan Tree*.

muddy in the rain. When the merchant asks how she managed to arrive without getting wet and she explains, he repents and becomes Kabīr's disciple. As David Lorenzen has observed, this legend 'combines protests against economic and sexual exploitation of poor low-caste people by local merchants with an insistence that even the poor owe charity and hospitality to religious ascetics.'[22]

One can certainly see the relevance, but why *only* this story? Why not the stories of Kabīr and the king Sikandar Lodī who persecutes him for daring to act as a religious teacher and challenging the authority of established leaders? In these tales, Kabīr miraculously survives multiple attempts on his life. One might posit that these low-caste people's experience of God is not of a God who saves His people by miracles. Instead liberation comes through human initiative and ingenuity coupled with unswerving devotion to God.[23] The story of Kabīr and Loi reflects such an experience of God, for their actions lead to the merchant's conversion and thus their freedom from his exploitation, rather than miraculous intervention by God.

The religion and the God we find revealed in these Kabīr songs sung by Meghvāls show remarkable parallels with the reflections of Christian liberation theologians and base communities, suggesting that social positioning plays a distinct and perhaps interreligiously similar role in shaping religious experience within theistic traditions. Kabīr calls his listeners into a dignity grounded in their basic humanity as wondrously created by God with the potential for spiritual realization and relationship with the divine. He counters the claims of others to religious (and social)

---

[22] Lorenzen, *Kabir Legends and Ananta-Das's* Kabir Parachai, Albany, NY 1991, p. 49.

[23] It seems that their experience may be not unlike that of the black Christian Womanist theologians and their ancestors, who do not articulate their experience of their God as one who 'leads them out of the land of Egypt'. These black women have chosen to tell the story of Hagar, the slave woman who encountered God in the wilderness and, rather than being liberated, was initially told to go back to her abusive mistress (Sarah) in order to survive. Delores Williams writes, 'Liberation in the Hagar stories is not given by God; it finds its source in human initiative' (Williams, *Sisters in the Wilderness: The Challenge of Womanist God-Talk*, Maryknoll, NY 1993, p. 5).

superiority based on birth status, wealth, education, specialised and privileged knowledge, or outward religious actions, affirming the indwelling of the divine in every person. And he advocates a respect for body and soul coupled with a realization of the transitory and relative nature of all our usual sources of security and grounds for self-worth—wealth, youth, status, love of family and friends. What is unshakable is our relationship with God. And he speaks alternately in the language of analogy between the human and the divine (God as weaver, washerman, potter, spinning woman) and of overwhelming mystery and love in the encounter with God.[24] This is not a limiting vision; it is one without boundaries. The greatest danger is that we will waste the opportunity of this life, only half-heartedly pursuing the truth, becoming distracted or beaten down by circumstance. 'Wake up!' says Kabir, as he weaves his cloth of dignity and protest, wake up to a life that is hard, yes, but filled with meaning and joy.

---

[24] Gustavo Gutiérrez identifies a similar experience of mystery and gratuitious love in his analysis of Job's culminating encounter with God (*On Job: God-talk and the Suffering of the Innocent*).

Kabīr-Panthīs in Kanpur: From *sampradāya* to Dalit Identity

Maren Bellwinkel-Schempp

It is generally acknowledged that Kabīr was the most outstanding figure in the bhakti movement of northern India.[1] Medieval bhakti as loving devotion was preached by a number of low caste and untouchable saints like Raidās, Pīpā and Sen.[2] It opened up the access of low castes, women and untouchables to a devotion that did not depend on wealth, status or knowledge. Kabir's strict monotheism and the teaching of a purely spiritual religion with God as an all pervading reality that is invisible and does not need any representation,[3] made him attractive for protestant missionary scholars who sensed Christian thought in his teachings.[4] Among them was George Herbert Westcott, an Anglican missionary, who wrote one of the first comprehensive books on Kabīr and the Kabīr-panth in 1907.[5] The following paper tries to trace the Kabīr-panthīs in Kanpur. Although the reception of Westcott's book and the contextual setting is well known,[6] its genesis is not. Besides, there are hardly any references to

---

[1] Charlotte Vaudeville, 'Sant Mat: Santism as the Universal Path to Sanctity', in: Schomer, Karine and W. H. McLeod (eds.), *The Sants: Studies in a Devotional Tradition of India*, Delhi 1987, p. 23.

[2] David N. Lorenzen, 'The Kabir Panth and Social Protest', in: Schomer, Karine and W. H. McLeod (eds.), *The Sants. Studies in a Devotional Tradition of India*, Delhi 1987, p. 286.

[3] Charlotte Vaudeville, *Kabir*, Oxford 1974, p. 106.

[4] Vaudeville, *Kabir*, p. 11; see also the contribution of Bandyopadhyaya in this volume, pp. 9-31.

[5] George Herbert Westcott, *Kabir and the Kabir Panth*, 2nd ed. Calcutta 1953 (1st ed. Cawnpore 1907).

[6] Vaudeville, *Kabir*.

Kabīr-panthīs in Kanpur,[7] whereas the veneration for the untouchable Sant Raidās is fairly well covered.[8]

The present study dwells entirely on the Dalit community of Kanpur. It will touch the crucial issues of Kabīr's reception, which centres around the notion of caste and untouchability, as they are refracted amongst the Dalits themselves. Western and Indian scholarship has generally accepted that although there is a revolutionary potential in Kabīr's teachings, he was primarily concerned with the relationship between man and God: 'Kabir was a poet, a radical reformer, though society was only the outermost skin of what he wished to reform.'[9] The Dalit view on the other hand holds that the reform of society was a major concern of Kabīr.[10] A staunch advocate for this position was Dr. Ambedkar himself: 'There have been many who have worked in the cause of the abolition of Caste and Untouchablity. Of those who can be mentioned, Ramanuja, Kabir and others stand out prominently.'[11] Here I explore the attitude of the Kabīr-panthīs to caste and untouchability.

Although it is generally accepted that the bhakti movement included brahmanical traditions and low caste movements, there were bhakti saints like Sant Raidās whose followers were exclusively from untouchable castes. Sant Raidās became the figurehead of the Ād Dharm

---

[7] Nandini Gooptu, 'Caste and Labour: Untouchable Social Movements in Uttar Pradesh in the Early Twentieth Century', in: Robb, Peter (ed.), *Dalit movements and the Meanings of Labour in India*, Delhi 1993, p. 289.

[8] Arthur Niehoff, *Factory Workers in India*, Milwaukey 1959, pp. 68-74; Maren Bellwinkel, *Die Kasten-Klassenproblematik im städtisch-industriellen Bereich. Historisch-empirische Fallstudie über die Industriestadt Kanpur in Uttar Pradesh, Indien*, Wiesbaden 1980, pp. 205-212.

[9] Linda Hess, 'Kabir's Rough Rhetoric', in: Schomer, Karine and W. H. McLeod (eds.), *The Sants: Studies in a Devotional Tradition of India*, Delhi 1987, p. 23, in: 1987, p. 144.

[10] For further elaboration on this point, especially Dharmvir's position see Monika Horstmann's paper in this volume, pp. 000.

[11] Bhimrao Ambedkar, 'Annihilation of Caste', in: *Dr. Babasaheb Ambedkar Writings and Speeches*, vol.1, Bombay, Government of Maharashtra 1936, p. 74.

movement in Panjab[12] and for the Ādi Hindū movement in Uttar Pradesh.[13]

Today, sharing the broad label of bhakti, progressive social movements as well as Hindu fundamentalist notions are grouped together.[14] In the Kanpur context I would like to show how Kabīr is interpreted in the concert of different political and religious discourses within the Dalit community. What kind of importance is attributed to Kabīr vis-à-vis the other bhakti saints? In the representation of the different discourses, I follow the argument of Rajendrenath Ahervar who has been at the forefront of the Dalit movement in Kanpur.[15] For the history of the Kabīr-panthīs, I rely on the narrative of Munni Devi, who is daughter and granddaughter of two eminent Kabīr-panthīs. Fortunately she has kept all the books, papers and documents of her father's and grandfather's times.

When the Westcott brothers came to Kanpur in 1889, the town was still struggling to overcome the trauma of the Mutiny.[16] But miraculously, it was transformed into a prosperous industrial town, the first in India altogether. British enterprise, ingenuity and diligence had made Kanpur a centre of leather and textile industry and the main supplier for the British Indian Army. An industrial labour force developed, which consisted of Chamars, Koris and Muslims.[17] The city was well connected by water, rail and road to all major ports of India. It had public water works, a sewage system, garbage collection and night soil disposal, streetlights and a

---

[12] Mark Juergensmeyer, *Religion as Social Vision: The Movement against Untouchability in 20th-Century Punjab*, Berkeley 1982.

[13] R. P. Khare, *The Untouchable as Himself. Ideology, Identity and Pragmatism among Lucknow Chamars*, Cambridge 1984; Gooptu, 'Caste and Labour'.

[14] David N. Lorenzen (ed.), *Bhakti Religion in North India. Community, Identity and Political Action*, New York 1995.

[15] He was the founder of the 'Bharatiya Bauddh Mahasabha', long time president of the 'Ravidas Julus Committee', founder and president of the 'Swami Achchutanand Smarak Samiti'.

[16] Zoe Yalland, *Boxwallahs. The British in Cawnpore 1857-1901*, Wilby 1994, p. 2.

[17] Bellwinkel, *Kasten-Klassenproblematik*, pp. 38-40.

tram.[18] The population of the town according to the Census of 1891 was 188, 000.

Canon George Herbert Westcott was sent by the Society for the Propagation of the Gospel to Kanpur. He was an Anglican and as such represented the majority of the Protestant Christian denominations in Cawnpore.[19] But he and his brother set out to be 'clergymen of all citizens of Cawnpore',[20] which gained them tremendous popularity. Altogether George Herbert spent twenty-one years of his life in Kanpur. Well versed in Hindi and Urdu, he took a keen interest in the religious orientation of the lower classes, which led to the publication of *Kabir and the Kabir Panth* in 1907. In the introduction to the first edition he states: 'For help in this undertaking I am principally indebted to my Mali, Badlu Dass, who is himself a member of the Panth. He has visited all places of interest in connection with the Panth and introduced me to many Mahants and conducted inquiries with great intelligence.' If Westcott relied for his research on the knowledge of the local Kabīr-panthīs, Kanpur itself must have had a substantial number of them.

When I came to Kanpur in October 1998,[21] the city had a population of over two million. All the old industrial enterprises were closed. The erstwhile working class population had gone over to vegetable selling and private labour. Only shoe and leather factories, together with *pān kā masālā* flourished. Kanpur's eminence as a railway junction was gone. The Ganga had deserted Kanpur and taken a different course. After fifteen years of the Indo-Dutch Environmental and Sanitary Engineering Project (IDSEP), the sanitary problems of Kanpur were not solved. The Ganga barrage is still under construction and water supply is irregular.

---

[18] D.N. Majumdar, *Social Contours of an Industrial City. Social Survey of Kanpur 1954-1956*, Bombay 1960, pp. 16-18.

[19] The Anglicans apart, there were Baptists, Methodists and American Presbyterians. Orthodox Christians and Roman Catholics had their own congregations. See A.B.K. Sebastian, *A Sociological Study of the Protestant Church Organisation in Kanpur*, DPhil thesis, Kanpur 1982, p. 6.

[20] Yalland, *Boxwallahs*, p. 331.

[21] From 1972 to 1974 I did fieldwork on industrial labourers in Kanpur. The present study is part of a larger project on 'Identity Construction and the Meaning of Communal Dimensions for Scheduled Castes in Kanpur'.

Electricity cuts are frequent, especially in the hot months. Garbage disposal has reached a new abomination as the municipally assigned garbage collection spots are used as feeding grounds for cows and pigs. Pig husbandry has become a flourishing private enterprise on public grounds.[22] Violence still occurs in present-day Kanpur. The 1931 Hindu-Muslim riots were said to have been the most severe in pre-Independence times.[23] In the aftermath of the destruction of the Babri Masjid in Ayodhya in 1992, it came to a three-day, nearly unrestrained killing in Kanpur.[24] Since then, minor disturbances have flared up and on all public occasions the police is alert.

George Herbert Westcott remains unforgotten. Kanpur's middle class knows him as the founder of Christ Church College and even the common man is familiar with the 'Westcott' building next to the college. But even among local intellectuals it was not known that George Herbert Westcott wrote a book on Kabīr, although Kabīr is highly thought of by Kanpur's upper middle class.[25]

When I asked about the Kabīr-panthīs in Kanpur, even the aforementioned Rajendrenath Ahervar was at a loss. To his knowledge there were none. But quite willingly he pointed out four Kabīr Mandirs of which the oldest at Karbala is defunct. It was the home of the renowned Mahant Sevak Das, who was amongst Westcott's informants. His grave is on Sanval Das Ghat, constructed in the 1880s by the rich tannery owner, leather merchant and Kabīr-panthī Sanval Das (1864-1908). He was a

[22] Maren Bellwinkel-Schempp, 'The Khatik of Kanpur and the Bristle Trade: Toward an Anthropology of Man and Beast', in: *Sociological Bulletin*, 47.2 (1999), pp. 187-206.

[23] Vibhuti Narain Rai, *Combating Communal Conflicts. Perception of Police Neutrality during Hindu-Muslim Riots in India*, Allahabad 1999, pp. 31-5.

[24] Paul R. Brass, *Theft of an Idol. Text and Context in the Representation of Collective Violence*, Princeton 1997, p. 214.

[25] I discussed Westcott's heritage with Dr. Munishwar Nigam and Mrs. Santosh Mahendrajit Singh. Dr. Munishwar Nigam is the chairperson of the Kanpur Historical Society. Mrs. Singh is chairperson of a number of charitable institutions, Spastic Centre and the Inner Wheel Club and also a member of the Kanpur Historical Society.

Chamar by caste, and his wealth, generosity and benevolence were so great that he even found mention in Arora's *Kānpur kā itihās*.[26]

The second Kabīr Mandir is situated in the Idgah Colony. The brothers Makkan Das and Dakkan Das built it in 1915.[27] They were Kureels like Sanval Das, rich tannery owners and devout Kabīr-panthis as well. Inside the house there is a shrine, showing Kabīr with his two main disciples Dharmdās and Surat Gopāl (ill.1). They were famous for the religious celebration, the *caukā* on Kabīr's birthday in August.[28] For that event they invited 25,000 villagers from Unnao district to attend the celebration and the following meal.

The third Kabīr Mandir is in Juhi Labour Colony near Swadeshi Cotton Mill. It was set up in the 1930s and is a simple structure housing the graves of the two mahants, Laldas and Balakdas. The present officiant is a young Kabīr-panthī who looks after the Mandir.

At Cooperganj, the main grain market in Kanpur, the Kabīr Mandir looks like a feeding place for water buffaloes. It was set up in the 1940s with a dharmshala for marriage parties. It has also served as an office of the Republican Party. The Kabīr Mandir is an interesting structure with a decorated front. Stretching over the wall beneath the flat roof, two friezes of male statues are to be seen, approaching the oversized figure of Satyapuruṣ, the primordial man, who nearly covers the whole of the front of the building. Underneath, Hanumān stretches out his arms. A white-clad nun with short-cut hair told us that Baba Sahib was not here. During three consecutive visits I never managed to meet him. Obviously he hadn't much of a parish left in need of his services.

Only when I met Munni Devi did I come to know the history of the Kabīr-panthīs in Kanpur. Her grandfather Hulasi Das left his village in Unnao at the age of ten. He entered Cooper and Allen Tannery and Leather Factory just when it was opened in 1880. Intelligent, hard working and reliable, he became a *mistrī* after nine years. The expression *mistrī* (derived from Portuguese *mestre* in the meaning of gentleman) is

---

[26] Narain Prasad Arora, *Kānpur kā itihās*, Kanpur 1954, pp. 296-9.

[27] Interview with Makkan Das's grandson Kishan Kumar on 5 May 1999.

[28] David N. Lorenzen, *Praises to a Formless God*: Nirguṇī *Texts from North India*, Albany, NY 1996, p. 237.

misleading, because his responsibilities far exceeded supervisory functions. He was a labour contractor, recruiting, employing and maintaining labourers for the factory. He lived for his men and on them. His job was so remunerative that he was able to buy eighteen houses, which he rented out. He was a patron, looking after his workers in sickness and death, marrying off their daughters and caring for the old.

Besides, he became the disciple of Mahant Lal Das in Dalelpurwa, from whom he took the *pañjā* as priest in 1903. This enabled him to resign his job. It is stated in his work certificate,

> This is to certify that I have known Hulasi Dass Mahant for about 26 years. He worked under me as mistry for the last 17 years in Cooper & Allen Factory. I always found him honest, hard working and a man with a certain amount of tact, dealing with the men under him. I was very sorry to part with him. He left about ten years ago on his own request to take up the calling of Padri amongst his class. I very often see him and judging by the esteem in which he is held by his followers, he must have kept up the reputation I had of him years ago, Cawnpore, July 3rd 1914, J. H. Sannester.

Kanpur's Kabīr-panthīs all belonged to the Dhamakhera line of Madhya Pradesh.[29] In the time of Westcott, there were five *gaddī*s in Kanpur which attracted substantial followings among the Untouchable castes, which is very much in line with the social composition of Kabīr's following of Sudras, tribal people, and Untouchables.[30] The *sampradāya* was closely knit and strict in its commandments of honesty, faithfulness, cleanliness,[31] vegetarianism and *ahiṃsā*, education and a self-reliant income. Transgressions were reprimanded and led to excommunication,[32] even in irrelevant cases. Vegetarianism and the strict rejection of any intoxicants set the *sampradāya* very much apart from Untouchable

[29] Hulasi Das's son Prem Das wrote a history of the Kabīr-panthīs in Kanpur.

[30] David N. Lorenzen, 'The Kabir Panth and Social Protest', in: Schomer and McLeod (eds.), *The Sants*, p. 283.

[31] I was told by Rajendra Kumar (Interview on 29 March 1999) that his father, a devout Kabīr-panthī, even used to wash the firewood before burning.

[32] George Herbert Westcott, *Kabir and the Kabir Panth*, Calcutta 1907, p. 81.

culture.[33] Although Kabīr is considered to be the pre-eminent figure of 'the transcendent and formless nirguna aspect of divinity',[34] his Kanpur followers were quite evasive and blended the belief in the spiritual representation of God with worship of the Devī.

Westcott's research is still remembered by the disciple of Mahant Sevak Das who was amongst those who were summoned by Westcott's Mali. Mahant Jaigur Das does not remember Westcott's name but he told the following story: 'The Angrez Sahib wanted to thank the mahants for their help. So he called them for a meal. But they could not easily accept the invitation because the Angrez Sahib was not a Kabīr-panthī. They gave him the *kaṇṭhī* and made him a Kabīr-panthī. So they could eat together.'[35]

Hulasi Das was too young at that time to be among Westcott's discussants. What little we know of his biography is paradigmatic of the industrial situation of Kanpur at the turn of the century. Hulasi Das was a Kureel from Unnao. The Kureels are Chamars and were treated as Untouchables. They originated from the districts of Kanpur, Lucknow, Rai Bareilly, Unnao and Hardoi.[36] Traditionally landless labourers, tanners and leather workers,[37] the Kureels moved to Kanpur even before the Mutiny to work in the harness depot of the British army[38] and were the first to join the newly-established leather factories. But not all of them were industrial labourers. Many became leather merchants and tannery owners. As the British had a great demand for leather for the requirements of the Army as well as for export, people like Sanval Das became exceedingly rich. And the *sampradāya* lived on the patronage of such entrepreneurs and labour contractors. Kabīr was not the only Sant

[33] David N.Lorenzen, 'The Kabir Panth: Heretics to Hindus', in: Lorenzen, David N. (ed.), *Religious Change and Cultural Domination*, Mexico 1981, p. 161.

[34] Karine Schomer, 'Introduction: The Sant Tradition in Perspective', in: Schomer and McLeod (eds.), *The Sants*, p. 5.

[35] Interview with Mahant Jaigur Das on 2 April 1999.

[36] H. R. Nevill, *Cawnpore, a Gazetteer*, Allahabad 1909, pp. 105ff.

[37] George Weston Briggs, *The Chamars*, Calcutta 1920, pp. 10ff.

[38] Yalland, *Boxwallahs*, p. 21.

venerated by the Kureels. Sant Raidās, a Chamar cobbler by birth,[39] was held in equal esteem and gained increasing popularity in Kanpur.

Migrating from Bundelkhand, the Koris entered the textile industry and were preferred by the British.[40] Although they are performing a non-polluting task,[41] in Kanpur they are classified as Untouchables.[42] The Koris considered themselves natural adherents of Kabīr, as he was a weaver like them. But there was no Kori mahant to my knowledge. They gave up worship of the Devī in the Bundelkhandi fashion as little as the Kureels gave up Kālī worship.[43] Followers of a *nirguṇa* Sant, image worship was still followed, and this they did not perceive to be in contradiction to Kabīr's teachings.

Unlike the Kureels, the Koris had, apart from industrial labour, no entrepreneurial gifts, although there were quite a number of labour contractors among them who built substantial houses or *ahātā*s (enclosed wards). Besides, a section of them were even forced to work in the informal sector. They were employed by Khatik pig breeders and bristle manufacturers to do bristle dressing.[44]

The religious notion of equality before God tallied well with the initial experience of Koris and Kureels in industry. The different castes

---

[39] Winand M. Callewart and Peter G. Friedlander, *The Life and Works of Saint Raidas*, New Delhi 1992, p. 22.

[40] Stefan Molund, *First we are people... : The Koris of Kanpur between Caste and Class*, Stockholm 1988, p. 47.

[41] Vaudeville, *Kabir*, p. 83.

[42] It has been suggested that the untouchable status has been attributed to them because they once broke off from the Chamars (see Stephen Fuchs, *At the Bottom of Indian Society. The Harijan and other Low Castes*, Delhi 1981, p. 178), a theory which is nowadays repeated by the educated Chamars, because most of them have read George Weston Briggs's book *The Chamar*, either in English or in Hindi. Briggs mentions, among the Chamar subcastes, also the Koris (p. 30).

[43] Interview with Kripa Shanker on 4 April 1999 and with Rajendra Kumar on 28 March 1999.

[44] Molund, *First we are People*, p. 119.

worked 'cheek by jowl'[45] as a report from 1906 said. For those Untouchable castes impoverishment and expropriation did not accompany the process of proletarization, because they had little to lose except their home village. And industrial work was not the only mode of living as long as the contact to the village was maintained. In the pre-war period, workers changed industry freely when they were discontented with the working conditions.[46] And for a few gifted ones like Hulasi Das it led to wealth, esteem and a *samādhi*.

Hulasi Das's only son, Prem Das, was born in 1908. Educated privately by a pandit and a maulwi, he was trained to become a *vaid*, which secured him an income over and above his remunerations as a Kabīr *mahant*. During the Hindu-Muslim riots in Kanpur in 1931, with the power of his moral command, he saved two Muslim families from the rioters. He also put a ban on *balidān* (animal sacrifice) at the Kālī-temple in Parmat, much to the dismay of his Kureel brothers.

Only after World War I did a radical trade union movement and a nascent Dalit movement emerge. In 1925 Swami Achutanand (1879-1933), founder of the Ādi Hindū movement,[47] chose Kanpur as the centre of his agitation. And in 1927 the Acharya from Dhamakhera organised a big meeting in Kanpur to propagate the teachings of Kabīr.[48] Kanpur became the focus of agitation because it had a well-developed working class, which as for its Untouchables, was certainly freer in their contractual relationships than their bonded caste brothers in the village. The trade union movement and the Dalit movement were not interrelated at all, because Dalit identity had to be negated by the communist trade union movement.

In 1935 there was a disputation on the publication of the *Kabir Mansoor*. Amazingly, the invitation was phrased in English and among the honoured guests were, Mahant Prem Das apart, two missionaries from

---

[45] S. H. Fremantle, *Report on the Supply of Labour in the United Provinces and Bengal*, Lucknow 1906, p. 25.

[46] Chitra Joshi, *Workers' Protest, Managerial Authority, and Labour Organization. Kanpur Textile Industry 1919-1929*, New Delhi 1985, pp. 5 ff.

[47] Khare, *The Untouchable as Himself*, pp. 81-7.

[48] Information received from Mahant Gyan Das, Shuklaganj, on 3 May 1999.

the American Presbyterian Mission. The APM had been present in Kanpur since 1901 and mainly worked among Untouchables with the intention to convert them to Christianity and secure them jobs in industry.[49] Obviously they were also instrumental in forming a 'Dalit Mazdoor Sangh'[50] which was used against the dominant communist trade union by the British employers as strike breakers with the argument of the brahmin dominance in the trade union movement. The British used caste as an argument to pursue their capitalist interests, though factually they were right. Besides, in the 1930s the caste composition of the industrial labour force had changed considerably. Koris and Chamars had lost their numerical dominance in the textile industry, as upper castes took up industrial work in large numbers after World War I.[51] The Hindu-Muslim riots of 1931 had additional economic repercussions on the Chamars. They were evicted from Hiramankapurwa where they had their godowns and workshops.[52] This was a great financial setback for them. Giving up the leather business was generally a deliberate Chamar act, in obedience to Ambedkar's teachings.[53] Only nowadays do they realize the economic consequences of this which they voice with an undercurrent of hostility towards the Muslims.

Prem Das was also among Swami Achutanand's followers. There was a lively spiritual exchange between them, mainly on religious matters. When Achutanand established Raidās as the saint of his movement, the Kabīr-panthīs fell behind in public attention. Girdhari Lal, a Kureel like Makkan Das and Dakkan Das, who lived in the same ward, became

---

[49] Sebastian, *A sociological study*, p. 18.

[50] Shiv Mohan Pandey, *As Labour Organizes: A Study of Unionism in the Kanpur Cotton Textile Industry*, New Delhi 1970, p. 61.

[51] Bellwinkel, *Die Kasten-Klassenproblematik*, p. 40.

[52] Interview with Krishna Kumar Rahi, grandnephew of Sanval Das, on 6 May 1999.

[53] Interview with Madan Mohan Chaudhury and Babu Lal Ahervar on 10 March 1999.

Swami Achutanand's patron.[54] He was a rich tannery owner and leather merchant and he gave Achutanand a house to live in. It was surrounded by a beautiful garden, where later on Girdhari Lal had his grave constructed in the form of a little temple, depicting him in veneration at the feet of Sant Raidās. Patronage was an individual affair, but the Swami made it clear that he wanted to be supported by the untouchable community as a whole. He used to go from house to house to collect food for his meals. And the caudharis from the different untouchable castes in Kanpur understood his message. Through contributions of all untouchable castes in Kanpur, the first Raidās temple in Harbans Mohall was erected in the 1920s. It served as the meeting point of annual processions, which set out on Raidās Jayantī. When during the 1930s in retaliation to the communist-inspired militant strikes the British recruited 'docile' Jaisvara Chamars from eastern U.P.,[55] they brought with them a deeply felt veneration for Sant Raidās which gave a new turn to the movement. The *caukā*s of the Kabīr-panthīs, Makkan Das's conspicuous consumption apart, were a private affair. The Raidas procession was not.[56] It was an appropriation of public space, a representation of Dalit culture, which had a provocative effect when the Untouchables went drum beating through wards inhabited by upper castes.

After Swami Achutanand's death in 1933, there was a void which was filled by Dr. Ambedkar. He came to Kanpur in 1944 for the second meeting of the Scheduled Caste Federation.[57] In Dalit narratives, this historical event has gained a legendary quality. Everybody claims to have had an important function at that meeting, be it as bodyguard, usher or participant in the *sahabhoj*.[58] This community meal was organised on the request of Dr. Ambedkar to abolish untouchability. But few caudharis

[54] I am following Rajendrenath's narrative and the booklet by Swami Achutanand's son-in-law Mangal Singh entitled *'108 Svāmī Achūtānand kī jīvanī'*.

[55] Bellwinkel, *Die Kasten-Klassenproblematik*, p. 41.

[56] Rajendrenath Ahervar, 'Sri Ravidas Birthday Celebration in Anwarganj'.

[57] Dhananjay Keer, *Dr. Ambedkar, Life and Mission*, Bombay 1954, p. 362.

[58] Interviews with Rajendrenath Ahervar, Madan Mohan Chaudhuri, Nawal Kishor, Vijay Sagar Sonkar and Suresh Chand Sonkar in October 1998.

accepted the invitation and the ones who did were ostracized—*hukkā pānī band*—by their respective castes. Praise to the Kabīr-panthīs who solved their issues of commensality with Westcott more elegantly!

Prem Das attended the meeting but not the meal. He considered himself part of the Dalit movement, although he leant towards the Congress. He wanted to improve the educational and moral standards of his brethren. In 1947 he founded the 'Depressed Classes Educational Society' and set up a girls' school in Parmat. For this purpose he rented the Kureel panchayat building. Unfortunately the school did not last long.

Tilok Chand Kureel, Municipal Corporator from 1936 and President of the Scheduled Caste Federation and next-door neighbour of Prem Chand, tried to appropriate the school building. A court case began, which lasted for thirty years and ended before the Allahabad High Court. The school had to close down. The same happened with the 'Nehru Chattravas', a students' hostel for Scheduled Caste students studying in DAV College, which Prem Das opened in 1950. Tilok Chand Kureel withdrew the financial support given by the Municipal Corporation and it closed in 1962. Times had changed. Politics in independent India endowed its politicians with new means of patronage.

The 1950s and 1960s witnessed the resurgence of the Raidās movement. A number of Raidās temples sprung up which were served by *bhagat*s. The patrons of these temples were not any longer rich tannery owners, but clerks[59] and babus employed in the telephone exchange and government services. The Raidās procession was celebrated with pomp and splendour, but apart from that Raidās never made an entry into life-cycle rites as in Panjab.[60] Devī worship was still prominent among the Kureels, and it was taken over by the *savarṇa* castes. The old Kālī temple

[59] Interview with Meera Dohre on 13 December 1998. Her father Bhagat Singh was a devoted Raidāsī who built three temples in Adi Nagar, a ward predominantly inhabited by Kureels and in close proximity to the area where Swaṃi Achutanand used to live.

[60] Communication by Kapil Dev, former District Magistrate of Kanpur and devout Raidāsī from Panjab.

in Parmat used to have a Kureel *purohit*. When he died, a brahmin family took over.[61]

Prem Das knew that he had to lead the Kabīr-panthīs out of the private realm into a public domain. Just at the end of his life he started a unification move amongst the *sampradāya*.[62] In 1969 he called for an 'Akhil Bhāratīya Kabīr Ācārya Sammelan evam Satsaṅg' in Kanpur. It was held in the Brijendra Swarup Park, named after a leading Ārya Samājī family of Kanpur. The objective was to generate equality, love and good will among the *ācārya*s, Sants and *mahant*s for the development of the Kabīr-panth. The meeting was well attended and a great success. The second conference of the All India Kabir Panthis took place in Kudar Mall in Madhya Pradesh, the seat of the Dhamakhera *gaddī*, in 1971 and could claim to have welcomed delegates from Maharashtra, Gujarat, Madhya Pradesh, Uttar Pradesh and Bihar. The third conference took place in New Delhi in 1973. Prem Das's detailed report tells us of the difficulties he had in organising a meeting of that significance in the capital city and of the reluctance of the Gujarat *ācārya* to attend.

For the heirs of the brothers Makkan Das and Dakkan Das the economic decline only started after Independence. Their urban property was sold to the municipal corporation, which erected a labour colony at that place. To the 1960s they still excelled in conspicuous consumption on behalf of the Kabīr-panthīs. Nowadays Krishan Kumar, their grandson, is struggling to get his harness business going.[63]

In 1974 Prem Das died and soon after his wife, a Brahmin widow whom he had employed as school teacher in his Depressed Classes Girls School, followed him. Theirs was a great love. Prem Das took her as second wife as his first wife was issueless. Munni Devi, their only daughter, was left alone with her stepmother, unable to finish her MBBS studies. She married a close relative of her stepmother and became a mother and housewife. After her father's death the Kabīr-panthīs in Kanpur lost their focal figure. And Munni Devi became more and more

[61] Communication by Dr. Anand Srivastava from Parmat.

[62] Mahant Prem Das, *Let the Kabirpanthis of the World Unite. A Brief History of All India Kabir Panthi Sangh, registered 1971*.

[63] Interview on 5 May 1999.

isolated within the Kureel community, being left with her grandfather's *tāj* and *kaṇṭhī* and the memories of a more distinguished past.

Buddhism in Kanpur has an interesting history, because even before Dr. Ambedkar's conversion in 1956, there was a Buddhist congregation in Kanpur[64] which goes back to Acharya Ishwardatt Medharthi, a Garheria (shepherd) by caste. In the 1940s, during his quest and search for a new religion for the Dalits,[65] Ambedkar visited Ishwardatt. But when Ambedkar converted to Buddhism in 1956, there was little response in Kanpur. The Census of India in 1961 records only 610 Buddhists. The educated Dalits used to go to Sarnath or Bodh Gaya to take *dīkṣā* there.

In 1973 Jagjivan Ram inaugurated the first Ambedkar statue in Nanarao Park. This was a big success for the Dalit movement. The Nanarao Park was the former Memorial Garden of the British, commemorating the outcome of the Mutiny. After Independence, the colonial image was put aside and the Indian hero of the Mutiny set up. Erected in an historically charged public place, Ambedkar's statue now attested to the new significance of the Dalits.

Thereafter, in every Dalit ward Ambedkar statues came up, like the Raidās temples in the 1960s. The Ambedkar movement became powerful when it finally linked with Buddhism. This happened through Bhikshu Deepankar who set up a monastery in 1980 in Juhi Labour Colony. Against all odds he started preaching Buddhism with considerable success.[66] Nowadays, there are about five thousand committed Buddhists in Kanpur. For them Buddhism is a complete negation of Hinduism and

---

[64] Niehoff mentions a Buddhist temple, built in the 1920s. According to his estimate there were twenty-five Buddhists in the 1950s. See *Factory Workers*, p. 70.

[65] His book, *Bhārat ke ādimvāsi-pūrvjan aur sant dharm*, claims Buddha to be the fountainhead of the Sant Dharm, which was the non-literate religion of the original inhabitants of India.

[66] Interview with Bhikshu Deepankar on 3 May 1999. He told me that there was an attempt to poison him. This is an interesting hagiographic detail, as Swami Achutanand is said to have been poisoned by the *savarṇa*.

the caste order. Although they prefer to marry among themselves, they still have not formed an endogamous group. Buddhism has developed its own life-cycle rites and rituals and has transformed the political Dalit culture into a splendid representation of perfection and grandeur. Besides, the former Dalit woman chiefminister of Uttar Pradesh, Mayavati,[67] set unprecedented standards with the creation of 'Lord Buddha Parks', of which Kanpur's park was completed on 26 July 1997.

Kabīr and Raidās, as *nirguṇa* bhaktas, are considered the predecessors of Buddhism in their teaching of love, brotherhood, equality and their attack on the caste system and the *savarṇa*, although their public representation within Dalit culture has taken different paths. Although the Raidās procession has lost its splendour in comparison with the Ambedkar Jayantī, the Raidās temples are well kept, and one of them, built in the 1950s, was renovated in the 1990s.[68] In public representation Raidās is depicted as the founding father of a Dalit lineage with his 'son' Buddha and 'grandson' Dr. Ambedkar. Although Kabīr was considered to be the 'fountainhead' of bhakti culture, within the present Dalit discourse in Kanpur, he has receded into the background.

Sadhvi Kumari Bandhni, self-styled president of the 'Satya Guru Raidās Pariṣad', tries to establish a personal Dalit religiosity with the focus on women. In the labour colony Allenganj, she has transformed one quarter into a temple. She sings songs on Raidās, Kabīr, Buddha and Ambedkar. When I asked her to allow me to take a picture of her altar, she quietly put the picture of Kṛṣṇa away, to maintain the purity of the Dalit pantheon, consisting of Kabīr, Raidās, Mīrā Bāī, Buddha and the Rājā of Benares.

The Kabīr-panthīs were the puritans of the early Dalit movement. With their strict emphasis on truth, cleanliness, vegetarianism and *ahiṃsā*, they considered themselves the elite of their community. As long as they

---

[67] Oliver Mendelsohn and Marika Vicziany, *The Untouchables: Subordination, Poverty and the State in Modern India*, Cambridge 1998, pp. 228-31.

[68] This goes to the credit of educated Dalits from the Panjab, as in the case of the Raidas temple in Kalyanpur, in which Om Prakash, former Professor of Psychology at IIT, and Kapil Dev, former District Magistrate of Kanpur, were instrumental.

were rich and could give freely to their caste brothers, their moral superiority was accepted. Prem Das's life set an example in that respect. Their religion was basically inwardly oriented and there was no scope for public representation, which is essential in present day political discourse. Besides, the uncompromising righteousness of the Kabīr-panthīs does not fit into modern politics, which is based on networks of shifting alliances. What was handy, has been absorbed into Dalit culture: Mayavati has named a whole district after Kabīr.

Where have all the Kabīr-panthīs gone? They have moved to Shuklaganj on the other side of the Ganga, where the river still has water. In new suburbs *pān kā masālā* is produced and plots are cheap. The *mahant*s followed their disciples. Mahant Jaigur Das holds his *caukā* there. Mahant Gyan Das, a great yogi who took *samādhi* for six months, has also moved to rural Unnao, just opposite the Karbala and Sanval Das Ghat.[69]

In Chamanganj Koriana there were ten Kabīr-panthī families twenty years ago but now there is only one.[70] Kabīr is not forgotten. The educated young generation learns about Kabīr in school and college. They take 'Kabīr' as their family name,[71] like so many educated Chamars take Ambedkar's name. The surname becomes a caste marker. Kabīr and Ambedkar are signifiers of dalitness among Koris and Chamars. The 'Korī Samāj Sevā Samiti'[72] places Kabīr, Ambedkar and Jalkārī Bāī[73] in their pantheon. As Buddha's mother, Māyā, belonged to the Koli lineage, the

[69] Mahan Gyan Das went to school in Budhpuri, where Acharya Ishwardatt Medharthi had established a school.

[70] Interview with Lalta Das on 28 March 1999.

[71] Interview with Swami Maiku Lal's granddaughter Suchitra Kabir on 10 March 1999.

[72] Interview with K. K.Verma, R. K.Verma and Gauri Shanker on 10 April 1999.

[73] Vīrānganā Jalkārī Bāī was the servant of Rāṇī Lakṣmī Bāī of Jhansi, who fought with her in 1857 against the British. Jalkārī posed as Rāṇī Lakṣmī Bāī, misled the British, and helped Rāṇī Lakṣmī Bāī escape from Jhansi Fort with her adopted son on her back.

Koris were originally Kshatriyas[74] and have a natural adherence to Buddhism.

Kabīr is considered to have incorporated the remnants of Buddhist teachings of his times, Vaudeville suggests.[75] Some subscribe to this view.[76] Rajendrenathji puts it more cautiously: '*Kabīra dharma Buddha kā jānā, kara ācaraṇa gayo śabda gyāna*' ('Kabir understood the religion of Buddha, he acted accordingly and he obtained the knowledge of the word'). On the other hand, as Ambedkar has shown in his autobiography, paradigmatic for the educated Dalits of Kanpur, there was a personal development of Ambedkar as son of a Kabīr-panthī, to Buddhism. Buddhism is the ultimate rationale, the stringent logic of that development, because only Buddhism sets you free from the caste system, oppression and discrimination.

Buddhism is a liberating religion for Rajendrenathji. Only Buddhism leads the Untouchables out of caste and untouchability. For Munni Devi that is different. The Kabīr-panthīs were free of caste within their *sampradāya*. But the *sampradāya* has dwindled away. Discussing caste with Munni Devi, Rajendrenathji holds that unless one changes religion, one cannot escape caste and untouchability. For Munni Devi liberation is only possible as a spiritual aim, as unification with Satyaguru Kabīr. In her view, present-day Dalit culture is only paying lipservice to Buddhism. For her, the daughter of a Kureel father and a Brahmin mother, the Dalits as the Other drink alcohol and eat meat; they maintain all the vices of untouchable culture. Unless one changes one's behaviour, a spiritual quest is meaningless. And Kabīr, although he is good to quote, but difficult to live by, has disappeared from the public representation of the Dalits. But out of sight is not out of mind. Kabīr has been superseded by Raidās and both have been absorbed into Buddhism.

---

[74] Article in *Kuṭumbikā* entitled 'Pride of Kabir Sahib and Koli Society'.

[75] Vaudeville, *Kabir*, p. 85.

[76] D. C. Ahir, *Heritage of Buddhism*, Delhi 1989.

The Sants and the Struggle against Brahmin Dominance

Shukdeo Singh

Brahmins did the intellectual and religious work for the ruling classes. They were responsible for the creation of the structure of the society and religion, but on the other hand they also legitimated the oppression of the working classes. Under Brahmanical Hinduism, the lower castes were subjected to all sorts of mistreatment. They were not allowed to read books, meditate, or live with dignity in the society. They were often treated as criminals, slaves and untouchables. Their treatment was recorded in Brahmin texts which prescribed various punishments to be used against them. While writers like Vasiṣṭha, Vālmīki, Vyās and Raikva are all said to have been born into these neglected classes, their achievements were ultimately used to the advantage of high-caste persons. Their exemplary lives, codified in hagiographical stories, never influenced the status of their fellow low-castes nor were they able to create any class affinities which would combat the abuse heaped upon the low castes by the Brahmanical system. Nonetheless, there were always those among the lower castes who were conscious of their own dignity in the divine order. They developed parallel systems of ideology, philosophy, and meditation, hoping to achieve a proper place in the social structure.

In ancient history, the greatest intellectual opponents of caste ideology were referred to as Lokāyatas, who argued that the present is our first and only birth. They were also sometimes called Carvāka or Brihaspat. No texts of the Lokāyatas exist that we know of, so it is only through references in Brahmanical and other texts that we can find out something about who they were. In the *Prajñānaśāstra* of Candraketu as well as in the Buddhist *Dīghanikāya*, *Aṅguttaranikāya* and *Divyāvadāna*, Lokāyata texts and philosophies are mentioned. Similarly, in Medhātithi's commentary on the *Manusmṛti*, there is reference to a philosophy or text called *Lokāyata*.

The Buddhist *Dīghanikāya* mentions the names of six radical philosophers who were most likely popular amongst the downtrodden classes. Puraṇa Kaśyapa, Ājivika Gośāla, Ajita Keśakambalin, Prakruddha Kātyāyana, Niganthanāthaputta and Sañjaya are remembered as great philosophers who were opposed to the caste system, untouchability, the use of Sanskrit and the supremacy of the Brahmins. The lives of these philosophers recall the lives of ordinary people. They often lived naked, using blankets of human hair. They had no faith in purity or pollution nor in ritual in which the presence and guidance of a Brahmin priest was deemed necessary. Because of this, these six scholars are remembered as Śūdras. In the commentaries of the Jain *Āgama*s, they are mentioned as untouchables. The Hindu *Vāyu-Purāṇa* likewise calls them Śūdras, but also mentions their popularity amongst the poor, accusing them of ensnaring ignorant people like fish in the net of their philosophy. It is also said that they disagreed with the prevailing customs of writing holy books and establishing monasteries or *maṭh*s. We refer to these figures as Siddhas and now know that there were both Hindus and Buddhists in this category.

Free from the barriers imposed by Brahmanical texts and the caste system, the Siddhas convinced others to free themselves as well. Unlike the Māyāvādins, they believed that this world is the ultimate world. Faith in a deity was seen as a kind of *pākhaṇḍa* or hypocrisy, created to cheat human beings and digress from the truth of this immediate reality. In the later Buddhist texts it is indicated that the eighty-four Siddhas lived on the outskirts of populated areas in cremation-grounds instead of monasteries. The Hindu Siddhas also practised cremation-ground rituals and kept a distance from society, but were sought out by members of the society for their extraordinary powers.

Medieval Hindi dates from the time of these Siddhas. Their thinking was philosophical and the language symbolic. In their own way they fought for the downtrodden, combining their meditation systems with yoga and tantra. Many of their symbolic terms referred to the lower castes. The terms *ḍombī*, *caṇḍālī* and *śabarī* are used; *caṇḍālī*, for example, referring to the internal power of the meditator. Their songs are named after various low castes. For example, *Naṭnārāyaṇ* referred to the Naṭas, a caste of jugglers; *Ahīrbhairava* to the Ahīrs or milkmen; and *Śabarī* to

Śabars. These poem-songs functioned like sermons for the masses and illustrated their acceptance of low- caste persons for *ādhyātmik* (spiritual) activities such as meditation and worship of a deity beyond name and form. Using the vernacular languages, the Siddhas were opposed to Sanskrit and its supremacy in the religious world. Idol worship, Brahmin initiations and the caste system were attacked.

The Siddha tradition existed within the larger Nāth tradition, the folk religious culture that included yogis and householders alike. The thousand names of God were not in their vocabulary. They searched for a new name for the God beyond all name. *Alakh* or *Alakhnirañjan*, meaning the unseen and uncoloured, was the name they came up with. By the period of the eighth to tenth century, when these sects were most influential, Muslims were already present in north India and the Sufi saints were popular among the lower castes. The Sufis spread a message of love and social equality and thus aided in the mass conversions to Islam which took place during this period. Nāth yogis moved about begging and singing the songs of what would later be termed the Hindu tradition, but in fact their teachings were not very different from the Muslim Sufis. Today, many of the Bengali Bāuls and other yogis are actually converted Muslims, but they are popular among Muslims and Hindus alike because they are against formalities of both traditions, the caste system and any type of communal prejudice and hatred.

The tradition of the Nāths and Siddhas with its similarities and borrowings from Sufism and certain other Islamic features eventually gave rise to the *nirguṇ* bhakti in which both Sufis and Sants were the leading figures. In this movement, elements of folk Hinduism and Islam mix together. Hundreds of Sufi saints, including Jāyasī, Dāud, Mañjhan and Nūr Muḥammad based their poems on Hindu mythology. Their philosophy is Muslim in character while their linguistic expressions and stories are closer to Hinduism. Similarly, Sants like Kabīr, Raidās, Dhannā, Pīpā, Trilocan, Sadhanā, Dariā, Dādū, Rajjab, Malūkdās and Śeo Nārāyaṇ advocated Hindu-Muslim unity. Like the Nāth Siddhas before them, they opposed idol worship, Sanskrit texts and Brahmin authority. They envisioned a society where every man and woman is equal and free of caste and religious prejudice. Gender discrimination remained, but even this was modified and softened. Legendary texts like the *parcaī*s, *janamsākhī*s, *bhaktamāl*s, the *Bhaktivijay* and *Padprasaṅg* show that, while these Sants actively resisted the Brahmanical order, some were nonetheless worshipped by Brahmins and members of the other high castes. Raidās says 'I curse the four Vedas but Brahmins bow to me' (*cāro veda ko kiyo khaṇḍauti/ tā ko vipra karaiṁ deauti).*

In India there are now approximately 10,000 monasteries (called *maṭh*, *āśram*, *til*, *jhompaṛ* and *caurā*) related to Kabīr. Similarly, there are many Sikh *gurdvārās* and other religious sites related to Raidās, Dādū, Dariā and Śeo Nārāyaṇ. Significantly, by contrast there are no shrines or *maṭh*s related to Tulsīdās, whose writings foster the interests of the upper strata of society. Although there are, of course, many temples, *maṭh*s and other religious centres of the orthodox tradition, it is clear that during the medieval period, religious movements representing the emerging philosophy of the lower castes and downtrodden people were of increasing importance.

The Sant tradition has survived and flourished due to the singers, living-language poets, professional beggars, yogis, *sāī*s, *māṁgtā*s, *bhagat*s and other singer and dancer castes. The influence of these people is important because their daily functions and ceremonies accurately reflect the social behaviour of much of Indian society. Precisely because the lower castes were so influential in the bhakti movement, people of upper caste birth often followed lower caste Sants and struggled in their own way for the upliftment of farmers, labourers and other poor men. For example, Jagjīvandās and Śeo Nārāyaṇ were both born in upper castes but created for themselves honourable places among the neglected and outcaste. The poetry of the oppressed segments of society was transmitted both orally and through written manuscripts. Many texts were produced, hailing the importance of the poet-saint as Guru, for Supreme Knowledge could only be gained in his presence. The Guru, however, does not only exist outside, but within the self as well. Among such texts are the *Gurū granth*, *Kabīr-bījak*, *Kulzam svarūp*, *Sarvāṅgī*, *Guṇgañjnāmā*, *Pañjī panth prakāś*, *Guru anyās*, *Rām jahāj* and the *Pañcvāṇī* of the Dādū-panth. In these the poems and sayings of Sants are collected in an order which in itself holds philosophic meaning. The basic structure is according to *aṅga*s and *rāga*s. The constituent parts are often referred to as *sākhī*, *sabad*, *ramanī*, *salok*, *pad*, *bāṇī*, *cāṁcarī*, *belī*, *birhulī*, *cauṁtīsā*, *bāvan akharī* and *vipramatīsī*. These parts often number fifty-nine or eighty-four, numbers identified with mystical significance. Most importantly, they express an ideology of resistance to the orthodox caste hierarchy, systems of logic, emphasis on Sanskrit, and the paraphernalia of temple ritual.

It is interesting to note that all these poets wrote critically of rituals, for example, of the *ārtī*, the lamp waving ceremony conducted in front of images of deity. Some of the poets' songs are not dissimilar to those used in *ārtī* in the mainstream tradition. But the meaning of these *ārtī* poems contradicts the custom of *ārtī* and suggests that the ritual is part of a hypocritical system. Raidās writes:

> What have you brought for *āratī*, what do you see?
> It astonishes your servant and slave!
> You have made fifty-two golden lamps –
> Fool, you have not even glimpsed renunciation!
> The brilliance of His hair is ten million suns –
> how can you perform His *āratī* with smoke and fire?
> The five elements and the three *guṇ*s of Māyā –
> whatever is visible is all His creation.
> Raidās says, I have seen within,
> all your flames cannot equal a single hair.[1]

Another important form of protest were poems that highlighted the greatness of the lower-caste professions. They uplifted the vocabulary of labour to the heights of poetic language and even to the height of *ādhyātmik* (spiritual) philosophy. Kabīr, for example, used the language of weavers, frequently employing words like *julāhā* (weaver), *tānā* (warp), *bānā* (woof), *sūt* (thread), *karghā* (loom), *carkhā* (spinning-wheel), *cādar* (shawl).

---

[1] आरती का ले करि जोवै सेवग दास अचंभै होवै। टेक।।
बांवन कंचन दीप घडावै जडि बैराग द्रिष्टि न आवै।।
कोटि भान जाकि सोभा रूंमैं कहा आरती अगनि र धूंमैं।।
पंच तत अरु त्रिगुंनीं माया जो दीसै सो सकल उपाया।।
कहै रैदास मैं देष्या मांहीं सकलहि जोति रोम संमि नांहीं।।
Winand M. Callewaert and Peter G. Friedlander, *The Life and Works of Raidās*, New Delhi 1992, p. 159 and p. 225.

That the vocabulary of cloth weaving could be used to convey a religious message was a new and radical idea. Similarly Raidās used the vocabulary of a cobbler, Dhannā used agricultural terms and Dharmdās and Palṭūdās used the shopkeepers' language to describe meditation and religious philosophy. Instead of using Sanskrit terms, they used the language of everyday life. Through the use of '*ulaṭbāṁsī*', or 'upside down language', Sant poetry and ideology, as it appeared in texts like the *goṣṭhī*, *saṃvād*, *sāgar*, *bodh* and *tilak*, offered straightforward alternatives to the abstract philosophy of Sanskrit culture. Even the sound of their verses captured the artistry of their work. The rhythm of Kabīr's poetry reminds one of the rhythm of weaving. Thus the experience of work is deeply woven into the Sants' poetry.

The Sants' view of renunciation is very different from that of the upper castes. Without giving up family and caste, as labourers and householders, they dedicated themselves to God. Despite the fact that manual or physical work was polluting in the eyes of Brahmins, the Sants maintained that all work is worship. Every type of labour, from shoe-making to cloth-weaving and to harvesting crops can be a kind of meditation and offering to God. Like the Siddhas, whose poetry was called *caryā* or 'life behaviour', the Sants' poetry is based on their everyday experience, and to see this as sacred is in itself a protest against the caste system. Although the Brahmins were totally dependent on the working classes, because they themselves did very little physical labour, they claimed a right to be treated like Gods by the labourers. The Sants countered this by insisting on detachment from the world controlled by the upper strata. Despite their involvement in the householder's life, they remained detached from property and the everyday relations of society. Rather than sitting amidst the five burning fires, fasting as a kind of *vrat* or vow, or undertaking other kinds of ritual austerities, in a real sense their whole life was spent fasting because of poverty. Yet this poverty, ironically, became the very source of their power. Because they understood their condition and were able to express it through the profound message of their poetry, they were able to resist the meanings placed on them by the established order. In this way, the Sants not only helped their caste fellows to find dignity, they ultimately gained the respect of many among the higher castes as well.

Many of the major Sant lineages continue to this day, although since the medieval period there have been many shifts in their followings. Sects have merged and diverged. As mentioned already, nearly all the major poets and saints of the medieval period belonged to the lower castes. Raidās was a Camār, Kabīr a converted Korī-Camār, Sadhanā a butcher, Sen a barber, Dhannā a ploughman, Pīpā a Rajput who became a tailor. Their followers were mostly low-caste people. Muslims rarely followed Kabīr. In fact, at Magahar, where he died, there remains only one Muslim family with the name of Kabīrvaṃśī ('hailing from Kabīr'). They care for the grave of Kabīr and own some of the land. The Hindus of Magahar also own property and maintain relations with Kabīr-Caurā in Varanasi.

Regarding gender, there have been many female followers of the Sants, but they were mostly householders and not sadhus or nuns. One of the branches of the Kabīr Parkhī sect admits nuns, but they are clearly in a minority. Raidās has only one historically documented female disciple: Jamunā Raidāsinī. Jhālī Rānī of Rajasthan and even Mīrābāī are mentioned in texts as his disciples, upper-caste followers of a lower-caste Sant. It appears that the majority of Raidās's followers merged into the sect of Dādū. Raidās's followers in the Panjab were incorporated into the Sikh religion, yet some Raidāsī *dherā*s, which are not unlike *gurdvārā*s, still exist in the Panjab. Due to the effort of Jagjīvandās, a Rajput, as well as the Camār Ghāsīdās, many Raidās followers merged into the Svāmī sect or the Dharmdāsī subsects of the Kabīr-panth. Currently, the Śeo Nārāyaṇ sect is affiliating itself with Raidās. Parallel to the sectarian presence, there is also a mobile tradition of followers who have not organised themselves in any way.

Approximately eighty percent of medieval Indian literature is related to these poets. This largely oral tradition survives to this day and, through the *pad* and *sākhī* forms, continues to express the philosophy of the Sants in language accessible to the common people. Yet these literary forms remain relatively neglected by Indian and foreign scholars alike.

Today there is an increasing social awareness on the part of the members of backward and downtrodden castes. Many of them continue to use the Sants as symbols and inspiration for their struggle. In the medieval period, the Sants fought oppression using the weapons of poetry, meditation and lives of devotion. Although the form of struggle may have changed somewhat over time, I am glad to say that their fight continues.

CONTRIBUTORS

PRADEEP BANDYOPADHYAY is Professor at the Department of Sociology, Trent University, Peterborough, Ontario, Canada.

MAREN BELLWINKEL-SCHEMPP is a Research Fellow in Anthropology at the South Asia Institute, University of Heidelberg, Germany.

WINAND M. CALLEWAERT is Professor at the Department of Oriental Studies, Katholieke Universiteit, Leuven, Belgium.

THOMAS DAHNHARDT is a Research Fellow at the Oxford Centre for Islamic Studies, Oxford, U.K., and presently working as Lecturer for Urdu Language and Literature at the University of Venice, Italy.

PETER GAEFFKE is Professor of Modern Indian Literature at the University of Pennsylvania, Philadelphia, USA.

DANIEL GOLD is Professor of South Asian Religions at Cornell University, Ithaca, NY, USA.

MONIKA HORSTMANN (Monika Boehm-Tettelbach) is Professor at the Department of Modern Indian Studies, South Asia Institute, University of Heidelberg, Germany.

SADIQUR RAHMAN KIDWAI is retired Professor of Urdu at the Jawaharlal Nehru University, New Delhi, India.

DAVID N. LORENZEN is Professor at the Centro de Estudios de Asia y Africa, El Colegio de Mexico, Mexico.

NANCY M. MARTIN is Associate Professor of Religion at Chapman University, Orange, California, USA.

STUART MCGREGOR is Emeritus Reader in Hindi at the University of Cambridge, England.

KIRAN NAGARKAR is a free-lance writer living in Mumbai, India.

MARIOLA OFFREDI is Associate Professor of Hindi Language and Literature at the University of Venice, Italy.

BAHADUR SINGH retired from the post of language instructor in Hindi at the Institut für Geschichte Indiens und Tibets, University of Hamburg, Germany.

KEDARNATH SINGH, renowned writer of Hindi, is retired Professor of Hindi at the Jawaharlal Nehru University, New Delhi, India.

NAMWAR SINGH, renowned critic of Hindi, is retired Professor of Hindi at the Jawaharlal Nehru University, New Delhi, India.

SHUKDEO SINGH is retired Professor of Ancient Hindi Literature at the Department of Hindi, Banaras Hindu University, Varanasi, India.

INDEX